E-books in Libraries

A practical guide

E-books in Libraries
A practical guide

Edited by

Kate Price and Virginia Havergal

facet publishing

Published by Facet Publishing,
7 Ridgmount Street, London WC1E 7AE
www.facetpublishing.co.uk

Facet Publishing is wholly owned by CILIP: the Chartered Institute
of Library and Information Professionals.

British Library Cataloguing in Publication Data
A catalogue record for this book is available from the British Library.

ISBN 978-1-85604-572-8

First published 2011
Reprinted digitally thereafter

Text printed on FSC accredited material.

Mixed Sources
Product group from well-managed
forests and other controlled sources
www.fsc.org Cert no. SA-COC-1565
© 1996 Forest Stewardship Council

Typeset from editors' files by Facet Publishing in 11.5/14.5 pt
Garamond and Frutiger.
Printed and made in Great Britain by MPG Books Group, UK.

Contents

Preface

Despite the fact that e-books (electronic books) have been in existence for decades in various guises and added to library collections for several years now, there has been a noticeable lack of published manuals on the subject.

This is, we feel, due to the rapidly evolving nature of the market. There is now a plethora of different types of digital object which might be termed 'e-books' and a bewildering number of business and access models to match. It may be that many authors and publishers have been waiting for this situation to stabilize before committing to such a serious undertaking as a whole book on the subject.

However, the pace of change shows no signs of abating. If anything, now that e-books have come to the attention of the wider populace, the rate of growth is accelerating, with large collections of texts in e-formats becoming available to students, public library users and consumers alike, and with the revolution in internet-enabled mobile devices meaning that e-texts can be accessed at times and in locations that would have been impossible just a few years ago.

Therefore, the editors of this book felt that it would be timely to bring together a selection of practical information, best practice and case studies which would be of assistance to information and library professionals who are managing collections of e-books right now, even though it may be that some of the finer details will be out of date by the time of publication. We hope that it will be of interest to those who are just beginning to dip their toes in the water, as well as those who have been involved with e-books for years, and are interested to know what is happening at other libraries and in other sectors than their own. We also hope that it will be of interest to a wider audience, ranging from students of information and library studies to publishers who may currently be producing e-books or looking to do so in the future.

To bring together this work, we have drawn upon the expertise of a range of authors from diverse backgrounds, each of whom adds a valuable perspective. Inevitably, there is some duplication of subject matter across the chapters. However, since each can stand as an individual piece, we feel that it has been valuable to retain this cross-over, particularly where different sectors of the library community have approached aspects of the management of e-books from their own distinct viewpoint.

Following a scene-setting introduction from Chris Armstrong and Ray Lonsdale in which the history of e-books is described, the book is divided into six parts. The first part broadly examines how e-books come to be, and how they are sold or made accessible. The second part takes an in-depth look at the management of e-texts in three different sectors: public libraries, further education (FE) libraries and higher education (HE) libraries. The third part concentrates on the practical side of delivering e-books to readers, from cataloguing and technical issues to training and support. The fourth part addresses reader engagement, acknowledging that users must find e-books a valuable addition to their experience of leisure, study or work in order for it to be worthwhile for libraries to make them available. The fifth part looks to the future, asking two questions of our authors: 'What needs to change before e-books become universally and easily used?' and 'What will the e-book landscape look like in ten years time?' Finally, the sixth part offers a range of useful guidelines and reference material that we hope will be of practical assistance, including a list of very handy 'Top tips' from the contributing authors. Throughout the book, the authors offer web links and references to further reading for those who wish to research specific areas in more depth.

Acknowledgements

The editors wish to acknowledge the very substantial time and effort that the individual contributors have dedicated to this work, particularly as they have been attempting to write definitively about a topic where there are as yet no definitive standards.

Kate would like to thank the senior managers and staff of the University of Surrey Library for their support, and in particular the Resources Team who have ripped up their procedures and started again on several occasions during the University's long (and sometimes stormy) relationship with e-books. She would also like to thank Richard Price, without whose moral support and superb proofreading skills this book would definitely not have come to exist. Richard is now without doubt the only person working in the transport industry who is also an expert on e-books!

Virginia would like to thank her former employer John McKenzie, Manager of the Joint Information Systems Committee (JISC) Regional Support Centre (RSC) South West, for allowing her to embark on this e-book voyage and all the learning resource centre managers who gave their time and opinions. She would also like to acknowledge the support of her current employer Petroc and in particular her line manager Pené Prior for encouraging the work to its conclusion, and Robert Power for his support and forbearance as the book evolved!

Contributors

Chris Armstrong runs a consultancy, research and training company, Information Automation Limited (IAL). IAL specializes in library use of electronic resources and in electronic publishing, and Chris's research interests centre on electronic access to information – online and CD-ROM databases and internet resources. He has also worked as a research officer at the College of Librarianship Wales, now known as the Department of Information Studies, University of Wales Aberystwyth, and he continues to be involved in research projects with the department. He was a member of the Joint Information Systems Commitee (JISC) e-Book Working Group, and has undertaken training and consultancy work internationally on e-books in libraries, including work on the JISC National e-Books Observatory Project. Other projects have included a two-year Carnegie Foundation, pan-African project on the development of e-resources within university libraries, alongside Ray Lonsdale (fellow contributor to this book). Chris is a regular writer, and sits on the editorial boards of three professional journals.

Lee Bryant has been eLearning Training Manager at City of Bristol College since 2009. He has worked in the further education library and information sector since 1997 and became learning resource centre manager at City of Bristol College in 2000. His specialist interests are marketing and publicity and the evaluation of services. Until recently, he was a member of the national committee of CoFHE, the Colleges of Further and Higher Education subgroup of the Chartered Institute of

Library and Information Professionals (CILIP), and Chair of CoFHE South West.

Sue Caporn is Learning Resources Service Manager at City of Bristol College, where she has managed the learning resource centres since 1995. Previously she worked in special libraries. She introduced e-resources to the college soon after her arrival, and has a special interest in extending access to e-books, as well as in developing information skills programmes. From 2007 to 2009 Sue was a member of the Steering Group of JISC RSC South West.

James Clay is Information and Learning Technology (ILT) and Learning Resources Manager at Gloucestershire College, where he has been employed since November 2006. He is responsible for e-learning, libraries, digital and online resources and the strategic direction of the college in relation to the use of learning technologies. James' current interests include research on learning with handheld devices. Previously he was Director of the Western Colleges Consortium, where he was responsible for the development of e-learning, and prior to that he delivered hands-on science education and designed educational websites for At-Bristol, a Millennium project within the Harbourside of Bristol, and spent ten years as a lecturer in business and economics, employing a variety of learning technologies.

Joel Claypool of Morgan & Claypool Publishers has had a long career in publishing, encompassing roles from sales representative to editor and executive publisher. He has worked for several high profile scholarly publishers including Macmillan, Elsevier, CRC Press and Academic Press. In 2002 he joined Mike Morgan, founder and former president of Morgan Kaufmann Publishers, in starting a new company, Morgan & Claypool. M&C publishes 50 to 100 page peer-reviewed 'lectures' in engineering and computer science (the Synthesis Digital Library) and more recently in the life sciences (the Colloquium Digital Library). These short monographs are produced and made available primarily as e-books, but can be printed out in full by the user, or ordered as print-on-demand copies, effectively reversing the current process followed by most publishers, whereby the printed copy is the primary version.

Timothy Collinson is Faculty Librarian for Technology at the University of Portsmouth. He started his professional life in the Library of the Royal Geographical Society – a highlight of which was giving Michael Palin, now President of the Society, his library tour. Timothy then moved to the academic world of what would become Southampton Solent University, where he became subject librarian for technology. Among other things he was jointly responsible for 'The Alternative Library', a sideways vision of information services arrived at by employing creative thinking techniques. Timothy's particular interests are Web 2.0 developments, e-books and mobile technologies.

Jim Dooley is Head of Collection Services at the University of California, Merced (UC Merced), where he is responsible for collection development and management as well as technical services. He is Chair of the University of California Libraries Collection Development Committee and past chair of the Heads of Technical Services group. He has presented on various topics related to electronic resources at the American Library Association Annual Conference and the Charleston Library Conference. Prior to joining UC Merced in 2003, he held various positions in cataloguing and acquisitions in the J. Willard Marriott Library at the University of Utah.

Karen Foster has worked at Yeovil College as the Head of Learning Centres since October 2007, and leads the development of e-learning within the college as well as managing the learning resource centre. She previously worked at South Devon College in a similar role. Karen has a keen interest in e-learning and the ways that this can enhance the learner's experience in both further and higher education. She is always keen to investigate new and innovative ways in which the centre can encourage independent learning and research through the use of technology.

Karen Gravett has worked in the information profession since 2004 and is currently Academic Liaison Librarian for the Faculty of Health and Medical Sciences at the University of Surrey, where she is responsible for the delivery of subject specific support for learning, teaching and research. Karen's previous posts have included cataloguing and metadata and liaison support roles at the University of Surrey and Royal Holloway, University of London (RHUL). Karen has interests in electronic information and resources, developments in learning and teaching, and new technologies.

Anna Grigson is currently E-Resources Manager at Royal Holloway, University of London, where she is responsible for managing the Library's collections of online resources, including collections of over a quarter of a million e-books. She has a background in academic libraries, having previously worked in the e-resources team and as a liaison librarian at the University of Westminster, and as a music librarian at King's College, London.

Silvia Gstrein is project manager for the eBooks on Demand (EOD) network within the Department for Digitization and Digital Preservation at Innsbruck University, Austria. Since 2002 she has managed several national and international IT-related projects in the area of e-learning and digitization. Currently she is involved in several European Union (EU) projects such as ARROW (Accessible Registries of Rights Information and Orphan Works towards Europeana), EuropeanaTravel and Europeana-Connect as well as being EOD Co-ordinator.

Virginia Havergal is Learning Centres and e-Resources Manager at Petroc, a further education college in Devon. Prior to this role she was an e-Learning Advisor with JISC, with a particular focus on Learning Resources. Virginia specializes in library and learning resources, particularly e-resources such as e-books and e-journals. As both a qualified librarian and teacher her work has spanned over 30 years within the education sector, including work in public and school libraries and in further and higher education. She is also an experienced trainer and e-learning consultant, having run workshops for a number of national organizations within the learning and skills sector. Her research interests include informal learning and student interaction with e-resources focusing on accessibility and inclusion.

Ray Lonsdale is a Reader in Information Studies at Aberystwyth University. Formerly head of Education and Youth Services at Knowsley

Authority, Ray now specializes in the field of collection management and electronic libraries, and has directed a number of research projects focusing on e-books, most recently the JISC National e-Books Observatory Project. He has also been responsible for international training and consultancy work in e-resource collection management, including a recent two-year Carnegie Foundation, pan-African project on the development of e-resource collections within university libraries, alongside Chris Armstrong (fellow contributor to this book). Ray has published widely in the academic and professional press.

Günter Mühlberger is Head of the Department for Digitization and Digital Preservation at the University of Innsbruck. The focus of his professional interest is the design and implementation of innovative digital library technology and services. Günter has initiated and managed several EU projects such as LAURIN for the digitization of newspaper clippings, METAe – the Metadata Engine project for optical character recognition (OCR) and layout analysis of historical printed material – as well as BOOKS2U! and DoD (Digitization on Demand), the predecessor of the successful eBooks on Demand network. Currently, he is sub-project leader and member of the executive board for the IMPACT project (Improving Access to Text), funded under the European Commission's (EC's) Seventh Framework Programme (FP7).

Martin Palmer is Principal Officer for Essex County Council's Libraries Department. He has worked there since the mid-1970s in a variety of roles, including the introduction of e-book services as part of a Co-East project funded by the Laser Foundation in 2003. Martin is also a member of the Operations Board of Book Industry Communication (BIC), working to develop and promote standards in the use of technology in the library and book trades.

Kate Price is Head of E-Strategy and Resources at the University of Surrey. Having begun her professional career in further education librarianship, she has fulfilled her current role since 2003, and is responsible for the team that acquires and catalogues information resources in electronic, print and audiovisual formats, as well as for managing the strategic shift from print to online information resources. Kate is a member of the national committee of UKSG (United Kingdom Serials Group), an organization that exists to connect the information community and encourage the exchange of ideas on scholarly communication, and has chaired the Education Subcommittee of UKSG since 2009.

Emma Ransley has worked at the Learning Centre at Yeovil College since July 2006, initially as a subject librarian and currently as Deputy Manager. Emma began her library career in 2001 working as a library assistant in the public library service for the Royal Borough of Kingston upon Thames, and then worked at Kingston University as a senior library assistant and student advisor. She is particularly interested in improving the experience of learners at Yeovil College through the provision of information literacy workshops and the promotion of e-resources.

Anne Worden is Faculty Librarian for Humanities and Social Sciences (HSS) at the University of Portsmouth. She was previously languages librarian at both the Polytechnic of Central London and at Portsmouth. As the HSS Faculty is very keen to produce information literate graduates, Anne carries out a substantial amount of teaching and training, covering topics such as the use of e-resources, the evaluation of web resources and bibliographic referencing. Anne is also a committee member of the French Studies Library Group, which acts as a focus for librarians and others concerned with the provision of library resources and services in French studies in the UK.

Editors' note

It has become apparent as we have collated the contributions to this book that terminology has not yet reached the point of standardization, as befits a rapidly evolving area with applications to a diverse range of library services. Hence we have encountered many variants of the term 'e-book', as well as differing uses of the terms 'supplier' and 'vendor'. Different sectors of the library community also use variable terminology to denote the people who use their services: 'customers', 'users', 'learners', 'students', 'clients', 'readers' and so on.

Where it seemed sensible to do so, we have introduced an element of standardization, and hence the particular spelling of 'e-book' which has been used throughout the text. (That is, apart from where the term is a component of a service name or cited in a reference; in which cases the original formatting has been adhered to, as with '*eBooks* on Demand'.)

However, in other instances we have chosen to retain the terminology as given by the individual authors, in recognition of the usual practice within the sector in which they work. In these cases the context should make the meaning apparent. Notwithstanding slight differences in terminology, the information and practical advice given in the book is largely transferable between sectors and therefore should be of use to the library services community as a whole.

Kate Price and Virginia Havergal

Introduction

Chris Armstrong and Ray Lonsdale

Although Vannevar Bush (1945, 106), President Roosevelt's science advisor, wrote in the mid-1940s in his seminal *Atlantic Monthly* article of a device in which books could be stored, as well as other documents, it was nearly three decades before the first electronic books began to appear. In the late 1960s Alan Kay developed his Dynabook concept, seeing the notebook computer as an extension of the print medium: the technology was not in place but Bush's idea of a handheld reader was affirmed. Despite this early emphasis on portability, it was not until the 1980s that e-books moved far beyond the online reading of texts held on a remote server, and then it was simply a case of delivery on CD-ROMs and floppy disks; e-book readers came much later.

The generally accepted birth of the e-book lies with the Gutenberg archive of electronic texts, which was started in 1971 by Michael Hart. It began with volunteers keying in the US Declaration of Independence, and then the Bill of Rights, quickly followed by the whole US Constitution; The Bible was added book by book, and then the works of William Shakespeare, one play at a time. Project Gutenberg continues today by scanning older works, with the same philosophy of encouraging the creation, easy distribution and use of e-books.

Other text archives (or collections of free e-books) were developed later, for example, the Oxford Text Archive which opened in 1976, and the EText Center at the University of Virginia Library, set up in 1992.

Although the term 'e-book' was not used to describe them at the time, many reference books found their way onto CD-ROM in the 1980s, either marketed as databases or simply as '[title] on CD-ROM'. Examples include the *Oxford English Dictionary* on CD-ROM, Microsoft's Bookshelf (including *Roget's Thesaurus, Bartlett's Familiar Quotations* and the *World Almanac and Book of Facts* from the Central Intelligence Agency [CIA]) and the *Bible Library* on CD-ROM.

Also in the 1980s, university presses in the USA began to engage with the concept of electronic publishing, at least partly 'as a result of fears about the future of the [print] scholarly monograph' (Armstrong and Lonsdale, 1998, 18). The 1990s saw an international rise of both electronic reference and electronic fiction publishing, as well as, in the middle of the decade, the emergence of aggregators such as NetLibrary, Questia and ebrary. Similar to e-journal aggregators, these companies acquired the rights to titles from many publishers and brought them together in subject collections which customers could then directly license from the aggregator. Slightly later, collections of reference works were aggregated: XRefer Plus (which is now Credo Reference) and KnowUK, for example. From about this time onwards, commercial publishers (such as Penguin, Routledge and Oxford University Press) began making titles available electronically, and large numbers of individual e-books and limited publishers' lists began to appear on the web. Textbooks had been slow to appear but began to be made available from the early 2000s, and some publishers (for example, McGraw-Hill) now enable academics to generate personalized textbooks using chapters from a number of other titles in addition to their own material.

By the turn of the century it was clear that both publishers and libraries were treating the medium very seriously, and clear interest was evident in primary, secondary and tertiary education as well as in the legal and health sectors. In the UK, the Joint Information Systems Committee (JISC) of the Further and Higher Education Funding Councils had set up an e-Book Working Group in the early 1990s to support its collection development team, which has made available individual e-book titles or collections to tertiary institutions and also – in the last few years – to schools. Over the period, JISC has also commissioned a number of e-book research projects including, most recently, the National e-Book Observatory (NeBO), which includes a study on the management and economic impact of e-textbook business models on publishers, e-book aggregators and universities.

Effectively, JISC has always acted as a consortium for the education sector while the Museums, Libraries and Archives Council has a limited but similar role for public libraries in England. At the same time, consortia such as North West Academic Libraries (NoWAL) and Southern Universities Purchasing Consortium (SUPC) have made available substantial e-book collections to their member institutions at much reduced rates, more recently joining forces to purchase both e-book collections and single titles through a Joint Consortium Book Agreement. These consortia have together probably been the strongest driver for commercial e-book adoption. A related consortial activity has been the EU 'books2ebooks' or eBooks on Demand service described later in the book (see Chapter 3).

As has been suggested, fiction was being made available online from the early days of e-books and grew in popularity during the 1990s. Until very recently, there appears to have been a clear but artificial divide between fiction, which seems to be marketed towards individuals through purchase and downloading, and non-fiction, scholarly and reference material that is targeted at institutions by way of subscriptions, or other forms of licensing. Perhaps most typically, fiction has been made available from online bookshops and publishers which may offer it in a range of download formats to suit both computers and e-book reader devices. OverDrive – now used by over 20 public library authorities in the UK – flies in the face of the artificial divide and offers both fiction and non-fiction titles for virtual loan to library users, who may borrow using e-book readers.

Slightly behind the growth of e-books has been the growth of e-book reader devices. This short history suggests that e-books may be read on either handheld devices or on computers, but that has only been true since 1998 when the Rocket e-book and the Cybook became available. A second, more powerful, generation of readers was launched in 2006 with the iRex iLiad and the Sony Reader. This generation uses e-ink technology to give both exceptionally good battery life and visual (monochrome) screen clarity; these readers also offer the possibility of carrying several hundred titles in your pocket. More recently Apple's iPad appears to represent a further contender. Inextricably linked with downloading and devices (and to a lesser extent with reading online) are the format wars: there are at least a dozen formats of which variants of

Adobe PDF (Portable Document Format) and EPUB (electronic publication) seem the most popular – many e-book readers are compatible with more than one. Detailed discussion of e-book readers appears in several chapters in this book (see particularly Chapter 10), and consideration of the issues surrounding access is covered later in this introduction.

As the availability of commercial e-books has grown, so too has that of free e-books, with huge numbers made available for downloading or reading online. Free e-books can be found through archives and collections resulting from digitization projects, through gateways and specialized search engines, and from a small number of publishers, while some are made available as individual titles. While those resulting from digitization have the same publisher pedigree as their originals, other free e-books may suffer from a lack of quality control or from revenue-generating advertisements around the edges of pages; other issues such as managing access are taken up in a later chapter (see Chapter 4). As with their formally published cousins, there is no bibliographic control of free e-titles so, as we shall see later, sourcing new material remains problematic. A guide to free e-book sources is currently in preparation (Armstrong, 2010).

Thus far the e-books that have been discussed have been almost exclusively digitized versions of print books. Apart from convenience, one of the over-riding positive attributes highlighted by the NeBO project was the possibility of added-value features within e-books. Features found in the interface (such as note-taking) were less valued, but the possibility of built-in definitions, interactive exercises, rotating or enlarging images, and varying the data on which a graph is based were seen as invaluable. These attributes can only come with books designed (or significantly re-designed) for the medium: books which are born digital. It is worth noting at this point that this fundamental variation in the constitution of an e-book will necessarily also bring about a major change in the relationship between authors and publishers. Many born digital e-books are now available individually but few are available in the large collections available from aggregators or publishers. An excellent example of born digital fiction was produced by Penguin with the *We Tell Stories* website, while a long-standing example of a monograph is *City Sites*.

It is worth noting that a sub-genre of e-books, the social or networked book, is becoming increasingly important. These may be either simply developed within a social network such as a weblog, allowing readers to access, and comment on, chapters as they are written (for example L. Lee Lowe's *Mortal Ghost*) or developed from the outset using specialist software so that the text can be adjusted according to readers' input (for example McKenzie Wark's *GAM3R 7H30RY*). The end product may or may not be published subsequently by a conventional publisher. The Institute for the Future of the Book has released CommentPress, a free, open-source theme for the WordPress blog engine designed to allow paragraph-by-paragraph commenting in the margins of a text. Of more interest to libraries are social reading interfaces such as BookGlutton, which allow classes or reading groups to read, comment upon and discuss an e-book communally in real time.

It may be useful to reflect on the e-book provenance described above in order to understand the boundaries of the remainder of this book. What emerges is that e-books may be digitized or born digital, may be held locally or on a remote server, may come in a range of file formats, may span a range of genres, may come singly or in collections, and are designed to be read on conventional computers or using handheld readers. Our definition is that an e-book is any content that is recognizably 'book-like', regardless of size, origin or composition, but excluding serial publications, made available electronically for reference or reading on any device that includes a screen.

The array of commercial and free e-book publishing presents significant challenges for librarians in all sectors in terms of their management, promotion and use. Regardless of their origins and make up, the use of commercial e-books as provided for libraries will almost certainly be governed by licences and the complexities of these licences and of the business models they define mean that their administration presents librarians with a considerable degree of concern; consequently several chapters in this book touch on pricing models and the nature of licences, with reference to their administration, compliance and provision for archiving texts.

Business models referred to later in the book include outright purchase, sometimes known as perpetual access, and subscriptions, and a number of issues are raised around each, many of which are highlighted in the checklist in Part 6. Some aggregators will not deal with individual titles, and this may also be true of some publishers – meaning that the licence covers a package or bundle of titles. Licences giving access to large collections may imply a low per title cost while purchase gives perpetual access at higher per title cost. However, often the library has little or no control over the titles included and if some or most of a collection is either not core to the library's collection or irrelevant, the real per title cost may be higher. A mid-2010 report noted comments about a preference for one-off payment models as it is easier to budget, and ownership being important, as purchasing and collection development can then be managed in much the same manner as they are for print. Subscription models were preferred when e-books have frequent new editions, although it seems rare for new editions or updated content to be provided either automatically or free. No reported comments made reference to caps or usage limits which may circumscribe ownership (Eduserv, 2010).

The initial licence – often presented as a *fait accompli* or accepted as it stands owing to pressure of work – should actually be treated as an invitation to negotiate, and must be carefully examined and possibly amended before it is signed. Librarians should bear in mind the fact that licences may over-ride copyright exceptions and that signing such a licence may sacrifice their library's statutory rights under its national copyright legislation (Eblida, 2001). The licence will also contain a number of definitions (e.g. 'authorized users' or 'secure network') and it is important to ensure that these match the planned use. On the other side of the coin, the licence will bind the supplier to certain commitments, such as continuity of access – particularly important where aggregators or library suppliers, standing midway between the library and the publisher, may lose their rights to a title. Questions which are highlighted in a number of chapters include determining whether the supplier is using an archiving service such as CLOCKSS (Controlled LOCKSS [Lots of Copies Keep Stuff Safe]) or Portico; whether the library will receive notification of withdrawals in sufficient time to alert users; whether users can print, download, e-mail and copy-and-paste content; and whether the library is able to offer titles via interlibrary loan or to lend them for use on handheld e-book readers or laptops. In some cases extending the licence to e-book readers may involve additional cost; in other cases it may be only possible to pre-load library-owned readers. If the supplier has no escrow or archive in place, it is important to determine whether the licence allows the library to make archive copies and to consider whether the technical capacity is in place for this additional activity.

The functionality and elegance of the interface is dealt with later in this Introduction, but it is important to know whether it incorporates digital rights management (DRM), used by publishers and aggregators to protect the rights of the copyright holder. Many library users find its use problematic, particularly as it varies from platform to platform, and one author notes that there is a need to balance the restrictions against the needs of the user as it often inhibits legitimate use. It would almost certainly also prevent the sharing of e-books, for example in a study group (although ProQuest Safari has recently introduced this possibility).

Licences place the onus on the institution to ensure that their terms are followed, so authentication of users and access management on a secure network is a prerequisite discussed later by several authors.

The establishment of e-book collections has exacerbated the existing challenges for collection managers working with e-resources and Information Technology (IT) departments, and indeed they pose new challenges. The following sections explore the nature of some of the most prominent of these.

While it is fair to say that IT problems do not emanate only from e-book collections – other e-resources, such as e-journals, may produce similar issues – e-books are relatively new on the scene and the access and reading software may incorporate particular functions (such as DRM) that make IT issues more acute.

Difficulties in connecting to the e-book collections from remote locations and the complications of logging on to the system are often mentioned as disincentives for users, and several chapters touch on this (see, for example, Chapter 6). The need to ensure system security is not only a requirement of the publishers, but also a concern of IT departments. Those of a public or school library's parent authority tend to find that the library service's desire to offer their resources to an audience comprising all users is a fundamental challenge to the IT department's main role of protecting the security of the council's network.

The time taken for either the software or the book to load – as with web pages – also acts to irritate users and can cause problems in libraries when workstations are abandoned by a user without logging off correctly. Although the practice has largely disappeared, the need to download specialist software add-ons in order to read e-books stored on a remote publisher's server has been the source of considerable problems for libraries over the years. Some e-book formats still require their own local software (for example, DX Reader), and even where no purpose-built software is required, it may be necessary to load the Java runtime environment. In many institutions it is not possible to download the software over a network so each workstation has to be upgraded individually. Some security applications, such as firewalls (which are designed to protect computer networks from unauthorized access), pop-up blockers (which are intended to prevent unwanted advertisements appearing on the computer screen) and anti-virus software, may also interfere with e-book service interfaces; even Adobe PDF files can be problematic as not every library runs the latest software versions. This is not only a problem for small libraries: not every library is able to influence the institution's or the parent authority's IT policy in these respects. Experience suggests that the inter-relationship between the library and the IT department is critical, and must be fostered. Formalizing it in a service level agreement is often the best approach, enabling any conflicts to be understood and handled.

For those librarians charged with the responsibility of managing e-book collections, a range of issues are presented, only some of which are unique to the e-book format. Within academic institutions, the primary respon-sibility for selection, and consequently the major source of demand for e-books, remains the library (Armstrong and Lonsdale, 2009a). In this sector, the major factors that drive the need for e-books include students in remote locations who require 24/7 access, demand for multiple simul-taneous access to high use texts, and – where they are available – an array of added-value features. Reading lists themselves generate awareness and uptake of e-books if links to them are included. A number of the benefits identified in academic libraries are mirrored in the literature of public library provision, and throughout this book authors from both sectors explore in considerable detail the benefits and constraints of the e-format.

While there is evidence to demonstrate the need to develop academic staff's awareness of selection sources for e-books, there is some indication of growing demand from this quarter. The NeBO study also revealed that academic librarians perceive a small but significant increase in the selection of e-books by students, largely postgraduates. In the USA there has been a growing emphasis on patron selection within university libraries, where the decision to purchase an e-book title is driven by the user accessing the bibliographic record of the e-book in the online public access catalogue (OPAC) a minimum number of times. The mechanics of this approach, the financial implications, and the value and constraints are explored in some depth later in this book. Given the comparatively recent development of e-book collections within the public library sector it is not surprising that there is a dearth of information surrounding the selection of e-books and the role of the user – one might anticipate significant patron-driven selection in the future as the e-book reader and mobile technology market expands.

One important field of selection that has been identified by most library sectors concerns the need to establish selection criteria not only for the evaluation of individual e-books themselves, but also to assist in the identification of the most appropriate aggregator or publisher for the library. Given the proliferation of these companies and the varying business models discussed above, it is clear that choosing the most appropriate supplier offers new challenges for collection managers. Several of the chapters of this book enumerate and discuss the issues that need to be addressed, and offer valuable pragmatic criteria for librarians working in the academic and public sectors. Other potentially useful initiatives to aid selection concern the appearance of the e-book along with print books in book suppliers' online selection tools and approval plans and, again, these initiatives are considered by several of this book's authors

With respect to the selection of new titles, the lack of systematic bibliographical control of e-books is a matter of particular concern to librarians in all sectors in the UK, and one that has been reported throughout the literature since the inception of e-book collections within academic libraries at the end of the 1990s (Lonsdale and Armstrong, 2001; Armstrong, Edwards and Lonsdale, 2002; Armstrong and Lonsdale, 2005). Although the UK Legal Deposit Libraries Act 2003 was extended to embrace certain electronic formats, the enabling nature of this law means that new e-formats including e-books must be included through secondary legislation, and thus few e-book titles have been included in reality. Given the significance of the availability of free e-books mentioned earlier, the issue of control becomes more acute.

In the absence of a national bibliographical resource, librarians have recourse to using a disparate array of bibliographical and non-bibliographical sources to identify the existence of new commercially available titles as well as free e-books. However, research studies (Armstrong and Lonsdale, 2005) as well as anecdotal evidence gleaned from training workshops conducted with librarians from all library sectors in the UK reveal that many librarians remain unaware of these sources and services. To help facilitate an increased awareness, we have developed a bibliographical 'map' that outlines the major approaches that might be considered, and this is offered below together with a few examples of specific bibliographical resources.

Publishers' and aggregators' advertising, websites and catalogues constitute the most obvious and most highly used sources; indeed, many public or smaller academic libraries may rely solely on their chosen aggregator for new titles. Over the past decade there has been recognition by this sector of their responsibility to enhance their alerting services and, in some instances, aggregators have introduced an effective current awareness service. However, there are a few caveats – librarians still complain that there is a need for publishers to be more proactive in informing libraries about new e-titles (Armstrong and Lonsdale, 2009a), and some poorly designed publishers' catalogues still present challenges for librarians in their endeavours to locate new e-book titles!

For libraries which are already subscribing to e-journals, **subscription agents** such as SwetsWise offer a consolidated one-shop approach to identifying and selecting new e-book titles. Increasingly the major **union catalogues** (for example Digital Book Index and OCLC WorldCat [Online Computer Library Center World Catalog]) and **book trade bibliographies** (for example, Nielsen and Global Books in Print) are offering comprehensive listings of e-book titles and these constitute a significant source for those libraries that subscribe to them. Interestingly, Digital Book Index also covers an increasing number of free e-book titles. Note should be made of Eduserv's recently launched e-Book Finder, which is built on top of OCLC's xISBN service, which is in turn built on WorldCat and affords an effective means of searching for e-book titles, using the International Standard Book Number (ISBN).

Within the public library sector in particular, **internet bookshops** such as Amazon and **specialist e-book suppliers,** for example eBooks.com and LibWise, are proving to be a vital source for tracing new international fiction and general non-fiction, and the range of specialist suppliers is increasing greatly.

Understandably, considerable use is now being made of **search engines**, both general, for example Google Books, and also the more specialist, for example Inkmesh. **Professional and trade journals** are beginning to provide increased exposure to e-books, both in terms of listings and – in particular – reviews, and journals such as *The Bookseller* and the ICT@SLA section in *The School Librarian* are proving useful sources for public and school librarians.

For those working in university and college libraries, **educational organizations** also provide useful lists of newly available titles, for example the JISC Collections website has periodic lists of new e-books that they are trialling, and the JISC Regional Support Centres offer guidance for FE librarians. There is evidence that within this sector academic librarians also consult such sources as **subject gateways** (for example Intute) and packages specifically designed for **virtual learning environments** (VLEs).

The problems posed by free or open access e-book publishing were raised earlier in this chapter and, for those libraries who wish to develop such collections, there are a growing number of selection tools, including:

- E-books Directory
- The Assayer (which also contains reviews)
- Global Text Project
- Textbook Revolution.

There is ample evidence in the literature to suggest that librarians need to call on the support of a variety of more general and serendipitous approaches, including:

- discussion/mailing lists
- other library websites
- colleagues' websites (for example, Digital Librarian)

- newsletters (for example, eBooks Just Published)
- professional associations
- conferences/exhibitions
- trusted sources (for example, trainers, academics encountered at workshops and so on).

The literature that focuses on the development of e-book collections reveals certain fundamental changes in collection management activities. A common theme concerns the need for libraries to re-evaluate their staffing responsibilities and workflow patterns. Although there are commonalities, a myriad of approaches can be taken – often determined by the library sector – and considerable attention is paid to these topics in the ensuing chapters of this book.

Another critical dimension of collection management concerns the means by which institutions facilitate access to e-books. Libraries are presented with several access options, each possessing individual advantages and challenges. Across all the library sectors, internationally, there is considerable evidence to show that the OPAC is the preferred way of accessing e-resources and e-books by users, especially within academic libraries (Armstrong and Lonsdale, 2009a, Mundle, 2009). Given that many librarians see the OPAC as the most obvious access route, it is perhaps not surprising that, in most cases, the OPAC is also the recommended route in library training sessions. However, getting e-books into the OPAC presents a series of challenges, especially as the institution may be subscribing to many hundreds or thousands of titles within a single collection, and libraries report that changes to cataloguing policy are frequently necessitated. Although publishers and aggregators will usually provide MARC records (MAchine Readable Cataloguing records) for e-books, the literature is littered with evidence to show the problems that must still be addressed, many of which are associated with the quality of the records, the mode of updating and the deletion of records. Visibility of the e-book within the OPAC is another fraught issue and has been shown to influence the use or non-use of e-books (Armstrong and Lonsdale, 2009a). Thus, considerable effort is being put into the management of links. All these issues surrounding the cataloguing of e-books receive in-depth consideration in this book, with authors providing examples of practice within the different library sectors.

Whilst the use of the OPAC is preferred, considerable use is still made of the library's e-resources website in public and academic libraries. There are, nevertheless, certain constraints that must be addressed. One concerns the complexity of the structure of some of these sites – an issue reported on in some depth in the context of UK university and college libraries (Banwell et al., 2004), and which still appears to impact on use today; another centres on the fact that such portals may provide access only to collections of e-books rather than to individual titles.

As many academic libraries now offer a federated searching option, this may constitute another way of gaining access to e-books. There can be a considerable variety of e-books available through the federated search engines, including reference, textbooks and free e-books. However, there remain significant issues to be confronted, including – as with portals – the efficacy of the federated search in identifying individual e-book titles and the content within them rather than simply collections; something that receives due consideration later in this book. Perhaps the most challenging issue reported in recent studies of the use of e-books in universities in the UK concerns the apparent lack of awareness among users of the existence of federated searching (or what it is), and the confusion about what distinguishes it from the use of the OPAC (Armstrong and Lonsdale, 2009a).

Within university, college and, increasingly, school libraries, an important route to e-resources is the VLE – not least because academic championing of resources is probably one of the most effective ways of increasing use. Evidence taken from recent studies in the UK shows a strong correlation between page views of e-books and recommendations made by academics through links placed in the VLE (CIBER, 2008; Armstrong and Lonsdale, 2009a). The value of the VLE in further and higher education and the issues surrounding the embedding of e-books within it are well articulated in this book. An additional issue of concern that arises again and again in the literature (and in professional discussions) concerns the fact that the library may be excluded from the institutional deliberations on VLE development and content, and may even be ignored when it comes to providing links to resources (Armstrong and Lonsdale, 2009a). In some instances, it may not even be possible for librarians to access the VLE pages of academic departments, which may result in inappropriate copying or linking. It is essential, therefore, that the library be involved in any strategic, institutional e-learning discussions as well as in the day-to-day administration of teaching modules in the VLE.

Another potential means of gaining access to e-books is through the use of Google and other search engines. Librarians do need to respond to their users' inevitable use of these tools to find e-resources, and should facilitate OpenURL linking through search engines as well as library-supplied bibliographic databases as another mode of access to full-text resources.

Given the emphasis currently placed on the development of e-book readers as discussed at the outset of this chapter, there is extensive and ongoing debate in the profession about the practicalities of providing library access to reader devices. There are numerous issues to be resolved surrounding licensing, routines for loaning readers, procedures for loading content, access, security and DRM. The potential of e-book readers in secondary and tertiary education is great and receives due consideration later in this book. Up until recently there was little evidence of e-book readers being provided within the academic sector (Armstrong and Lonsdale, 2009a), although Princeton University undertook a semester long trial of the Amazon Kindle with mixed results (Cliat, 2010), and several university libraries in the UK have now begun to lend them on a smaller scale. In contrast, public libraries could find this a more pressing issue as so much fiction is available in e-book reader formats. The literature on the library's role in providing and managing e-book readers is scant (Clark, 2009; Drinkwater, 2010), and in 2010 there has been a constant flow of discussion within professional blogs such as TeleRead, which might offer the best source of current practice internationally.

The appearance of significant e-book collections only serves to underline the importance of promoting e-resources in general and, as we will see, whilst activity is reported across all sectors even within academic libraries there is evidence of the need to intensify promotion and marketing of texts in e-formats (Armstrong and Lonsdale, 2009b).

Ideally, the promotion of e-resources should be conceived within a strategic framework that embraces not only the library but the wider institution – for example, academic staff and students, and even other relevant players who are outside the institution or authority such as publishers and aggregators (Gold Leaf, 2003). The literature on promotion tends to focus on e-resources within academic libraries, and there is evidence to support the existence of such strategic thinking, although it appears to be confined largely to activities offered through the library (Schimdt, 2007; Woods, 2007). There is a small, but growing, body of evidence to demonstrate that libraries are beginning to formulate strategies for promoting e-books specifically (Pan, Byrne and Murphy, 2009).

A detailed account of the methods which academic libraries might employ to promote e-books is offered by Lonsdale and Armstrong (2010) who report on the findings of the NeBO study, and who place their critique within the context of international practice. The array of approaches in evidence at the point of writing could be classified as traditional with a strong emphasis on induction and information literacy training, approaches that may already be familiar to the reader. The significance attached to the OPAC as a means of promoting awareness of e-books is reported widely in the literature. However, awareness of the library's website as a promotional tool appears to be scant (Armstrong and Lonsdale, 2009b) – an issue that might be worthy of attention by the profession. Many of the approaches delineated in their article, especially training, receive detailed consideration by librarians from the USA and UK in this book. Although the literature on promotion of e-books within public, school and special libraries is comparatively scarce, it is intriguing to note that an array of other promotional methods are employed including the use of Facebook, pupil podcasts, blogs, dummy or surrogate e-books shelved with the main print collections, e-resource champions, plasma screens, road shows and library goody bags containing freebies advertising e-books. Further practical examples of promotional techniques used by libraries can be found in Chapters 5, 8, 9 and 12 in this book.

There is a strong, widely held and long established belief within university and college libraries that academics do play a hugely significant role in encouraging the take-up of e-resources among students, and increasingly this role is now focusing on e-books (Taylor, 2007; Wilkins, 2007). It is implicit in this belief that academics should receive appropriate training, and the challenges that this presents to librarians are discussed by us (Lonsdale and Armstrong, 2010) and also by several authors within this book. Additionally, some universities perceive an institution-wide responsibility to raise awareness of library services and resources, with their continuing professional development departments offering training for academic staff in e-resource use.

The strategic framework for promotion should also acknowledge the potential role that e-book publishers and aggregators have to play, whether in the offer of trials or use of the increasing array of promotional material and training packages. Whilst there are some thorny issues surrounding the use of these materials, such as the belief that the library should not promote one publisher over another (Lonsdale and Armstrong, 2010), there appears to be a strong consensus within the profession about the value and legitimacy of their contribution, and aggregators have expressed frustration that libraries do not make better use of their materials.

In developing a coherent and comprehensive strategy, librarians should give cognizance to the role which some other bodies or organizations might play in supporting library authorities and institutions in their endeavours to promote e-books, such as professional bodies (like the School Library Association), those with a national remit for e-resource development, for example JISC in the UK, or bodies with a remit for library strategy, such as CyMAL (Museums Archives and Libraries Wales) in Wales.

Implicit in promotion is the goal of increasing the use of e-books. How e-books are read and issues associated with their interfaces have received comparatively little attention previously, but have been specifically addressed by the NeBO project and the authors of several chapters in this book. The NeBO report on e-book use by academic staff and students had much to say on the positive and negative aspects of e-textbooks, and some authors in this work have linked specific findings on usage to quotations drawn from the NeBO reports (Armstrong and Lonsdale, 2009b).

It must be borne in mind that NeBO dealt with the use of e-textbooks in an academic environment, so some of the findings may not be generalized to other situations. However, it is worth noting that the use of e-textbooks was found to be primarily related to needs for brief information and quick fact extraction, and there was a clear suggestion that e-textbooks were not being used for extended reading, a finding reflecting earlier studies such as Abdullah and Gibb (2007–8), and one which receives discussion within this book. A corollary to this is that the e-textbook was usually preferred to the printed textbook only when it was to be used for short periods of time. Compared with these findings, one study reported in this book indicates that only 14% of survey respondents always print from e-books, while another reveals that year-on-year surveys show a decrease in the number of pages being printed. The 'discomfort of reading online', as one author expressed it, may explain the preference to print out material, but there is some evidence that other advantages outweigh the discomfort.

There are a multitude of factors influencing the choice between using e-textbooks and paper books identified by NeBO respondents, of which the most important seemed to be convenience, something that was seen as being considerably enhanced by tablet computers or use on smartphones and handheld readers. Convenience – including portability and 24/7 access, availability when heavily used print books are unobtainable, ease of search, and the ability to highlight and to copy and paste – also figure highly in this book, whereas there is little evidence of downloading of full text for later reuse or the use of the e-textbook's facility for note-taking. This echoes the NeBO findings, which added that there was still a preference for students and staff to take handwritten notes, even from e-textbooks.

In this book, several authors note that the way e-books are delivered and presented means that there are a number of barriers to their access and use. NeBO reported that most e-textbook interfaces – and this can be generalized to most e-books – make poor use of the available screen space, resulting in too little actual visible text, too much space given over to distracting navigational tools, and a poor reading experience. Indeed, there are several references here to the multiplicity of platforms and the problems that this presents to both the librarian and the user, who may well decide to stick with print. Although this book does not look in any detail at the success or otherwise of e-book interfaces, it is worth noting that NeBO respondents disliked a reading process that required two navigational activities: the need to both scroll downwards *and* click the next-page button to access further text. They also disliked within-page images and tables, which are often not handled well by the software, as the zoom function often destroys page formats or makes pages relocate slightly on screen. NeBO also noted that browsing to locate information in an e-book is not easy, and it was believed that the paper book is more conducive to certain forms of reading, such as scanning. Both students and academics accessed content in e-textbooks using search and tables of contents in roughly equal measure, although advanced searching and the expanding of the table of contents were almost never used.

This introductory chapter has attempted to provide an overview of the history and genesis of e-book publishing as well as some of the fundamental concerns surrounding aspects of business models, licensing, promotion and use of e-books in libraries. As such, it has been conceived as a precursor to the substantive chapters of this work.

Useful links

The Assayer www.theassayer.org

BookGlutton www.bookglutton.com

Bowker's Global Books in Print www.globalbooksinprint.com/bip

City Sites http://artsweb.bham.ac.uk/citysites

Digital Book Index http://97.107.129.173/logina.htm

Digital Librarian www.digital-librarian.com

e-Book Finder from Eduserv http://ebookfinder.labs.eduserv.org.uk

eBooks.com www.ebooks.com

E-Books Directory www.e-booksdirectory.com

eBooks Just Published www.ebooksjustpublished.com

*EText Center at the University of Virginia Library (*now *Scholar's Lab)*
    www.lib.virginia.edu/scholarslab

GAM3R 7H30RY www.futureofthebook.org/mckenziewark/gamertheory

The Global Text Project http://globaltext.terry.uga.edu/books

Inkmesh http://inkmesh.com

JISC National E-books Observatory Project www.jiscebooksproject.org

Mortal Ghost http://mortalghost.blogspot.com/2006/07/chapter-one.html

Nielsen BookData UK www.nielsenbookdata.co.uk

The Oxford Text Archive (OTA) http://ota.ahds.ac.uk

Project Gutenberg www.gutenberg.org

SwetsWise www.swets.com

TeleRead www.teleread.com

Textbook Revolution http://textbookrevolution.org/index.php

We Tell Stories from Penguin www.wetellstories.co.uk

References

Abdullah, N. and Gibb, F. (2007-8) Students' Reactions towards E-books in a University Library Collection, *The International Journal of the Book*, **5** (1), 107-12.

Armstrong, C. (2010) *The 2010 Guide to Free or Nearly-Free e-Books*, UKeiG, forthcoming.

Armstrong, C., Edwards, L. and Lonsdale, R. (2002) Virtually There: e-books in UK academic libraries, *Program*, **36** (4), 216-27.

Armstrong, C. J. and Lonsdale, R. (1998) *The Publishing of Electronic Scholarly Monographs and Textbooks: a supporting study in the JISC eLib Programme: report G5*, Library Information Technology Centre.

Armstrong, C. and Lonsdale, R. (2005) Challenges in Managing E-books Collections in UK Academic Libraries, *Library Collections, Acquisitions, & Technical Services*, **29** (1), 33-50.

Armstrong, C. and Lonsdale, R. (2009a) *E-book Collection Management in UK University Libraries: focus groups report, Information Automation Limited, final report*, November 2009, www.jiscebooksproject.org/reports.

Armstrong, C. and Lonsdale, R. (2009b) *E-book Use by Academic Staff and Students in UK Universities: focus groups report, Information Automation Limited, final report, November 2009*, www.jiscebooksproject.org/reports.

Banwell, L. et al. (2004) The JISC User Behaviour Monitoring and Evaluation Framework, *Journal of Documentation*, **60** (3), 302-20.

Bush, V. (1945) As We May Think, *Atlantic Monthly*, **176** (1), 101-8.

CIBER (2008) *E-Book National Observatory: deep log analysis report I*, University College London.

Clark, D. T. (2009) Lending Kindle E-book Readers: first results from the Texas A&M University project, *Collection Building*, **28** (4), 146-9.

Cliat, C. (2010) *Kindle Pilot Results Highlight Possibilities for Paper Reduction*, www.princeton.edu/main/news/archive/S26/64/38E35.

Drinkwater, K. (2010) E-book Readers: what are librarians to make of them?, *SCONUL Focus*, **49**, 4-9.

Eblida (2001) *Licensing Digital Resources: how to avoid the legal pitfalls*, 2nd edn, www.eblida.org/uploads/Pitfalls_web.pdf.

Eduserv (2010) *Eduserv e-Book Survey: August 2010*.

Gold Leaf (2003) *Promoting the Uptake of E-books in Higher and Further Education: a Joint Information Systems Committee report*, JISC E-books Working Group, www.jiscebooksproject.org/faq-links/ebwgreports/promoting-e-books.

Lonsdale, R. and Armstrong, C. (2001) Electronic Books: challenges for academic libraries, *Library Hi Tech*, **1** (4), 332-9.

Lonsdale, R. and Armstrong, C. (2010) Promoting Your E-books: lessons from the UK JISC National e-Book Observatory, *Program: electronic library and information systems*, **44** (3), 185-206.

Mundle, K. (2009) Integration of Electronic Books into Library Catalogs: the UIC Library experience. In Miller, W. and Pellen, R. M. (eds) *Adapting to E-books*, Routledge, 229-47.

Pan, R., Byrne, U. and Murphy, H. (2009) Nudging the Envelope: the hard road to mainstreaming UCD Library e-book provision, *Serials*, **22** (3), Supplement, S12-S22.

Schimdt, J. (2007) Promoting Library Services in a Google World, *Library Management*, **28** (6/7), 337-46.

Taylor, A. (2007) E-books from MyiLibrary at the University of Worcester: a case study, *Program: electronic library and information systems*, **41** (3), 217-26.

Wilkins, V. (2007) Managing E-books at the University of Derby: a case study, *Program: electronic library and information systems*, **41** (3), 239-52.

Woods, S. L. (2007) A Three-step Approach to Marketing E-resources at Brock University, *The Serials Librarian*, **53** (3), 107-24.

Part 1

The production and distribution of e-books

Overview

The development and availability of e-books for the library market have been growing in importance for the last ten years. The range of subject matter now available in e-book format is diverse, and includes textbooks at school, college and university level, self-help manuals, monographs and novels. Some e-books may have illustrations and charts embedded within the pages, whilst others may include interactive features and audio and/or video capability.

The most common distribution methods for e-books are payment and subsequent access through the website of the individual publisher or through third-party intermediaries; however, other methods of making this content available to readers can include consortium purchasing and hosting, in-house production and directing users to the many free e-books available. The authors contributing to this section consider the production and distribution of e-books from a number of perspectives.

Joel Claypool (Chapter 1) of Morgan & Claypool Publishers describes the process from the perspective of a book publisher, as well as highlighting some of the major challenges being faced by the industry in a world where so much factual information is now freely available via the internet.

Anna Grigson (Chapter 2) of Royal Holloway, University of London, provides some practical guidance for library and information professionals, addressing some of the factors to consider when selecting e-book providers, from identifying appropriate suppliers to negotiating licence terms.

Silvia Gstrein and Günter Mühlberger (Chapter 3) of the University of Innsbruck provide a fascinating insight into the eBooks on Demand (EOD) service, which allows readers to request digital versions of the print titles held in 30 member libraries. Gstrein and Mühlberger describe the process involved and consider the future for this impressive pan-European service.

Finally Kate Price (Chapter 4) of the University of Surrey discusses the role of free e-books in the library setting, reflecting on the advantages and disadvantages of managing a collection of freely available titles, and identifying some of the collections currently available.

1

Publishing e-books: challenges and perspectives

Joel Claypool

Introduction

This chapter deals with the transitions, opportunities and challenges for publishers, both large and small, arising from the expanding market for e-books. The aim of the chapter is to examine some of the fundamental business practices, cost structures and market forces that affect the ability to create a sustainable business model for e-books, whether in a for-profit, not-for-profit or 'not-yet-for-profit' publishing operation. A further aim is to provide an insight into the process of creating high quality books and e-books, to raise awareness of the effort and investment involved, and to examine the concept of value with regard to published information.

The observations that follow are primarily from the perspective of a publisher of professional and scholarly books in the science, technology and medical (STM) areas, but consumer (trade) publishing is also touched upon. The author also brings to bear the experience of founding a start-up publishing company in a market that expects online information to be both readily accessible and inexpensive. Overall, the chapter describes a fast-evolving and sometimes daunting environment for many of those currently working in publishing, and provides some background for library and information professionals who may not be aware of the pressures that are currently being faced by the industry.

The impact of digital technology on the publishing world

It would not be an exaggeration to say that the emergence of e-books will have the most profound impact on the book publishing business since Gutenberg's introduction of the mechanical movable type printing press in the fifteenth century.

In recent years a number of technologies have converged to allow the creation, sale and distribution of e-books: personal computers, page-making software, the internet, mobile communication devices, broadband wireless, e-reader devices and so on. However, the technologies alone do not greatly alter the traditional ways and means of the publishing business. In fact, perhaps the most important change is the potential for a dramatic restructuring of the financial model of the business. For the first time since movable type was introduced, the industry may be facing a situation where the technology available and the consumers who use it come together to create an environment where the price for books and information substantially decreases.

Book publishing may well be approaching a wall similar to that already encountered by the printed newspaper industry. This has transformed seemingly invulnerable publishing giants into companies in search of a survival scenario: there has been a reduction in circulation of 16.9% and an estimated loss of roughly 13,500 jobs in the USA over the past three years, following a migration of audiences and advertising to freely available websites (Project for Excellence in Journalism and Edmonds, 2010). Book publishing is being pressured by similar technological forces, consumer demand for easy online access and the deflation of the price of information in some quarters. These changes present some major challenges to existing publishing companies, both the mega-conglomerates and the many smaller publishing houses, but may greatly benefit consumers and provide equal access to more and better information for all throughout the world. There may be opportunities for new players to enter the market or convert existing content to e-book models. Similarly, new business models may emerge which could develop quickly into the industry standards of the future.

There is no doubt that e-books are gaining ground. In 2009 e-book sales made up 1.5% of total US book sales and grew to 5% of the market in the first quarter of 2010, according to a survey carried out by the Book

Industry Study Group (Holt, 2010). However, a number of crucial questions for publishers remain unanswered: when will individuals shift their purchasing preference over to e-books, how will they want them delivered, and, most importantly, what is the price they are willing to pay? Additionally, how is this influenced by the greatly increasing volume of free and open information in the scientific, technical and medical (STM) communities?

The economics of book publishing

In order to understand the viability of e-book publishing, it is important to have a basic understanding of the traditional printed book business, as, for the publisher, the basic tasks involved in creating e-books are very similar. Primarily these include the acquisition, financing, production, marketing, sales and delivery of books. Although the ways that these tasks and responsibilities are carried out have undergone quite radical change owing to technological, social and economic forces, the basic underlying functions of publishing remain the same: to facilitate the creation of content by an author, and then deliver that content to the interested reader.

Since the early 1980s, a number of internal and external forces relating to costs, pricing, discounts, sales channels and sales volume have led to the erosion of a profitable business model. Book publishing has never been an easy road to riches; it tended to be a business of rather well financed intellectuals who had the cash, patience and perseverance to survive. However, there has never before been a more challenging environment for publishers in which to make a profit.

Cashflow and profitability

The publishing of new and original content requires cash up-front for staffing, production and manufacturing, with sales revenues lagging behind initial investments by several years. At present, this seems to hold true for e-book publishing as well as for print. Publishing plans need to be developed; authors need to be recruited and publishing rights acquired. Then the creative process begins, with authors typically needing one to four years to produce the content. Only after the book has come to market can the publisher begin to recoup any costs.

Profits are constrained by supplier discounts and overheads. Books are generally sold by publishers to suppliers at an average discount, which now approaches 40% – a huge increase from the 20% levels of the 1990s. Also, the allocation for overheads (premises, equipment and staffing) has in some cases climbed above 30% of the list price. With discounts to suppliers and overheads taking up 70% of the revenue from the book, a thin margin of 30% remains to cover the production costs, royalties and profits. Hence, no matter what the price, numbers of books sold or net revenue, the margins of profitability are very slim.

Whether selling books at a cost of $10, $25, $75 or $150, it takes a great many sales before the revenue will cover expenses and yield a profit. It typically takes the production of dozens of published titles to optimize future income and revenues and absorb fixed costs. Publishing many more titles also spreads the risk of missed sales projections and the costs of production, sales and marketing. However, building up a portfolio of titles takes a tremendous amount of time, patience, labour and cash investment from the publisher, even before the time and efforts of the authors are taken into account.

Therefore, even the smallest start-up publishing company, needing to commission and acquire original content, may require over $1,000,000 in financing, along with revenues from ongoing sales, to reach a break-even point in around five to seven years. Even with a large amount of luck (or a perfectly-timed bestseller), this investment level and timescale appears to be similar for e-book, or predominantly e-book, publishing companies.

Content acquisition and editorial costs

No publishing operation, whether print or electronic, can exist without content. Therefore the first step in any publishing plan is to determine the costs of acquiring that content. In scholarly and professional publishing, this is likely to be nearly identical for print and e-book models of production. In a small company or start-up, content acquisition is often the function of the founder, but further editorial personnel may soon be required, owing to the time and energy demanded in order to forge a successful relationship with both existing and potential authors.

Commissioning editors may need to sign a large number of authors and publish a considerable number of books in order to achieve and maintain survivable margins, particularly in smaller companies which have not yet achieved brand recognition in the market. In some areas of publishing it may take the acquisition of three times as many book titles as are actually planned for publication, because of attrition caused by delays, titles that never get written, and those that are cancelled.

The salary cost for a junior commissioning editor is likely to be in the range of $75,000–$100,000 per year. Editors may need to travel both domestically and internationally to conferences, campuses and corporations in search of authors. The basic costs of travel can be $20,000–$30,000 per year. Add to this the costs of reviewing and editorial honorariums, and expenses begin to mount quickly. Bearing in mind that the editor's initial acquired titles may not be published for a minimum of two years and that the production of a truly substantial number of titles may not be seen for several more years, there will be significant lead time before that editor's salary is covered by sales revenue.

Pre-press costs

Pre-press costs for composition, copy-editing and formatting have reached their lowest point ever in real dollar terms. The move to digital desktop composition in the early 1990s, the introduction of online proofing and the creation of digital page formatting processes, together with the overwhelming shift to full production services offshore, have all led to greatly reduced costs. The pre-press cost of producing one page in 1985 could range from $30 to $50 for a standard one-colour book. Now, 25 years later, the pre-press cost of producing the same page ranges from $8 to $11, whether this is for an e-book or a physical copy. Once again, this is a cost that will not be reduced significantly by the shift to e-only formats.

Manufacturing costs

Perhaps the biggest misunderstanding from those outside the book publishing business concerns the relationship between the retail price of a book and the cost to the publisher of manufacturing a bound copy.

The cost for the printing, paper and binding (PPB) of a book has historically been as low as 10% of the listed price of the book. In some cases, with the high prices of STM monographs for limited markets, this percentage is even lower. A $100 book may cost as little as $2 per copy to produce. These levels will vary slightly according to the size of the print run, with higher per copy prices for print on demand (POD), for example.

Of course, if books are not printed at all there is lower usage of material resources such as paper, and less fuel is expended in transportation, so there is an environmental benefit. Also, the danger of overprinting and the need to maintain warehouses full of seldom- or never-purchased books is reduced, but not to the extent that profits are affected significantly. Therefore an e-book publishing model without the printing of any physical copies may only contribute 10% or less to either increasing profits or lowering prices. When this is coupled with continuing pressure from consumers and retailers for price reductions far greater than 10% for e-books, there may be no net gain to be had from a reduction in manufacturing costs.

Shipping and handling

In recent years, large online retailers such as Amazon have begun to offer free shipping and handling for consumers on what appear to be already discounted books. Unfortunately, this has resulted in even greater pressure on publishers from retailers and wholesalers to absorb their shipping and handling costs through the provision of even greater discounts. In the e-books-only publishing model, shipping and handling are reduced. This in turn reduces the impact on the environment and so is a benefit to society, but as profit margins are already being squeezed to provide discounts on the list price, the cost saving implied by the reduction in shipping and handling is unlikely to affect e-book business models substantially.

Royalties to authors and editors

In STM publishing, royalties paid to the authors or editors of monographs have traditionally ranged from 10% to 15% of net revenues from sales. In addition, the editors of series and advisory editors have received an average of 2%, and occasionally up to 5%, of sales income. It is likely that, for STM publishing at least, this percentage will not change substantially, owing to the high costs of bringing content to publication, as discussed above.

In the realm of popular publishing, some smaller e-book-only publishing companies are offering royalties of up to 50% (Teicher, 2010), and even major publisher Random House recently increased royalties for some high-selling backlist e-book titles from 25% to 40% as a result of negotiations with authors' agents (Deahl, 2010). This recognition that mass-market e-books with a large potential audience can generate substantial incomes and profits, and that authors therefore deserve an appropriate percentage of that income, is very positive for authors, but such conditions rarely apply in academic or STM publishing.

Sales and marketing

An e-book publishing plan would not be complete without a sales and marketing strategy. STM publishers generally hope to sell collections of e-book content to libraries, particularly in the education, health and business sectors. This requires either a sales representative employed exclusively by the publisher, or a contract with a third-party company which will represent the product on their behalf (this is particularly useful in overseas territories). If the representative works exclusively for the publisher then the returns on individual sales are much higher, as a third-party sales force will take an average of 20% to 30% commission.

In either case, the sales process requires travel and contact with potential buyers on location at the libraries, as well as through attendance at library conferences and meetings. It is important to note that it may take numerous contacts over the course of several years to achieve a sale of e-book content to a library, particularly for new publishing companies where content and reputation take time to build. Costs may also arise from the use of 'passive' marketing channels such as placing advertisements in relevant publications.

Retail pricing and discounts

At the beginning of this chapter it was mentioned that the biggest potential challenge for publishers caused by the move to e-books is the fact that the retail price for books and information may substantially decline under pressure from consumers. This is already happening in the more commercial sectors of the publishing industry that produce fiction and non-fiction 'trade' e-books. Some online retailers have for several years been routinely selling e-versions of novels and other popular titles for several dollars less than the paperback price.

Arguably, this is a workable business model for trade publishing, particularly if it follows the classic microeconomic model where, given a large enough potential market, a reduction in price will lead to an increase in sales and revenue. However, some larger publishing houses are rebelling against this practice, which they see as devaluing the content; for example, in the UK Hachette recently moved to a re-selling model where they, rather than the retailer, set the sale price, and other publishers are likely to follow suit (Neill, 2010).

The discount model also works poorly for textbooks, reference works and monographs in STM publishing, as, in comparison to trade publishing, the markets for these books, whether in print or electronic form, are very small. For many titles, the total interested audience worldwide may be counted in hundreds or at the most thousands of individuals. This creates an inelastic market where lowering the price does not necessarily result in increased sales. Furthermore, these readers may not continue to be willing to pay traditionally high print prices for the same material in e-book form, a factor that will be discussed later in this chapter.

In addition to direct sales to consumers, STM publishers have been experimenting with different pricing models for the sale of individual titles and e-book collections to the library market for a number of years, many of which are explained in detail by Anna Grigson in Chapter 2 of this book. However, this is still very much an evolving situation, with no single pricing model being preferred by libraries or publishers.

Additional processes required for publishing e-books

Up to this point, this chapter has concentrated on the processes and practices involved in publishing a book through the traditional route, and has compared the costs with the parallel processes involved in producing an e-book. However, there are additional factors to consider when moving into the e-book publishing arena.

Technological choices: supporting different devices

Most technologists and futurists would probably agree that there is a trend towards the development of multi-use devices, and that the consumer will eventually come to rely on having their information and communication needs served by only one or two devices. Because a larger format screen is preferable for comfortable reading, this need is likely be met by an emerging hybrid of a tablet-PC/e-reader for accessing e-books, word processing and additional applications where size of display matters, while a smartphone may also be required for communication and swift access to applications on a smaller device.

The front runners in the portable e-reader market are the Kindle and the iPad. Currently, the Kindle display (which uses e-ink) may be preferable for ease of reading text, particularly in daylight, whilst the iPad may be preferred for its colour display and web linking functionality. Much more information about the pros and cons of different devices can be found in Chapter 10 of this book. Ultimately, the market will decide, and it is likely that these devices and their competitors will converge in functionality very quickly.

Until such a convergence occurs, however, publishers will need to provide content for a variety of platforms and devices, from desktop PCs to e-book readers, iPads and other mobile devices. The cost of creating the digital document and page files necessary for an e-book to be readable on any popular device is relatively small, ranging from $50 to $200 per book. This cost is falling constantly owing to advances in software for content management systems and page-making programs. These services are provided to publishers by large content production companies, such as Aptara (www.aptaracorp.com), Innodata Isogen (www.innodata-isogen.com), Cadmus Communications (www.cadmus.com) and many others. In addition, software and hardware companies, internet commerce and delivery companies, content platform companies and search engines all have a role in ensuring that cross-platform access to e-books is possible.

Content platforms

Although the traditional costs associated with manufacturing and transporting physical goods are reduced in the e-book environment, there are many new requirements associated with the hosting and maintenance of e-book files. These represent significant expenses, and in some cases exceed traditional print distribution costs. In particular, STM publishers that make sales to university, corporate and government libraries will need to provide access to their e-books through an electronic content platform. This platform must provide a means of hosting the electronic files and delivering them to end-users through a series of web pages and/or a search engine. It may also provide administrative functions ranging from purchase requests from library staff to the download of COUNTER-compliant usage statistics. Typically, only the very largest journal and book publishers have developed their own platforms, at substantial cost, whilst smaller publishers will tend to outsource their hosting needs to a third-party company.

High quality hosting platforms can cost from a minimum of $50,000 to many hundreds of thousands of dollars annually, depending on the services required. An alternative, giving a lower up-front cost, is to provide the content to an e-book aggregator, which may both host and sell the e-books on the publisher's behalf, depending upon the contract. However, this might mean providing the content at a larger discount than would otherwise be the case. Another disadvantage is that the publisher's identity can be lost, or at best mixed with those of a wide variety of other companies. However, given the history of declining costs in software-related businesses, it is likely that the price for good quality hosting services will decrease in the future, and so ease of use and functionality will improve, even for those at the cheaper end of the market.

Content management systems

Many e-book publishers are now finding a need for content management systems (CMSs). These internal document-tracking and management systems have been the backbone of large corporations for years. They are also now becoming an essential tool to enable publishers to manage the multiple versions of files resulting from large numbers of book projects that are either in the process of editing and production or are already available in a variety of document formats for multiplatform delivery.

In addition to managing the workflow for internal documents, most CMS services feature a web content management system (WCMS). Features of WCMSs that are vitally important for e-book publishers include facilities to feed content and updated information direct to the websites of e-book platforms and vendors, transmit data to resellers using the ONIX (Online Information eXchange) standard, create online marketing materials automatically, and provide file storage and transfer functions. Overall, the costs of a CMS or WCMS can be in excess of $10,000 per year.

The value of information

Much of this chapter has been concerned with the cost of producing and selling books, whether printed volumes or e-books. However, when considering the evolution of business models for publishing, it is of equal importance to discuss the value of the information that is being produced. Value is defined in the Oxford English Dictionary as: 'That amount of some commodity, medium of exchange, etc., which is considered to be an equivalent for something else; a fair or adequate equivalent or return' (Oxford English Dictionary, 1989). Hence, value is determined as much by the consumer as it is by the producer.

Prior to the emergence of the internet, there were only certain specific places where specialized information was available. Encyclopedias, dictionaries, handbooks and directories were essential for quickly finding these pieces of information. The effort involved in producing these major reference works meant that a significant financial investment was required on the part of the publisher, and that they were therefore expensive to purchase. Libraries were the logical market for these resources, and were relied upon to provide good quality information sources to their readers through the development of comprehensive reference collections. Hence these collections and the books within them were perceived as a valuable commodity by those who used them, and the value of the information to the consumer was reflected in sales of books to libraries.

Now, in the internet-enabled world, the same information is easily available, by entering a few keywords, from networked computers in offices, homes and coffee shops, and from almost anywhere using a mobile device. In the space of less than a decade, the demand for major print reference works has withered away, and the widespread accessibility of basic factual information on the internet has led to serious questions about the value of other types of information presented in e-book form, most of which may only be answered in the longer term:

1   STM books (and e-books) are sold as packages of information, with the content being determined by the publisher and the author. Often only one portion of that package is of value to a particular reader: perhaps a section, a chapter, a table of data, a standard, a formula or an explanation of a method. Sometimes the reader only wants or needs that small piece of information, but is required to find, or buy, the entire package in order to gain access to that piece. With e-books, can it be assumed that the consumer will be willing to navigate through and/or buy the entire package, or will there be pressure to disaggregate books and sell the elements within separately?

2   With the sale of large packages of e-book content to academic and research libraries, and improvements in descriptive metadata for that content, coupled with improvements in the ability of search engines to pinpoint information within the text, will any information be uniquely available in any one portion of any one individual book? If significant proportions of books are found to be duplicating one another, will there be pressure to reduce the number of books published, or to reduce the cost price further?

3   Does the reader require information to be absolutely perfect at all times (which is the assumption behind the editorial efforts of most STM publishers), or are they in most cases willing to accept information that is simply 'good enough'?

Freely available alternatives to published e-books

If the consumer is satisfied with information that is 'good enough', then it is possible to find a vast amount of it available for free with even the most basic internet search. In the last ten years the advent of socially networked sites has resulted in a burgeoning of free information resources which can be seen as competitors to the traditional STM publishing industry, the most visible example of which is Wikipedia (www.wikipedia.org). A few years ago, most publishing professionals, including this author, felt that Wikipedia would not be seen by consumers as a reliable source of information because it was open to peer-editing, with the public being able to make additions and corrections. This perception was proved incorrect – although Wikipedia has not yet become the *de facto* source of citable and verifiable information, it has nevertheless become the place to go for a large proportion of general information needs.

Interestingly, Wikipedia is itself subject to economic forces similar to those affecting traditional publishers; even if the general public provides the content and factual editing for free, physical infrastructure is still required to host the information and make it readily available to a wide audience, and this entails a cost to the provider. Some 'free' information sources make a charge to advertisers in order to underwrite their costs, and in some cases make a profit. However, Wikipedia does not sell advertising, and founder Jimmy Wales has recently published an appeal for donations in order to keep it a 'community creation' that is advertisement free (Wikimedia Foundation, 2010).

In contrast to the articles on Wikipedia, which are intentionally made freely available by their authors, there is a growing issue of the unauthorized distribution of publishers' content through file-sharing websites. These sites are often also used for the legitimate sharing of original information, which makes it all the more difficult for publishers to trace and control their digital assets, and to determine whether or not they have been illegally copied. Many would argue that the free flow of information is to be welcomed, particularly in the academic world. However, it is difficult to make this case to those publishers who invest significant amounts of both time and money to bring this content into the world in the first place.

So, the publishing industry is undergoing seismic shifts as a result of freely available information on the web. While this may be extremely uncomfortable (to say the least), it does mean that there is scope for authors, publishers and technological innovators to come together and find new ways of ensuring that the information contained within e-books and other online resources is both valued highly enough to make it economically worthwhile for those who participate in its creation to continue doing so, and made available at a price low enough to satisfy the information needs and wants of the majority of consumers.

Conclusion

An examination of basic e-book publishing costs shows that the transfer of information delivery to electronic-only formats does not necessarily result in substantial cost savings. If the list prices of e-books substantially decline, and the availability of free and easily accessible information on the internet greatly increases, there may be difficulties ahead for current e-book business models. The challenge for publishers is to find models that enable them to make a profit in a world where the nature of demand for information is changing – and its perceived value is falling. However, there is no doubt that e-books are destined to be a dominant part of the future of publishing, and that the social, technological and economic changes that the industry is now undergoing are likely to result in some very interesting new businesses.

Useful links

Aptara www.aptaracorp.com
Association of American Publishers www.publishers.org
Book Industry Study Group (BISG) www.bisg.org
Cadmus Communications www.cadmus.com
Innodata Isogen www.innodata-isogen.com
ONIX www.editeur.org/8/ONIX
PW: Publishers Weekly www.publishersweekly.com
Wikipedia www.wikipedia.org

References

Deahl, R. (2010) Digital Royalties: Random House sets 40% bar for some titles. *PW: Publishers Weekly*, 30 August, www.publishersweekly.com/pw/by-topic/digital/copyright/article/44300-digital-royalties-random-house-sets-40-bar-for-some-titles.html.

Holt, K. (2010) E-book Sales Statistics from BISG Survey, *Publishing Perspectives*, 27 May,
http://publishingperspectives.com/2010/05/e-book-sales-statistics-from-bisg-survey.

Neill, G. (2010) Hachette UK to set e-book prices from Monday, *Bookseller.com*, 20 September,
www.thebookseller.com/news/128696-hachette-uk-to-set-e-book-prices-from-monday.html.

Oxford English Dictionary (1989) *Oxford English Dictionary*, 2nd edn, Oxford University Press [Online],
www.oed.com.

Project for Excellence in Journalism and Edmonds, R. (2010) Newspapers: summary essay in *The State of the News Media 2010: an annual report on American journalism*,
www.stateofthemedia.org/2010/newspapers_summary_essay.php.

Teicher, C. M. (2010) Rosetta Books Announces New Higher E-book Royalty Rate, *PW: Publishers Weekly*, 28 September,
www.publishersweekly.com/pw/by-topic/digital/content-and-e-books/article/44618-rosetta-books-announces-new-higher-e-book-royalty-rate-.html.

Wikimedia Foundation (2010) *An Appeal from Wikipedia Founder Jimmy Wales*,
http://wikimediafoundation.org/wiki/WMFJA1/GB.

2

An introduction to e-book business models and suppliers

Anna Grigson

Introduction

When an e-book is acquired, it must meet customers' needs, providing not only the content that is wanted, but also making sure that it can be made available where and when it is required, and at a price that provides best value for money. There are many different suppliers in the e-book marketplace, and it can be difficult to determine which can offer both the best value and the best content and service to their users, as well as meeting the terms and conditions for approved suppliers set by the library's parent organization.

This chapter aims to help the library make an informed choice by reviewing some of the issues to be considered when choosing an e-book supplier, including:

- the different types of suppliers and formats
- the content that they can provide
- the methods for discovering which titles are available as e-books
- the range of current business models
- the licence terms that require particular attention
- the quality of service and technical support provided.

It should be noted that the information in this chapter refers to suppliers and business models prevalent in the UK and US market.

Suppliers

There are many different suppliers of e-books to libraries. Some are established players in the library supply chain for printed books, including both major publishers and vendors such as Coutts (MyiLibrary), Dawsons (Dawson*era*) and Swets. Others are established as providers of other types of online content, including aggregators such as EBSCO Publishing, which recently acquired the NetLibrary e-book platform. There are also specialist e-book aggregators, such as Bloomsbury, EBL (EBook Library), ebrary and OverDrive. In addition, there are suppliers that focus on providing e-books to the consumer market, including e-book specialists, online retailers such as Amazon, and high-street booksellers such as WHSmith and Waterstone's.

As well as having different suppliers, the library and consumer markets also have different supply models. The consumer market is dominated by sales of e-book downloads. Primarily designed for offline mobile use, these are published in various formats suitable either for proprietary e-book readers, such as the Amazon Kindle, or for generic devices such as laptops. Downloads are sold outright for the user to keep, although further use may be controlled by DRM software. Consumer e-books therefore follow a retail model similar to online music sales and the role of the supplier is essentially limited to the sales transaction.

In contrast, the library market focuses more heavily on an online e-book supply model. Instead of buying e-book downloads and then making the files available for users to access offline at any time, the library pays for access to e-books that are hosted on a third-party website. In some cases, the e-books must be accessed fully online at this website, either because the supplier's business model does not allow downloads or offline access, or because the added features of the e-book depend on it being delivered while connected to the internet, for example reference books that depend on an online search interface. In other cases the library user may be able to download the e-book from the website to be read offline, although unlike retail e-books this is usually a temporary download in the form of a file, which can only be accessed for a limited period.

From the user's perspective, the experience of borrowing an e-book does not differ greatly from buying the same title. Rather than going to an online bookstore and downloading the text to keep, they go to the website where the library's e-books are hosted and download a file, which automatically expires in a few days. In some respects, library e-book loans could also be seen to work in a very similar way to print book loans, with a visit to the physical library simply being replaced by a visit to the library website.

However, for libraries, the e-book model for acquiring content and supplying it to users is fundamentally different from the print model. The supplier is no longer simply selling books to the library – they are also selling the service that supplies them directly to the library's users.

This mode of delivery appeals to libraries. It fits with the model of third-party hosting of e-resources, which has already become well established for e-journals and databases, and for most libraries it is much more cost effective than maintaining the technical infrastructure needed to host e-books themselves. It also appeals to publishers, as it gives them the means to retain greater control over the distribution and use of their content than if downloaded files were simply sold to libraries, something that is of particular concern given the size and value of the consumer market for books. However, this mode of supply leads to more complicated business models, which have more in common with those for the procurement of other types of online content than they do with print book supply. Because of this, there are also additional criteria to be considered, which may be more akin to the process of choosing an e-journal supplier than they are to identifying a suitable print supplier.

Although most library e-book procurement follows the online model, there are some libraries that purchase offline e-books and load them onto library-owned e-readers, which can then be loaned out to users, although the appeal of this model may be limited, both for the library that has to manage e-book reader devices, and for the user who has to visit the library in person in order to borrow the reader. There is also some cross-over in the consumer market. Although it is currently dominated by download sales, there are some online subscription-based e-book services aimed at individual users, for example Questia and Safari Books Online, and the forthcoming (at time of writing) launch of Google Editions with its online sales model, which is likely to result in the growth of online delivery in the consumer market.

However, these two supply models generally serve separate markets, to the extent that the terms and conditions of retail suppliers frequently limit their e-books to personal use only, prohibiting their supply to libraries. Therefore the first issue to address when choosing a supplier is whether they do actually supply to libraries, or whether their terms and conditions only permit personal use.

Another major consideration for libraries may be whether the supplier has a contract with one of the consortia of which the institution is a member (for example, the recently negotiated Joint Consortium Book Agreement covers several providers of e-books for university libraries) or provides an agreement through one of the national negotiating bodies such as JISC or Eduserv in the UK. Consortium purchasing can provide significant discounts, but there may also be limiting factors, such as a minimum threshold for spending before discounts are applied, or the necessity to sign a contract for two or three years.

Content

Once the range of potential suppliers has been established by the library, the next step is to evaluate the content that each of them can provide. Unlike print books, no single supplier will be able to supply the full range of e-books required. First, not all books are available in e-formats. In particular, many textbooks are not made available in this format as publishers are concerned that e-book sales to libraries could result in a loss of revenue from print book sales to students (JISC, 2009). Second, some books that have been published as e-books may be limited to retail sales. For example, although many new fiction titles are published in e-formats, some publishers may be reluctant to make them available to libraries for fear of a negative impact on sales (Hyams, 2009) – although other publishers see e-book availability as a driver for print book sales (OverDrive, 2010). Third, even when an e-book is available to libraries, it may not be available from all suppliers. The range of content available from a supplier is largely dependent on their role in the supply chain.

Publishers

Publishers may supply e-books directly to libraries, although they will usually only offer their own titles.

Vendors

Vendors sell e-books on behalf of publishers. The vendor's role is to provide sales support, and once the purchase is completed (or the subscription arranged), access to the e-book itself is provided via the publisher's website. As with major print book vendors, e-book vendors typically offer content from a range of different publishers. But whereas most major print book vendors will sell titles from most mainstream publishers, the range of publishers covered by an e-book vendor may be more restricted, because some publishers will only sell direct, especially when their e-books are available only as packages rather than as individual titles.

Aggregators

Aggregators such as NetLibrary or OverDrive also supply content from a range of different publishers. But unlike vendors who sell content on behalf of publishers, aggregators license content from them and then sell directly to libraries, hosting the e-books on their own platform rather than the publisher's website. As with vendors, they typically cover a wide range of publishers, including smaller companies that do not have their own e-book platforms. However, the content that aggregators can supply is limited by the licences that they can obtain; some publishers may choose not to license any of their content to aggregators, some may offer some or all of their content through all the major aggregators, and some may have an exclusive deal to supply through a single aggregator.

Some e-books are only available from aggregators, whereas others may be available from both the publisher and an aggregator. Indeed, it is common to find that an e-book is available both as an individual title from an aggregator, and as part of a collection available direct from the publisher. The situation is further complicated by the fact that some companies act as both vendors of print books and as aggregators supplying e-books, for example Coutts supplies through the MyiLibrary e-book aggregator, Dawsons supplies e-books through Dawson*era*, and Blackwells works in partnership with the e-book aggregator EBL. However, because of the limitations on which e-book aggregators can supply, there may be occasions where a company can sell a print book, but does not have the rights to supply the corresponding e-book.

So the range of e-book content available from any one company, whether publisher, vendor or aggregator, is likely to be restricted. Consequently, when looking at whether or not to use a new supplier, the following factors should be considered:

- How many e-books does the supplier offer?
- If it is an aggregator, how many publishers does it license content from?
- Does it cover a range of subjects, or does it specialize?
- How current are the books – are the majority new titles or backlist ones, and are the most recent editions available?
- Does it supply content from a range of countries and in a range of languages?
- Do the e-books include all of the material in the print versions, including graphical content?
- Is any material excluded because it is not licensed for digital format?
- Is any additional content included, for example accompanying multimedia content?

Using the same supplier for both print and e-book procurement may have advantages in terms of streamlining the administration of ordering and invoicing, but owing to the limitations on the range of content available, it may actually be necessary to work with several e-book suppliers. If a particular e-book or a particular publisher's content is only available from one source, this may even be a deciding factor in the choice of supplier.

Discovery

To purchase a book in e-format, it is necessary to identify not only whether it is available as an e-book, but also which company is able to supply it. Unfortunately, finding this information is far from straightforward. In the print world, finding tools such as Global Books in Print and Nielsen BookData can be employed, and most major suppliers will be able to supply most titles. In the online world, Eduserv's e-Book Finder or SwetsWise e-books may be of use to identify books that are available in e-formats, but they may not list specific suppliers. The title may also be available from multiple suppliers under different business models, some of which may offer better value for money than others, but which may be difficult to compare directly. Finding the relevant information can therefore be very time-consuming, and the difficulty in discovering available titles and comparing prices between different suppliers is a significant barrier to library acquisition of e-books.

When evaluating a potential supplier, it is important to consider not only the general range of content provided, but also to assess the ease with which it is possible to discover whether or not they offer a particular e-book title:

- How easy is it to find e-books when searching the database of available titles?
- Is there an option to narrow the search to look for e-books only?
- Does the database show whether the e-format is available when a print title is searched for?
- Does the supplier offer a title-matching service, allowing the library to send a list of ISBNs for print holdings and receive back a report of the titles that are available as e-books?
- Can alerts be set up to receive notification of new e-books on specific subjects?
- Are alerts sent for new editions of e-books that have previously been purchased?
- Are alerts sent when titles previously purchased in print become available as e-books?

Business models

Having established which suppliers can offer the content required the next step is to consider the business models on offer. There are a bewildering number of business models for e-books, each of which has advantages and disadvantages for different types of libraries. Comparing the models to work out which offers the best value for money can be difficult; however, most can be broken down into three key elements:

1 a choice between acquiring individual titles or packages
2 a choice between purchasing e-books outright or taking a subscription
3 a choice between a limited number of uses per annum or a limited number of simultaneous users.

Individual titles vs packages

As with print books, it is possible to acquire e-books as individual titles, usually from aggregators, either directly or through a library supplier such as Coutts or Dawson.

Many e-books are also available in packages, of which there are several different types. Publishers may offer packages of e-books grouped by subject (for example, Palgrave Connect) or publication date (for example, Springer eBooks). Aggregators such as ebrary may package together a selection of e-books from a range of publishers, or may offer mixed packages of e-books and e-journals. In some cases, the selection of titles in the package is made by the supplier (for example, PsycBooks from the American Psychological Association), whilst in other cases the supplier may offer the library a degree of choice over the content included (for example, Credo Reference).

Acquiring e-books in packages offers some advantages: the cost per title is usually lower than that for individual acquisitions and if the choice of titles is made by the publisher it can save staff time on selection, so this can be a quick and cost-effective way to build up the library's collections. However, a disadvantage of acquiring a collection is that the library is potentially paying for content that may not be used and therefore represents poor value for money.

A package that allows the library to have some choice over the titles included may address this issue, as it provides the opportunity to select content for which there is known demand, or to match existing print holdings. Some subscription-based packages allow the library to change the initial number and/or selection of titles. These may offer better value, since the library can adjust its selections in the light of actual usage and drop little-used texts in favour of new ones. Some packages may only allow changes once a year when the subscription is renewed, while others may permit adjustments during the subscription, allowing the library to swap the titles on their virtual bookshelf at more frequent intervals (for example, Safari Books Online). This gives the potential to maximize value for money by matching supply to demand, for example by adding content to reflect topics or authors in the news, or by adding or withdrawing particular textbooks at different points in the academic year.

Purchase vs subscription

Different business models offer different payment and ownership models, including outright purchase, temporary subscription, or even a mixture of the two.

Outright purchase

This is of course the more familiar way for libraries to acquire books and is offered by many suppliers. As with print books, payment is made once and the library can theoretically retain indefinite access to the e-book. However, there may also be an annual platform fee to cover the ongoing costs of hosting the purchased e-books on the supplier's website. This may be in the form of an additional charge added to the purchase price of each book, or it may be a flat-rate annual fee, which covers all of the books hosted on the site. In some cases the platform fee may be waived or reduced if a minimum amount of money is spent on new purchases each year.

Purchasing e-books is usually more expensive than paying for a subscription. In addition to a platform fee, the list price for an e-book may well be higher than that of an equivalent print copy, and in the UK it is currently subject to value added tax (VAT). However, although it is more expensive initially, a purchase option may represent good value for money in the longer term if the book is likely to remain in demand for several years.

If e-books are purchased with a view to long-term use, it will be necessary to consider how indefinite access is supported. For example what happens if, or more likely when, the original format becomes obsolete, or if the publisher goes out of business or decides to close their e-book service? The issue of the long-term preservation of e-resources goes beyond the scope of this chapter, but it is an important consideration if the library is building a significant collection of e-books, and one which the supplier should address in their licence terms.

Consideration also needs to be given to the fate of e-books in the event that the original supplier loses the rights to supply the content:

- If the e-book has been purchased, does the library retain access?
- If so, is access via the original supplier's platform, or through the new rights-owner's site?
- If access is lost, will there be a full or partial refund?
- How much notice is given that a title is being withdrawn?

Annual subscription

This is the other most common payment model for e-books. A subscription usually provides access only for a specific period, so that if the annual fee is no longer paid, the e-book or package is no longer accessible. For this reason, subscription prices are usually lower than purchase prices, and the pricing model may be simpler as platform fees are usually included. Although it provides only temporary access, a subscription may still represent good value for money. If the content has a short life-span (for example, law textbooks, computing books or tourist guidebooks), or if demand will be short-lived (for example, a book acquired to support a short course), then indefinite access to the content may be unnecessary, and paying a lower price for temporary access may therefore be more economical.

Alongside simple purchase and subscription models there are other options, which employ a combination of both. Some reference books may be available to purchase, but there may be ongoing annual fees for content updates (for example, Wiley-Blackwell Online Reference Works). Content fees may be included in the platform fees, or may be charged separately. In some cases the annual content fees may be optional, giving the library the option not to receive updates but to retain permanent access to content already paid for.

Rental

Some suppliers offer options for short-term rental of individual e-books (for example, Dawson*era* and EBL). In the rental model the library user is able to browse all of the e-books available from the supplier's website, including titles that are not in the library's collection. If the user sees a title they wish to read that is not owned by the library, they can request a rental. The library then pays a fee and the user is granted temporary access to the book for a set number of days or weeks.

This model is broadly equivalent to an interlibrary loan for a print book, providing a pay-per-view option for whole e-books. The fee is typically 10–20% of the list price of the book per rental, making this model appear comparatively expensive. But since content is only paid for when requested by a user, no funds are wasted on paying for titles that are never used; rentals thus may in fact offer better value for money than it would first appear. However, the content is only available to a single user for a limited period, so libraries may find themselves spending significant amounts of money without adding any content to their collections.

Demand-led acquisition

An extension of the rental model that is designed to address this is the demand-driven or patron-driven acquisition model (offered by, for example, Dawson*era*, EBL, MyiLibrary and NetLibrary). If the same book is accessed a certain number of times by library users, it will trigger a purchase request. The library is charged the full price for the book, which is then added to the library's collection.

This model offers several advantages. Once again, it maximizes value for money as the library only pays for content that is used, and no staff time is spent selecting titles for purchase. It also gives the library the means to respond very quickly to user needs, for example sudden demand for a title on a reading list, or for a book featured prominently in the mass media.

However, it does raise some issues for collection management policy. Allowing users to select titles could result in an unbalanced collection, which reflects the interests of a few users, although this risk can be reduced by limiting the range of titles made available to users for selection, or by increasing the number of requests required before a purchase is triggered so that only titles with broad appeal are purchased.

Allowing automatic approval of purchases also means that the library may have less budgetary control. Again there are options available to alleviate this concern, for example requiring more expensive books to be approved by a librarian rather than being purchased automatically. But very close monitoring of spending is required to manage the budget effectively and the demand-led acquisition model may therefore be less suitable for libraries with limited financial resources.

Selected chapters and pay-per-view

A further extension of the concept of buying only required content is the option to acquire only selected chapters of a book. Similar to the custom-publishing model for textbooks, this new option may be particularly suited to the academic sector, as it fits well with demand for short extracts of online content for inclusion in VLEs, as well as aligning with trends towards article-level purchase models in the scholarly journals market. However at the time of writing very few publishers are offering libraries the option to purchase content in this way, possibly because they fear a potential loss of revenue if they are only selling sections of books, and where chapter-level (or even page-level) purchasing is available it may be restricted to sales to end-users on the pay-per-view model.

Usage limits

As mentioned above, a major concern of publishers supplying e-books to libraries is that one copy of an e-book in a library provides potentially unlimited usage, possibly reducing overall sales of multiple copies to libraries or end-users. Therefore it is common to find that e-books for libraries have some form of limit on the level of usage, and the nature of this limit is another factor in the choice of a suitable business model.

Unlimited usage model

Some e-books offer unlimited usage, typically major reference works (for example, Oxford Reference Online), specialist research monographs (for example, Springer eBooks) and database-style packages of books that have traditionally been sold principally to libraries, so the publisher may be less concerned with the possible loss of print book sales.

However, most business models impose a cap on usage, limiting either the number of users who can access the e-book at the same time, or the number of times the book can be accessed within a set time period.

Limited user model

Where there is a limit on the number of simultaneous users it may restrict the total number of readers able to access the supplier's platform as a whole, but it is more common to limit the number of users who can access a particular book at the same time. Access may be limited to just a single user, or to a small number of users, but once the limit is reached any other readers trying to access the book are turned away and will have to try again later (for example, MyiLibrary and NetLibrary).

This method of limiting usage may be suitable for titles that are not in high demand, as it is unlikely that more than one user will need access to the work at any one time. It may also be suitable for titles with higher demand but where that demand is spread throughout the year, because although only one user can access the book at a time, there is no limit on the total number of times the book can be used. It is less suitable for titles where usage is concentrated into periods of peak demand, for example new fiction or books on reading lists. Users may find that the e-book they want is already in use, a situation that may be particularly frustrating for users who equate online access with immediate availability. As with print books, if the library wishes to increase access to meet demand it will have to purchase additional copies.

Limited usage model

An alternative model that addresses this problem is to allow many users to access a book simultaneously, but to limit the number of times the book can be viewed within a given time period, usually a year from the date of purchase (for example, Dawson*era* and EBL). If an e-book reaches its limit it cannot be used again until the start of the next year, when the usage count is reset to zero. If further access is needed in the meantime, the library must purchase additional copies to provide more usage credits for that title. This model provides more flexibility to meet peak demand, but it may be less suitable for books with high demand throughout the year, as there is a risk that the book will hit its annual usage limit very quickly. Some suppliers give an additional option to 'opt out' a single chapter from the usage count, providing unlimited use of a part of a book for a limited period, and this may be a useful option if there are works with chapters in very high demand, for example where reading lists of textbooks cite key chapters to be read.

There are advantages and disadvantages to both methods of limiting access (limiting usage and limiting user), and as to which represents best value for money; both the overall level of demand for a title and the distribution of that demand throughout the year need to be taken into account. Usage statistics will demonstrate these patterns, showing how many times a title was accessed, whether the usage was concentrated into a short period or spread throughout the year, and whether any readers were turned away, and this information can help to decide which option is best for the library. Some suppliers offer both options while others will offer only one or the other, so this will be another key factor in the library's choice of supplier.

Licence terms

Most suppliers will apply a licence to the use of their service. Some may simply display a web page stating the terms and conditions, but most will supply a formal licence, which defines who can use the e-books, where they can use them and what they can do with them.

Licences can be very complex, so before taking on a new e-book supplier it is essential to ensure that the terms are acceptable, and that the library and its users are able to comply with the requirements. Some key elements are common to all licences, although some details may vary considerably depending on the nature of the library service, and whether it is intended for public, academic or other libraries.

Authorized users

The licence may define those who can be given access to the service. As already noted, the key consideration is to ensure that the service allows library use, and is not limited to private use only. The library will also need to ensure that any definitions of authorized users cover all of the groups that need to access the service, such as alumni, external members, business users and visitors or non-members, often termed 'walk-in users'. The exact nature of the user groups that need to be covered will depend on the policy of the individual library.

Authentication and access

The licence will usually place some limits on where and how the service can be accessed. Most licences will stipulate secure network access requiring the use of a login and/or password. Many will also contain geographical restrictions, for example overseas usage may not be allowed, or in some cases access by users based in specific countries may be prohibited by a supplier, according to the trade law of the company's country of origin. Walk-in access may only be permitted within the library building, and if the library operates over multiple branches or campuses, the licence may not cover all sites, or at least not without the payment of a higher fee.

Authorized usage

The licence will also define the acceptable uses of both the e-book titles and the supplier's interface. For example, it may specify that use is for non-commercial purposes only, and it may limit the printing, copying and downloading of extracts or their use for the purposes of interlibrary loan. For academic libraries, the licence may state whether sections of the book can be uploaded for use in a VLE.

Supplier responsibilities

As well as imposing terms on the library, the licence also determines the responsibilities of the supplier, for example, to maintain website availability, to provide technical advice to the library and its users, to support authentication systems and/or to supply usage statistics. As noted above, the licence may also commit the supplier to guarantee continuing access to the e-book, perhaps by preserving content in a secure archiving service such as CLOCKSS or Portico.

Before using a new supplier, it is essential to ensure that the terms of the licence are acceptable. If any of the terms are unclear, ambiguous or contradictory, clarification should be sought from the supplier and if possible from a legal professional. If some of the terms are unacceptable, it may be possible to negotiate more appropriate terms. Whilst the supplier may not agree to major changes, they may well be prepared to accept minor amendments such as a change of wording. However, if the supplier is unable or unwilling to compromise and the terms remain unacceptable, it will be necessary to seek an alternative source for the required material.

Quality of service and technical considerations

As well as the core issues of content availability, business models and licence terms, the quality of service the supplier offers to the library and its users will also influence the choice of supplier.

For e-books intended to be read online, the quality of service to library users will depend largely on the quality of the supplier's interface. The library will need to evaluate the features available to readers as follows:

- Is there a good range of search options?
- Are the search results clearly presented?
- Are the books easy to read, and in a suitable file format?
- Can users print or copy selections from the e-book easily?
- Does the supplier use DRM software to enforce limits on printing and copying?
- Does the interface offer any personalization features such as the ability to add notes, reviews or bookmarks to help the reader return to text of particular interest in the future, or tags to identify key topics?
- Does the interface offer any additional tools, such as embedded dictionaries or study support materials?

The library will also need to assess whether the interface is technically compatible with its systems:

- Does it meet accessibility requirements?
- Does it support the authentication systems in use?
- Does it support any federated searching or web-scale discovery systems that are in use?
- Is it compatible with any link resolver system in use?

Although limited in scope to suppliers to the academic market, the JISC Academic Database Assessment Tool (ADAT) provides a useful overview of the features of a range of different e-book platforms.

The quality of service that the supplier can offer to the librarian is also an important factor:

- Is ordering via electronic data interchange (EDI) or via the supplier's website possible?
- Are COUNTER (Counting Online Usage of NeTworked Electronic Resources) compliant usage statistics provided?
- Are good quality catalogue records provided, and if so is there a charge?
- Is good support provided, ideally from a local office or re-seller to account for any time zone differences?
- Are marketing materials for the promotion of e-books provided?
- Are training materials that can be repurposed by the library provided?
- Is personal training provided, either on-site or online, and is this offered to library staff and/or library users?

Conclusion

Choosing an e-book provider involves balancing many different criteria to find the best value option for the content required. Acquiring e-books can be more complicated than acquiring print books, and restrictions on content availability in particular have hampered the take-up of e-books in libraries. However, more content in e-formats is now appearing, and new practices are being introduced to address problems in the supply chain, for example developing standards for the consistent use of e-book ISBNs, and building new services to provide e-book metadata and better information about the availability of specific titles.

This complexity is not wholly negative. It also gives the potential for greater flexibility, with new suppliers and evolving business models giving libraries the opportunity to find innovative new ways to supply content to users. A shift from local provision to an outsourced model offers a new approach for library services, with the potential for significant cost-savings, and models such as demand-driven acquisition offer the opportunity to move from a 'just-in-case' mode of collection building towards a more cost-effective 'just-in-time' mode of content supply.

This is a time of rapid change in the wider e-book market. The growing popularity of e-book reader devices is driving a rapid increase in the number of titles available in e-formats, and new suppliers and business models are challenging the established economics of the publishing market. In the longer term, the eventual settlement of the Google Book agreement could lead to further fundamental changes (see Chapter 4 'E-books for free'). These will no doubt drive further evolution in library e-book business models, which will offer both new opportunities and new challenges to librarians.

Useful links

Eduserv e-Book Finder http://ebookfinder.labs.eduserv.org.uk

JISC ADAT www.jisc-adat.com/adat/adat_ebooks.pl

TeleRead (blog): news and views on e-books, libraries, publishing and related topics www.teleread.com

The UKSG E-Resources Management Handbook www.uksg.org/serials#handbook

References

Hyams, E. (ed.) (2009) Divergent Views on E-book Lending Emerge from Publishers, *Library and Information Update*, March, 11.

JISC (2009) *National E-books Observatory Project Final Report*, www.jiscebooksproject.org/wp-content/JISC-e-books-observatory-final-report-Nov-09.pdf.

OverDrive, Inc (2010) *How Ebook Catalogs at Public Libraries Drive Publishers' Book Sales and Profits*, www.overdrive.com/files/PubWhitePaper.pdf.

3

Producing eBooks on Demand: a European library network

Silvia Gstrein and Günter Mühlberger

Introduction

Following the creation of the European Commission's digital strategy in recent years, European libraries have been meticulously digitizing parts of their cultural heritage. At the same time they have witnessed increasing demand from researchers and readers for access to digital resources, particularly historical books. This was the impetus behind the eBooks on Demand (EOD) network, which provides a trans-European digital document delivery service for readers all over the world. Currently the EOD network consists of almost 30 libraries from 12 European countries. Since 2007 between 4000 and 5000 e-books have been generated, delivered to users worldwide and subsequently made available to the public through the repositories of the participating libraries. User reactions have been very positive and more libraries are interested in offering the service. This chapter examines the service in general, the libraries involved, the experience from both user and library points of view, and future developments.

Background

In 2005, the European Commission launched i2010, a policy framework for the information society and media, which aimed to promote 'the positive contribution that information and communication technologies (ICT) can make to the economy, society and personal quality of life' (Europa, 2010). Recently the i2010 strategy has been superseded by a new initiative, the Digital Agenda for Europe 2010–2020, which aims to 'maximize the benefit of the Digital Revolution for all'. In line with both of these initiatives, European libraries and other cultural institutions are gradually digitizing and making available their cultural heritage to a wider public. However, it will still take decades for the majority of books, journals and other library material to become available in digital form owing to the sheer volume of source material, despite the digitization efforts of Google Books.

In an ideal world, all of the works in a collection would be considered for digitization. In practice, however, this is rarely feasible and difficult choices must be made. Lists of criteria have been developed for identifying the most appropriate titles. According to the MINERVA Good Practices Handbook (Minerva Working Group 6, 2004), material should be prioritized for digitization when:

- it would otherwise be unavailable/of limited availability
- it is very popular and could be more widely and easily accessed digitally
- it is delicate and could be preserved by making digital versions available as an alternative
- it is suitable for the physical process of digitization
- it is appropriate for online viewing
- it has a theme/subject matter identified as of interest to researchers/the general public
- it can be legally digitized, taking into account copyright and intellectual property rights (IPR) issues
- it has not already been made available digitally
- it can feasibly be digitized within the funds available.

In reality, the approach chosen is often determined by the availability and source of funding, in combination with the institution's digitization policy. This method of deciding which material to digitize only very rarely acknowledges user interests other than the influence of popularity, as mentioned above. This raises the following questions: how can the process take account of the individual users' needs, and what happens to the material not covered by any of the criteria? For example, who will digitize books in minor languages or those from smaller or more specialist collections and institutions?

All of these considerations form the starting point for the eBooks on Demand network: an electronic document delivery service initiated and part-funded by the user. The service meets the need for a model of ongoing rather than project-led digitization, and is a co-ordinated European initiative. The selection of material for digitization works bottom-up rather than top-down – the individual reader begins the process by requesting that a certain book be digitized, and then contributes financially towards the scanning process. Subsequent costs for storage, access, long-term preservation and migration are not funded by the reader, and will not be addressed in detail in this chapter.

The eBooks on Demand service

It was recognized that it would be difficult to maintain a user-orientated library service such as EOD within the context of the usual methods of mass digitization, as additional resources for order management, customer communication and payment procedures would be required. Therefore, a structure allowing for efficient processing of orders was designed for the service. This employs elements of both centralization and decentralization, where some processes such as the optical character recognition of scanned images and online payment for completed orders are hosted centrally, but other processes such as the scanning itself are managed by the individual libraries that are members of the network.

From October 2006 to June 2008, a pilot Digitization on Demand project was carried out, with funding from the European Union eTEN programme (Europa, 2006). This involved 13 national and university libraries from eight European countries: Austria, Denmark, Estonia, Germany, Hungary, Portugal, Slovakia and Slovenia. After the pilot project was evaluated, the self-sustaining eBooks on Demand network was set up by the 13 founding libraries. Since then EOD has attracted further associated members (Mühlberger and Gstrein, 2009).

Ordering books through EOD

Briefly, EOD functions as follows. The starting point is the online catalogue of the participating library. The EOD button is visible on the catalogue entry for all items available for digitization. Presently these are books that are in the public domain and not yet digitized by any of the network libraries. Any user interested in obtaining a copy of a book simply clicks on the EOD button to initiate the process (see Figure 3.1). From 2011, a search engine covering as many as possible of the online catalogues of participating libraries will go online, which will make it easier to search from one single point. The link will be made available on the network website at http://books2ebooks.eu.

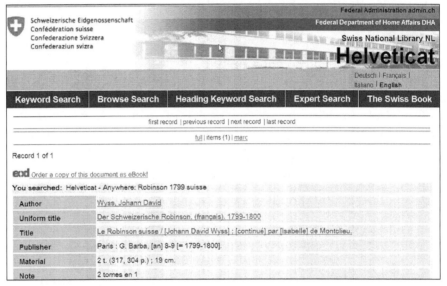

Figure 3.1 *Example of EOD button in the Swiss National Library online catalogue*

Next, the user fills out the order form, where they can choose the type of delivery they require. This may take the form of a download or can be delivered via a data carrier such as DVD (Digital Versatile Disc) (see Figure 3.2). After this, the user is invited to follow the progress of the order on their personal tracking page.

Fulfilling the order

The relevant library receives the order in real time, then scans the requested book and transfers the scanned images via File Transfer Protocol (FTP) to the central server located at Innsbruck University,

Figure 3.2 *Example of order form after clicking on the EOD button*

which is the network co-ordinator. Each library manages and processes its own orders using a central database, the Order Data Manager, accessible via their web browser (see Figure 3.3 overleaf).

The workflow for the creation of the digitized book is also tracked via the Order Data Manager (see below). After completing the payment process, which supports online credit card payment, the user downloads the PDF from their personal tracking page. After a period of time, the library adds the digitized book to its digital library or repository and thus makes it available to the general public.

The Order Data Manager includes another core component: the Digital Object Generator, which is used to create e-books by applying OCR and generating the PDF file (see Figure 3.4 overleaf).

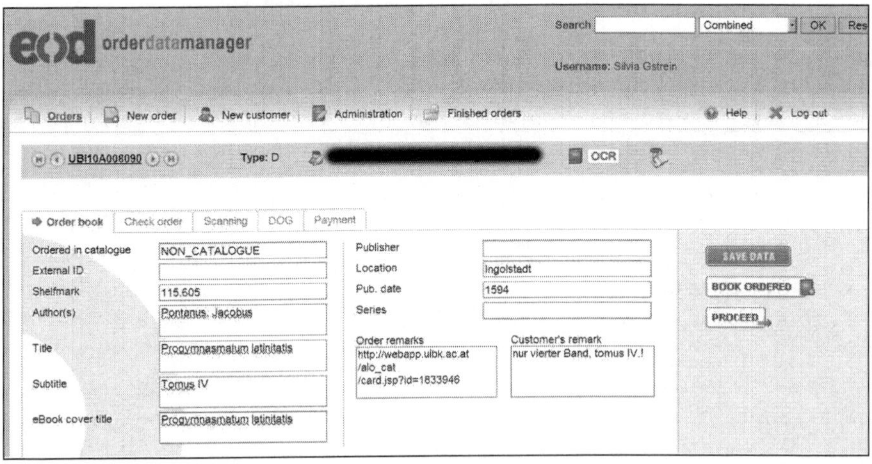

Figure 3.3 *The Order Data Manager database*

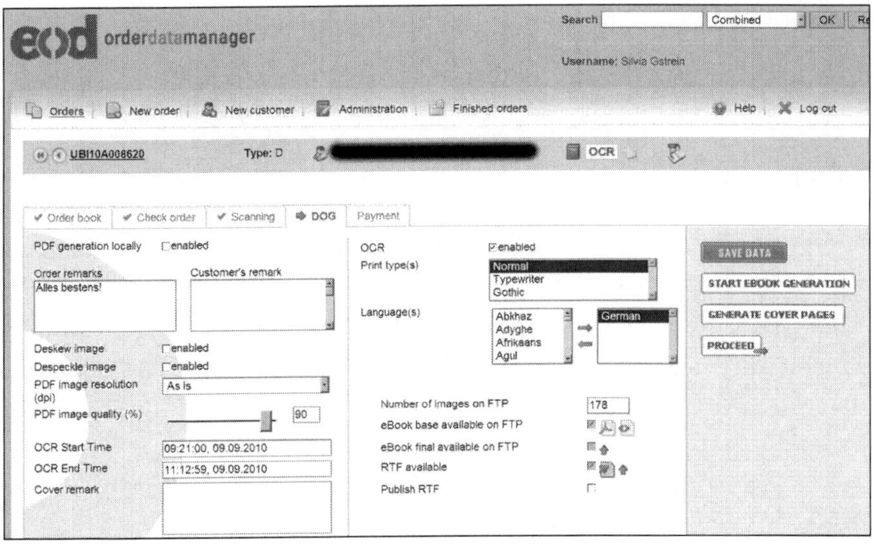

Figure 3.4 *The Digital Object Generator*

The Digital Object Generator supports OCR of all common typefaces from the 18th century to the 20th century, including Roman and Gothic fonts as well as Cyrillic, Hebrew and Greek scripts, all of which are important when digitizing a wide range of historic texts. It is also possible to generate a cover automatically, including the relevant metadata and displaying the logo of the delivering library. The creation of output files such as PDF, RTF (Rich Text Format) and OCR XML (EXtensible Markup Language), as well as the generation of the streaming link for downloading, is rendered during the process. The PDF e-book delivered to the user consists of two layers: the first containing the scanned images and the second containing the automated recognized text.

Multilingual access is a very important aspect of a pan-European service. All generic content, such as the text on the order form, is offered in all the national languages of the participating libraries, meaning 11 different languages currently. All other library-specific text is provided in the respective national language as well as in English, as a minimum. According to its needs and objectives, any participating institution can adapt and customize different content, such as the information linked from the order form and tracking page as well as automatically generated e-mail text.

The EOD network – participating libraries

Currently almost 30 libraries from 12 European countries offer the service, ranging from Portugal in the far west to Estonia in the East. For up-to-date information about network members see www.books2ebooks.eu/partner.php5. Several types of libraries are currently involved: national libraries, university and state libraries as well as research and academy of science libraries (see Table 3.1 overleaf).

Efforts are also being made to include archives and other cultural institutions in the network, with the aim of providing digitization on demand far beyond the world of books in the narrow sense. For example, the St Pölten Diocese Archive (Austria) began to implement the service in 2010.

User experience

To date, between 4000 and 5000 books have been digitized and delivered to customers through the EOD – books that may not otherwise have been digitized. Over a million scanned pages have been produced, and nearly 2500 readers have used the service worldwide. The three libraries that process the most digitized texts receive one request per working day on average and deliver 250 to 350 books per year each. The average delivery time is one week.

Table 3.1 *Libraries involved in the eBooks on Demand network (September 2010)*

Country	Library
Austria	University of Innsbruck Library (co-ordinator)
	University Libraries of Graz and Vienna
	Vienna City Library
	Library of the Medical University of Vienna
	St Pölten Diocese Archive
Czech Republic	Moravian Library in Brno
	Research Library in Olomouc
	Library of the Academy of Sciences in Prague
	National Technical Library
Denmark	The Royal Library
Estonia	National Library
	University Library of Tartu
France	Medical and Dental Academic Library of Paris
Germany	University Libraries of Regensburg, Greifswald, Leipzig and Humboldt-Universität zu Berlin
	Bavarian State Library
	Saxon State and University Library (Dresden)
Hungary	National Széchényi Library of Hungary
	Library of the Hungarian Academy of Sciences
Portugal	National Library
Slovakia	University Library in Bratislava
	Slovak Academy of Sciences
Slovenia	National and University Library
Sweden	Umeå University Library
Switzerland	The Swiss National Library

The average price of an e-book ordered via EOD is 50 EUR. This is calculated by starting with a minimum fee (on average 10 EUR) and adding a cost-per-page-scanned (generally 0.15 to 0.30 EUR). At the moment the pricing system is fairly heterogeneous, as each library sets its own prices depending on national and local policies and conditions; however, harmonization of prices would be desirable in the future.

As mentioned above, revenue from the customer only partly funds digitization, whilst the customer-orientated service provided by EOD is more costly on a per-book basis than mass digitization, which places huge emphasis on efficiency and economies of scale. However, given that the master files remain with the library and are later made freely accessible to the public, the overall benefits greatly exceed those to the individual who initiated the process, so it is felt that the customer should not be required to pay the total real cost of digitization.

In 2008 a survey of EOD customers was carried out to collect feedback on the service, and to find out what users thought about the pricing policy. The findings were that 30% of customers felt the price was high or very high, but overall value for money was still found to be acceptable by the majority.

The overwhelming majority of users are either researchers or readers requiring e-books for professional or scientific use (over 60%). The second largest category of users (16%) is made up of book collectors and readers from special interest groups such as amateur historians, collectors or ethnographers (see Figure 3.5).

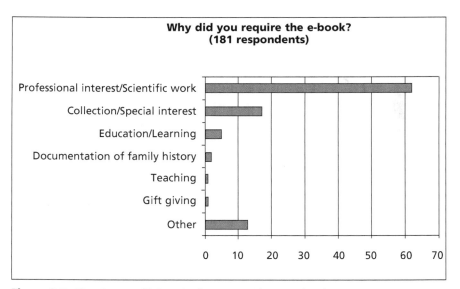

Figure 3.5 *Users' area of interest when requesting an e-book*

Asked why they had opted for the EOD service, almost half of the interviewees answered that without EOD the book would have been 'impossible or difficult to access'. This shows that EOD has achieved one of its main goals, that of being a practical alternative to accessing printed books in a library or archive collection (see Figure 3.6).

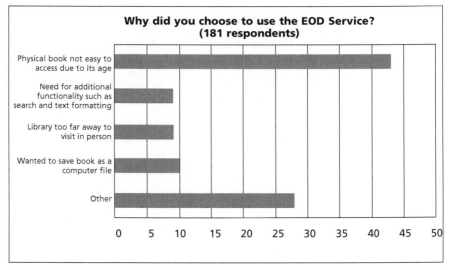

Figure 3.6 *Reasons for ordering an eBook on Demand*

In the same survey, 60% of customers said that they usually print out selected pages or even the whole book. Thus, there is an obvious demand for 're-materialization' of digital material. In response to this, the EOD network has recently begun to offer 'reprints on demand': the provision of historical books in paper format supplementing the digital file. This option can be selected during the ordering process, in addition to requesting the PDF. From the perspective of the participating library, the service is straightforward. Each library carries out the scanning of the images and provides some additional metadata. All other processes, such as image enhancement and the creation of pre-press PDFs and related files, are carried out by the central co-ordinator at the University of Innsbruck Library.

Infrastructure and other organizational aspects

Staff and departments involved

Depending on the structure of the individual library, EOD may be run by a variety of different departments including those focusing on digitization, document delivery and user services. In almost all cases local library staff carry out the digitization; only rarely is scanning outsourced.

Equipment

Owing to the wide range of different institutions offering the service, many different types of hardware and software are used, depending on the local infrastructure already in place. Scanning is carried out largely using overhead scanners, but automatic or semi-automatic book scanners and photo cameras are also used in some libraries.

The member libraries have agreed common minimum digitization standards in order to guarantee good quality reproduction, with a focus on optimizing OCR results. The accuracy of OCR depends not only on the quality of the scan, but also the print type and language of the original; for example, there are very severe difficulties in accurately converting image to text for texts published prior to 1850. The European project IMPACT tackled these difficulties through comprehensive research into OCR and language technology in relation to the processing and retrieval of historical documents, as well as by promoting the sharing of expertise to build digitization capacity across Europe.

Use of fees

Most of the revenue from the fees paid for digitizing books is put directly back into the digitization services of the member libraries and only rarely into general library funds. As mentioned above, the fee covers the scanning and order handling costs, but not the infrastructure or costs of subsequently providing the e-book to the general public.

Life after digitization

After the books have been scanned and successfully delivered to customers, the EOD network libraries make them publicly available by uploading them into their own repository after a certain period (in most cases about two months), and then providing a link to the full text from the records in their catalogue.

Currently, the option of providing a central repository for all books digitized via EOD is being discussed within the network, and this would be of particular benefit for those libraries without a repository of their own. Additionally, from 2011 onwards the metadata of books digitized via EOD will be made available through Europeana, the library of digital objects created by cultural institutions throughout Europe. This is because EOD acts as the content aggregator for its member libraries for the European Commission project EuropeanaConnect, which aims to share best practice in the area of digital libraries.

Currently there is no centralized provision for digital preservation; each library makes its own arrangements for the long-term care of the scanned images and resulting files.

Holdings offered

Currently, only books in the public domain that have not previously been digitized are offered through the EOD digital document supply service. Within the new 'Reprints on Demand' service, works already digitized will also be offered in print format. In the future, the network may also be able to offer out-of-print books. However, in most European countries the copyright status of each individual item still needs to be checked, making the digitization of out-of-print books that are still in copyright time-consuming and costly.

To avoid duplication of effort, a tool to check whether a book has already been digitized by a member of the network is in development. However, this is still a work in progress, particularly as various European libraries use different identifiers in their catalogues for the same book title, making it difficult to match results accurately. As a result, identifying whether a specific book has already been digitized by another member library is still labour intensive.

Communication

Within the network, meetings are organized at least twice a year. There is a general meeting in spring where overarching objectives and the methodology for collaboration are discussed. This is followed by a session in autumn, which focuses more on practical and technical issues such as scanning workflow, hardware issues and so on.

Between the main meetings, communication takes place via e-mail and an internal wiki. If necessary, face-to-face meetings between the co-ordinator and partner libraries are held. On occasion distinctive national features need to be discussed, in which case it has been highly effective to bring together all of the library representatives from the same country, with or without the network co-ordinator.

Difficulties of running a pan-European service

Despite the various methods of communication described above, difficulties are still encountered at times. The various local, regional and national contexts have to be taken into account, and problems tend to arise in areas where there are a variety of practices in use. In a decentralized network this is particularly the case in the area of pricing, which varies according to both national and individual library policies. It can also be seen in the need to handle different currencies, languages and terms and conditions.

Future developments

Recently a new EOD project began, within the framework of the European Commission Culture Programme 2007–2013. The project focuses on the larger scale involvement of three main target groups: participating libraries, individual users and the general public. Twenty libraries from ten European countries are concentrating on the following objectives: first to enlarge the EOD network by the inclusion of additional European libraries, especially those from countries not yet represented; second to take EOD as a best practice model for other Europe-wide networks of this kind and to train stakeholders (libraries, museums or other cultural organizations) to run a multinational cultural service based on state-of-the-art information technologies; and finally to support intercultural dialogue among readers and users of historical books with the help of Web 2.0 technology.

During recent years the internet has become noticeably more participatory in nature. Users not only create and edit information, but take part in the digital community by sharing texts, images, videos, opinions and reviews with other users. Whereas many sites such as library catalogues and repositories are only visited occasionally for the purpose of retrieving clearly defined data, individuals frequently log in to their personal accounts at Web 2.0 applications such as Twitter and Facebook, and use them as they might read a newspaper, meet friends in a café or visit a museum. It follows that cultural organizations need not only to make their cultural heritage accessible via the internet in a passive way, but also to proactively feed Web 2.0 platforms with their content, since these are the sites where many users are actively engaging in social and academic discourse.

As a way of moving towards this, Web 2.0-based social platforms such as Wikipedia (www.wikipedia.org), LibraryThing (www.librarything.com) and Goodreads (www.goodreads.com) will be supplied with information about selected historical books. Readers all over the world who are interested in a specific book will be able to interact easily with one another, exchange information and share reading and research experiences independently of their geographical location and professional, social or academic background. Initially EOD will explore the technical feasibility of automatically generating Wikipedia source-code for selected digitized books, and then will add metadata to articles about the relevant authors. Other social platforms will be tackled at later stages of the project.

Conclusion

European libraries host millions of print books published from 1500 to 1900. Because of their age and value they are often only accessible to users who are prepared to visit these libraries in person. With the eBooks on Demand service these hidden treasures are now becoming available to all, with just a few mouse clicks.

The experience of running the EOD network has shown that such services are a desirable means of providing researchers and other customers with the material they need 'here and now'. However, this is just a first step. In the future, it may be possible to establish further on-demand services, such as digitization for visually impaired people (see 'Accessible e-book services in public libraries' in Part 6 of this book) and the creation of fully navigable e-books rather than simple image files, with corrected full text of up to 99% accuracy. This would pave the way for the transfer of e-books onto mobile devices, making the written word available anytime, anywhere.

Acknowledgements

This work programme has been funded with support from the European Commission. This publication reflects the views only of the authors, and the Commission cannot be held responsible for any use that may be made of the information contained therein.

Useful links

Culture Programme 2007-2013 http://eacea.ec.europa.eu/culture/programme/about_culture_en.php

Digital Agenda for Europe 2010-2020 http://ec.europa.eu/information_society/digital-agenda/index_en.htm

eBooks on Demand www.books2ebooks.eu

Europeana http://europeana.eu

EuropeanaConnect project www.europeanaconnect.eu

IMPACT: Improving access to text www.impact-project.eu

Bibliography

Europa (2006) *eTEN Digitisation on Demand Project Factsheet*, http://ec.europa.eu/information_society/activities/eten/cf/opdb/cf/project/index.cfm?mode=detail&project_ref=ETEN-518635.

Europa (2010) *i2010 - a European information society for growth and employment*, http://ec.europa.eu/information_society/eeurope/i2010/index_en.htm.

Mezö, Z., Svoljsak, S. and Gstrein, S. (2007) EOD – European Network of Libraries for eBooks on Demand. In Kovács, L., Fuhr, N. and Meghini, C (eds), *Research and Advanced Technology for Digital Libraries 11th European*

Conference, ECDL 2007, Budapest, Hungary, September 16-21, 2007. Proceedings, 570-2.

Minerva Working Group 6 (ed.) (2004) *Good Practices Handbook*, Version 1.3, www.minervaeurope.org/structure/workinggroups/goodpract/document/ goodpractices1_3.pdf.

Mühlberger, G. and Gstrein, S. (2009) eBooks on Demand (EOD): a European digitisation service, *IFLA Journal*, **35** (1), 35-43, http://archive.ifla.org/V/iflaj/ IFLA-Journal-1-2009.pdf.

Svoljsak, S. and Gstrein, S. (2007) EOD - eBooks on Demand. In: *Users and Use of DL & Economics of Digital Libraries: Libraries in the Digital Age (LIDA) Conference 2007, Dubrovnik and Mljet, Croatia, May 28-June 2, 2007*, 229-30.

4

E-books for free: finding, creating and managing freely available texts

Kate Price

Introduction

Most of this book concentrates on acquiring and managing e-books that are commercially available. But there *are* other options. Almost as soon as the internet came into existence, it was being used to freely disseminate full textbooks and reports. At first these were created through typing in basic ASCII (American Standard Code for Information Interchange 2) text, then with desktop publishing and word-processing applications, and by scanning in existing text and using OCR to instantly create keyword searchable text files. Now graphical, audio and video elements are embedded in books and documents through the use of cheap and widely available hardware and software.

Today, there are millions of texts freely available online through myriads of small scale efforts right on up to the behemoth that is Google Books. However, few libraries are currently making full use of this fantastic resource. This chapter aims to raise awareness of a small fraction of this content, explain the pros and cons of free e-books, address some of the issues involved with managing ongoing access to a collection that contains freely available texts, and also introduce the option of creating e-books in-house, by writing them from scratch or through digitizing existing published or unpublished works.

Making use of free e-books

Advantages

Free e-books have one rather obvious advantage – they do not require an acquisitions budget. But the following should also be considered:

1 Some essential reference resources that a library might already receive in print are also available freely online. These include government statistical publications and accounts, census data, government reports, and publications and statistics from non-governmental organisations (NGOs) and international bodies such as the United Nations (UN), the World Health Organization (WHO) and the EU. It is therefore a fairly easy matter to include a link from the catalogue record of the print publication to the online version, quickly making this material much more easily available to library users without the need for them to search across the web for it. In addition, the factual information within this type of reference material is often more quickly and simply accessed online through a search interface tailored to the resource in question.

2 There is usually no need to log in (advantageous for the user, and meaning that there is no need for the library to maintain access and authentication systems or provide instructions on how to log in, much reducing the need for user support and troubleshooting). These are very real advantages to libraries that have a fluid user population, such as cultural institutions that often host visiting researchers and therefore find managing authentication and access to e-resources a challenge. However, some government data in formats aimed at the academic audience does require registration and login via Athens or Federated Access (Shibboleth), so some guidance may still be necessary for these users.

3 Free e-books are not usually subject to DRM software. Again this makes life easy for users, as they do not encounter barriers such as limits on the amounts that can be downloaded or printed.

4 There are generally no limits on the number of simultaneous users, which reduces the incidence of frustrating lock-outs.

5 The lack of usage restrictions has great advantages for researchers using data and text mining techniques, such as those working on

various projects currently being supported by JISC in the UK. For these techniques to function, large amounts of text and other data must be downloaded, processed and then manipulated by sophisticated software programs, an activity that is rarely allowable under the licence terms of commercially available e-books, even if the file formats were to be suitable.

Disadvantages

However, there are also many real or perceived disadvantages:

1   Free resources (including free e-books) may suffer from a certain lack of credibility. There may be worries that the content is of poor quality or is pushing a specific agenda without this being immediately obvious, particularly if the item lacks the recognized stamp of a mainstream publisher. In the library setting, there is also an understandable tendency to concentrate staffing resources on paid-for resources in order to make them available to readers as quickly as possible, so that the expenditure can be justified. As with unsolicited print donations, free e-books can therefore languish on the 'to do' shelf for longer than might be the case if money had been spent acquiring them.
2   There may be issues of quality and standardization. Resources may have been created by volunteers working as individuals, without the layers of rigorous editing and proofreading available within large organizations. This may be of some concern if absolute accuracy is crucial for library users, although free texts available through sources such as Project Gutenberg may prove invaluable as a starting point for gaining an overview of various versions of the same text if they are not available in the physical library. In a college or university environment, it is wise to be aware that there may be issues such as lack of pagination or corrupted text, and it is therefore prudent to check with tutors before recommending such resources.
3   Some freely available resources are created by entities (such as government-funded or privately supported projects) that may not exist indefinitely. There may be uncertainty over who will take

ownership of the material once the project is finished, or even if there will be a location for the material to be hosted in the future. In some cases funding may be stopped unexpectedly, with potentially serious consequences. For example, the Arts and Humanities Data Service (AHDS) ceased to be funded by the Arts and Humanities Research Council (AHRC) and JISC in March 2008 after 11 years of existence, on the basis that individual HE institutions in the UK should now have the expertise to provide digitization and preservation services without central support (Arts and Humanities Data Service, 2007). Fortunately, the substantial number of texts made freely available by the AHDS Language and Literature Service continue to be hosted by the Oxford Text Archive, based at Oxford University Computing Services. Of course mainstream publishers are also vulnerable to commercial failure, mergers and takeovers, although their assets are usually sold on and therefore remain available, albeit with changes of branding or business model.

4   Free e-resources may lack a defined revenue stream, unless they are supported through advertising, as with Google Books. This lack of revenue creates many disadvantages: there is unlikely to be a substantial promotional budget, so awareness of the resource may be low amongst potential users; it is unlikely that services such as free MARC records will be provided, which makes it more time-consuming for libraries to make free e-books available through their catalogues; and it is likely that less money will be spent on creating and continuing to develop a visually arresting and user-friendly platform interface, which again reduces the appeal to readers.

5   Similarly, low or no budget operations are unlikely to be able to offer technical support or comprehensive training and guidance materials for their resources over the long term. It is also unlikely that they will provide institution-level usage statistics, making it difficult to judge the scale of usage for these resources by the users of a specific library, unless in-house server logs can be interrogated, which is a time-intensive task requiring technical expertise to develop.

6   Both the lack of a revenue stream and the short-term nature of

some digitization initiatives have potential consequences for long-term access and preservation of free e-book content. Digital media formats shift with frightening rapidity; as software versions move on and new formats are created, so old file formats and storage media become unsupported and unusable. At the same time, digital files can degrade rapidly and unless they are constantly repaired, the content within them also becomes unusable over time, even if an appropriate software programme can be found to access it. Small scale digitization projects may not have the expertise or budget to address these issues, although there are open-source initiatives such as LOCKSS that allow for cheap, distributed digital preservation (see http://lockss.stanford.edu) as well as national digital archiving initiatives that aim to identify and preserve important materials for the future, such as the Internet Archive at www.archive.org.

7 Finally, although no budget is required to access free e-books, in the library context there may be staff costs associated with tasks such as selection, cataloguing, maintaining access and deselection.

Case Study: Google Books – the ultimate library?

No chapter on free e-books would be complete without a section about Google Books, a project breathtaking in scope but mired in controversy since its inception. Google's well known mission to '[o]rganize the world's information and make it universally accessible and useful' (Google, 2010b) took a leap beyond the purely online world with the announcement in late 2004 that the company had partnered with a number of high profile libraries, as well as some major publishers, to make the content of huge numbers of books available to search through the Google interface. By early 2010, over 12 million books had been digitized, and metadata from over 174 million unique works made available for searching (Oder, 2010). From the start, the opinions of librarians, authors, rights-holders and researchers have been deeply divided on the desirability of this development.

On one hand, the directors of major libraries such as those of Harvard, Cornell, Oxford, Princeton, Stanford, California and Keio Universities, the New York Public Library and the Austrian National Library were deeply committed to bringing the full text of their unique holdings to anyone who needs or wants it, and Google in its dominant position as the world's preferred internet search engine was one way to bring this about (Google, 2010a). Researchers reliant on unique or otherwise difficult to access texts have already reaped the benefit of this approach, as texts that are no longer in copyright have been fully digitized on a massive scale, and are now available without payment anywhere in the world (subject to government restrictions in certain countries). Rights-holders such as publishers who have bought into the project have also made their books available for full-text searching and limited preview, although the text itself is usually not fully available unless payment is made for either the online text or a printed copy – hence for them this is an excellent opportunity to maximize sales.

On the other hand, Google is a commercial entity, which plans to make revenue by selling both advertising and access to the full text of books that are not commercially available but still in copyright. By digitizing large amounts of library books that are still in copyright, prior to asking the permission of rights-holders, Google Books is in serious breach of copyright law, as its actions cannot be seen in the context of fair use. Accordingly, a class action was filed in the USA against Google in September 2005, led by the Author's Guild. The details of the case are complex, and at the time of writing it is still ongoing, despite a proposed settlement, which was first published in late 2008 and amended in late 2009, but is still to be approved by the US Department of Justice. The terms of the proposed settlement involve giving rights-holders, including individual authors, the chance to opt out of Google Books entirely, and also the setting up of a mechanism called the Books Rights Registry (BRR) through which a percentage of revenue will be allocated to rights-holders who did not opt out. The settlement also provides for unrestricted access to non-commercially available books through terminals in public libraries, and through institutional subscriptions aimed at universities – although the terms of the settlement will initially only apply in the USA, and would have to be renegotiated in other geographical areas according to national and regional copyright laws.

Further to the primary concern with breach of copyright law, there are concerns that Google Books is effectively setting up a monopoly over online book supply (particularly of texts that are not currently commercially available but still in copyright) and thus may breach US antitrust law; concerns from representatives of photographers and artists that their rights are being breached unless an appropriate mechanism for compensation is put in place;

and concerns about who holds the rights to the digital files should Google decide to divest itself of that part of the business, and questions about how the digital files will be preserved for future generations should this happen. In addition, some non-Anglophone countries and groups maintain that Google Books is culturally divisive since its efforts are primarily concentrated on books available in the English-speaking world.

On a purely practical level, some researchers and librarians have found that there are deep flaws in Google Books' metadata, rendering searches at best non-comprehensive. In a post to the *Language Log* blog in August 2009, Geoff Nunberg cites numerous examples of dating and subject classification errors, noting that:

> To take GB's [Google Books'] word for it, 1899 was a literary *annus mirabilis*, which saw the publication of Raymond Chandler's *Killer in the Rain*, *The Portable Dorothy Parker*, André Malraux' *La Condition Humaine*, Stephen King's *Christine*, *The Complete Shorter Fiction of Virginia Woolf*, Raymond Williams' *Culture and Society*, Robert Shelton's biography of Bob Dylan, Fodor's Guide to Nova Scotia, and the Portuguese edition of the book version of *Yellow Submarine*, to name just a few.
> (Nunberg, 2009)

In a response in the same blog, Jon Orwant of the Google Books Metadata Team explained that Google had imported 250,000 records from a Brazilian metadata provider that used 1899 as an automatic placeholder in the date field, a flaw that has since been corrected. He goes on to argue that no set of metadata is comprehensive or perfect, including the catalogues of OCLC and the Library of Congress, and that given the huge scale of the enterprise, the amount of imperfect data is correspondingly magnified (Orwant, 2009). However, the company says that it is committed to improving metadata wherever it can, and according to an affidavit submitted in support of the Google Books agreement, receives metadata from 48 different libraries and 21 different commercial databases, on which it spends $2.5 million per annum (Oder, 2010).

In summary, Google Books has huge potential to provide access to book content when and where readers want it, but many information and publishing professionals, as well as researchers, are treating the service with caution because of the issues raised above. Therefore, Google Books is not yet 'the ultimate library', but there is a very real chance that it could become so, at least in the eyes of some readers.

Managing access to free e-books in the library context

Overall, the process of managing free e-books offers similar challenges to that of managing commercially available e-books, which are explained elsewhere in this book, although the procurement and budget management aspects of the process are omitted. Paradoxically, there may be additional challenges simply because these resources are free, and therefore the familiar workflow from purchase, to cataloguing, to enabling access and troubleshooting, to weeding and de-selection, is somewhat disrupted and new prompts to carry out the next stage in the process may need to be added where they are lacking.

There is also a real concern that since there is no sales contract in place, and therefore no direct relationship between supplier and library, free e-books are in much more danger of simply disappearing or changing without notice, and that any staff time spent painstakingly tracking down and adding free e-books to the library catalogue may ultimately be wasted. However, this concern may be balanced out by the rapid expansion of high quality resources being offered to library users, particularly for library services where acquisitions budgets may be very restricted, as in the case study below.

Case study: free e-books at the Heinz Archive and Library, National Portrait Gallery

The Heinz Archive and Library of the National Portrait Gallery (NPG) in London is primarily an image library holding prints, photographs and reproductions of British portraits in collections worldwide. Supporting this collection is a reference library of 35,000 books, 150 periodicals and a number of special collections. The clientele of the Library consists of internal users such as NPG curatorial and educational staff, and external users such as commercial gallery owners, biographers, amateur family and local historians, academics and research students.

The Library catalogue, dating back to the foundation of the gallery in 1856, has only recently been made available online, with the installation of the EOS. Web library management system in 2008, and the launch of the OPAC to the outside world in 2009. Catalogue records from an in-house database dating from 1994 were transferred into EOS.Web, and retrospective cataloguing of pre-1994 material is still ongoing, with the involvement of both salaried and volunteer staff.

The Library makes available some relevant online databases including the Dictionary of National Biography (a benefit in kind, as the Gallery supplies many of the images within), specific collections from JSTOR (Journal Storage) and Early English Books Online, both of the latter at rates negotiated by JISC as part of a pilot study into consortium negotiations at a national level on behalf of cultural institutions.

Because of the diverse nature of the clientele and the costs and complexity involved in setting up Athens or Federated Access, access to online resources is IP-address (Internet Protocol-address) authenticated, and therefore accessible only within the Gallery's buildings, or through authenticated access to a remote desktop service provided for Gallery staff. IT support for the library management system (LMS) and the Library website is currently provided by a small department, which services all of the Gallery's administrative departments, including the Archive and Library.

The Library currently has four salaried staff, plus from six to eight volunteer staff at any one time engaged on various projects. There is £7500 per annum available for purchasing books, although it is estimated that 30–40% of that figure again is added in the form of books that are deposited with the Library by publishers as a condition of the use of images from the Gallery.

The Library does not currently purchase any individual e-books. However, it does add links to over 100 free e-books to its catalogue. This came about in late 2009, as a consequence of one of the Gallery staff noticing that a local library had set up a Google Bookshelf, and suggesting that their organization could do the same.

Now, as well as adding links to their own Google Bookshelf, staff systematically search for the online full text of the books that they are cataloguing (both new acquisitions and retrospective additions to the catalogue), and create links from the relevant print catalogue record on the OPAC. This is achieved by searching for the print record in conventional sources such as the English Short Title Catalogue (ESTC) via the British Library, the Library of Congress, and Senate House Library via the Z39.50

protocol, and at the same time routinely querying the Internet Archive and Google Books, usually by using an ISBN number search through the conventional web interface. The MARC record is then uploaded to EOS.Web, and, if available, a link to the e-book is created within the 856 field, with a note added to explain the level of access: for example, 'Full text available', 'Preview available' or 'Keyword searchable' in the case of items on Google Books where only snippet view is available. It is estimated that this adds very little workload to the process – perhaps only one minute per record, but is potentially adding substantial value to the catalogue as a whole.

Examples of the formats in which free e-books are added to catalogue records can be found via the EOS.web catalogue by searching for 'The Annals of Covent Garden Theatre from 1732 to 1897' by Henry Saxe Wyndham and 'Biographical history of Gonville and Caius College, 1349–1897' by John Venn.

It is interesting to note that a specialist library that is primarily focused on image-based material, which only recently made its OPAC publicly available, and which does not have a clientele that specifically wants or demands online information resources, is systematically 'collecting' free e-books. However, in some ways the Heinz Archive and Library is very well placed to carry out this development. It has a well defined collection development policy, and a process already under way (retrospective cataloguing) that enables it to systematically interrogate likely sources of free e-books for specific titles. As an organization with a small number of staff all focused on the same subject matter, it is perhaps easier to quickly come to agreements about new policies and procedures that may cause more debate within a larger organisation with a more diverse remit in terms of collection development.

As mentioned above, linking to free e-books is not a development that has been specifically requested by library users, nor has it been particularly promoted as a service, because staffing resources are currently concentrated on the cataloguing effort. Therefore awareness of the service is low and there is little feedback from users on how e-books are being used (if at all). In addition, within an environment focusing on the visual arts, electronic faxes are not a viable direct replacement for original volumes offering large, high quality images and the physical experience of type and print on the page. However, e-books in general are still seen as an increasingly valuable and convenient reference source by library staff.

As Joseph Ripp (2010), Librarian of the Heinz Archive and Library, says: 'Anything that we can do as librarians to reduce the mediation between the reader and the information that they need is a good thing.' Thus, in common with librarians the world over, he is developing the reference collection by anticipating the implicit and future needs of the Library's readers as much as he is responding to their explicit requests at the present moment.

Creating digital content

An issue that is commonly identified with e-books is the lack of availability of the particular texts desired by the library and its readers. In response to this problem, librarians could attempt to find suitable alternative material, and lobby publishers to digitize their past and present portfolios as soon as possible, but it is also well within the technical capabilities of many larger libraries or their parent organizations to create and host their own e-book content. This can be achieved in two ways – by digitizing existing print collections, and by creating new 'born digitial' material with no print analogue.

Digitizing books or other materials in the library collection

Over the last 15 to 20 years there has been a boom in digitization projects, many of them concentrating on library or archival collections of material that is unique and/or physically difficult to access, creating digital surrogates that both encourage wider access to the content and preserve the original for the future. In the UK, the Heritage Lottery Fund and JISC have been major sources of funding for projects as diverse as the digitization of 520,000 wills and testaments registered with the Scottish Commissary Courts from 1500 to 1901 (a fantastic resource for family history, which can be searched via www.scotlandspeople.gov.uk), and the large collections of British Parliamentary Papers and related material scanned by the BOPCRIS Digitization Centre (formerly British Official Publications Collaborative Reader Information Service) at the University of Southampton's Hartley Library.

BOPCRIS began digitizing material in 1994, and today is home to a sophisticated array of technical infrastructure, including specialist book scanners suitable for fragile material and a high speed robotic scanner capable of processing 500 pages per hour (Kirby Smith, 2009). However, expensive infrastructure is not always necessary to provide a valuable service to library users, and much can be achieved with a desktop scanner and access to a web server for hosting purposes.

It is not the intention of this chapter to go into detail about the technical aspects of digitization, as there are several excellent books on this topic. However, there are a number of issues that should be considered with care before embarking on the process, including:

- clarifying the copyright status of the material
- choosing the appropriate equipment, software and file formats for scanning, giving due attention to accessibility for disabled users
- recruiting or training appropriate staff
- ensuring quality control throughout the scanning process
- creating or enhancing metadata
- making arrangements for long-term access, hosting and preservation.

Creating 'born digital' e-books

The option of creating born digital texts may particularly appeal to teachers, lecturers and researchers early in their careers who are frustrated by the lack of online material that exactly fits their requirements in the classroom or lab or who feel hindered by the time it takes to publish research through traditional routes. However, it may be of interest also to those academics now late in their careers who have little to lose by making their wisdom freely available to all.

There is always the possibility that self-created digital texts could be seen as vanity publishing. However, the Open Access (OA) movement, which has the aim of removing subscription barriers to the content of peer-reviewed academic e-journals, and the parallel Open Educational Resources (OER) movement, which enables lecturers and teachers to share self-created course materials and teaching exercises through repositories such as Jorum (www.jorum.ac.uk), are raising the profile of open content services, which are now being increasingly regarded as sources of high quality information.

These initiatives are now extending to e-books and e-textbooks. For example, the Community College Open Textbook Collaborative (CCOTC), a joint effort by a number of colleges and universities in the USA has collected together links to over 500 open textbooks and ensures quality control by providing reviews written by a number of academics and publishing professionals (see www.collegeopentextbooks.org). Meanwhile in Europe, university presses are also beginning to make peer-reviewed scholarly monographs freely available through the OAPEN (Open Access Publishing in European Networks) project (www.oapen. org). Although technically not self-publishing, releasing open content through a local university press may be an acceptable compromise for academics and readers who prefer books to bear the stamp of credibility from an established scholarly publisher.

Authors may also be concerned about their intellectual property being misused if it is made available openly online, whether inadvertently or maliciously. However, Creative Commons (http://creativecommons.org) licences at various levels can be appended to texts in order to assert the author's moral and legal rights, whilst simultaneously making it clear what use can be made of the material, for example allowing educational use but prohibiting commercial use.

Whilst there are understandable concerns about open e-books, there are also exciting possibilities. Social media (Web 2.0) tools allow for tagging, reviewing, text mining and collaborative authoring. For example, Wikibooks is hosted on the same platform as Wikipedia, and currently contains almost 2500 'textbooks, annotated texts, instructional guides and manuals' (Wikibooks, 2010b), which can be added to and edited by the general public. As with articles available via Wikipedia, this approach means that books ('modules') are always considered to be works in progress, and can be the result of a social effort by a group of strangers rather than the work of a particular author. Peer review is not carried out by a panel of experts in the subject, but rather by the consensus of those who take the time to read the material and comment upon it. The collaborative and fluid nature of the texts might lead some readers to view the content with suspicion, although the Wikibooks policy states clearly that it is not the place for publishing primary research or for polemics. Nevertheless, it does contain some unique and intriguing material - for example *Na'vi*, an explanation of the history and development of the language spoken by the fictional inhabitants of the moon Pandora, in James Cameron's 2009 movie *Avatar*. The text includes a comprehensive grammar, lexicon and dictionary and, as with other Wikibooks texts, the content can be exported and turned into a customized downloadable or printed book.

Conclusion

The advent of the world wide web has resulted in an explosion of different types of information freely available to those with access to an internet connection, and books have been no exception. Many libraries have been slow to exploit these resources for a number of understandable reasons: lack of awareness; concentration of already scarce staffing resources on paid-for resources; concerns about quality; and a lack of trust in the permanence of free resources. However, there are treasures to be found, and some time spent investigating free e-books and considering how they might be integrated into a library collection may prove invaluable to readers in the future.

Useful links

British Library Online Gallery: virtual books
    www.bl.uk/onlinegallery/virtualbooks/index.html
British Library Treasures in Full www.bl.uk/treasures/treasuresinfull.html
Digital Book Index www.digitalbookindex.org/about.htm
Gallica http://gallica.bnf.fr
Google Books http://books.google.com
Internet Archive Ebook and Texts Archive www.archive.org/details/texts
Manybooks.net http://manybooks.net
National Portrait Gallery EOS.web OPAC
    http://librarycatalogue.npg.org.uk/EOSWeb/OPAC/Index.asp
National Portrait Gallery Google Bookshelf
    http://books.google.com/books?uid=7090843886902795013
The Oxford Text Archive http://ota.ahds.ac.uk
Project Gutenberg www.gutenberg.org
Wikibooks www.wikibooks.org

Bibliography

American Library Association Office for Information Technology Policy (2009) *Google Book Settlement 2 Page Super Simple Summary*, http://wo.ala.org/gbs/2-page-super-simple-summary.

Arts and Humanities Data Service (2007) *Supporting Research in the Arts and Humanities: JISC to review its services*, www.ahds.ac.uk/exec/news/ahrc-news-may07.htm.

Google (2010a) *Google Books Library Partners*, www.google.com/googlebooks/partners.html.

Google (2010b) *Google Corporate Information: company overview*, www.google.com/corporate.

Google (2010c) *The Future of Google Books*, http://books.google.com/googlebooks/agreement.

JISC (2009) *Data & Text Mining*, www.jisc.ac.uk/en/whatwedo/topics/datatextmining.aspx.

Kirby Smith, K. (2009) *BOPCRIS Digitisation Centre: experimentation with sustainability and partnerships for library digitisation projects*, http://sca.jiscinvolve.org/wp/files/2009/07/sca_bms_casestudy_southampton.pdf.

National Portrait Gallery (2009) *Information for Visitors to the Heinz Archive and Library*, www.npg.org.uk/assets/files/pdf/archive-and-library/NPG_VisitorLeaflet.pdf.

Nunberg, G. (2009) *Google Books: a metadata train wreck*, Language Log, http://languagelog.ldc.upenn.edu/nll/?p=1701.

Oder, N. (2010) Google Book Search by the Numbers, *Library Journal*, 2 December, www.libraryjournal.com/article/CA6718929.html.

Orwant, J. (2009) *Comment on 'Google Books: a metadata train wreck'*, Language Log, http://languagelog.ldc.upenn.edu/nll/?p=1701.

Ripp, J. (2010) Telephone interview, 6 August.

Wikibooks (2010a) *Na'vi*, http://en.wikibooks.org/wiki/Na%27vi.

Wikibooks (2010b) *What is Wikibooks*, http://en.wikibooks.org/wiki/Wikibooks:What_is_Wikibooks.

Part 2
Planning and developing an e-book collection

Overview

At a time when library and information services are under pressure through budget cuts, the need to maintain highly relevant, accessible and innovative services whilst ensuring cost-effectiveness is a major concern for library managers.

Whilst e-formats provide the potential to extend services far beyond the walls of the library, planning and developing an e-book collection introduces complexities over and above those associated with traditional collection management. The authors contributing to this section discuss the introduction of e-books into their library services and highlight some of the issues that were addressed in the process.

Martin Palmer (Chapter 5) of Essex Libraries asks what relevance e-books have within the public library sector, offering cogent arguments both for and against e-book provision. Palmer reflects on the over-riding requirement to ensure that public libraries provide value-for-money services whilst considering the ways in which e-books can reach new audiences effectively, as well as offering practical guidance on matters from promotion to staffing.

Karen Foster and Emma Ransley (Chapter 6) of Yeovil College discuss the strategic drivers that have influenced the ways in which FE has employed technology in teaching and learning over the last ten years, and explain how this has directly impacted upon the provision of e-books by learning resources centres. Foster and Ransley discuss the practicalities of managing an e-book collection within the further education environment, from selection to budget management.

Jim Dooley (Chapter 7) of University of California, Merced, discusses the acquisition of e-books from the unique perspective of a new HE library that was created *after* the internet revolution. Dooley provides a clear picture of how the Merced collection has evolved, and describes the strategic, budgetary and staffing considerations that have influenced the management of e-books within the collaborative environment of California University Libraries.

5
E-books for public libraries

Martin Palmer

Introduction

The common perception of the modern public library service in the UK tends to involve cuts to book funds, long waiting lists for the latest titles and reductions in opening hours. Consequently, the view of some critics that whatever resources remain available to public library managers should be devoted to providing the best 'traditional' service possible, rather than fragmenting effort and funds in exploring ways of diversifying service provision, is one that strikes a chord with many members of the public.

Yet, against this background, public library provision of e-books has begun to gather pace. A comparatively early survey commissioned by Resource (Dearnley et al., 2002) found that only one public library in the UK (Blackburn with Darwen) was actively providing an e-book service. Five years later, there were still only a couple more, but, by 2010, the number had risen to around 20, with more in the pipeline. Meanwhile, in the USA growth followed a similar pattern, beginning with the take-up of NetLibrary by a small number of public libraries in 1998 to a position in 2010 where OverDrive alone had over 9000 services as customers.

So, at a time when most libraries in the sector struggle to balance budgetary constraints with demands to help fulfil a multiplicity of agendas, how is it possible to justify branching out into such a service, where levels of take-up are uncertain, when the technology is still unstable, and which threatens to dilute already diminished funds even further? This chapter aims to make a sound case for the introduction of e-books into the public library environment, as well as examining some of the practical issues involved in such a development.

The strategic case for e-books

Is the current push for e-books simply yet another example of public library managers ignoring what the public want and jumping on the latest bandwagon, driven by a fear of being seen to be behind the times?

If so, it would clearly be difficult to defend such a position. However, in the light of their successful engagement with electronic reference material, it is perhaps surprising that more UK public libraries have not adopted e-books sooner. Since the first appearance of the *Encyclopædia Britannica*, the *Dictionary of National Biography* and a host of other staples of the traditional public reference library in online form, library managers have been keen to exploit the many advantages offered by the electronic versions of such titles, from enhanced currency and easier searching to remote access for readers. There has often also been a financial incentive to make the change, with savings being realized as standing orders for multiple print copies are cancelled.

As a consequence, most UK public libraries have now shifted their reference services significantly towards electronic provision, to the extent that nationally negotiated contracts for the provision of these titles, under the auspices of the Museums, Libraries and Archives Council, are now an integral part of the service offered by most authorities around the country.

Unfortunately, however, the public library manager looking to justify such an approach to what are traditionally seen as lending services will find it much more difficult to find supporting arguments. In fact, the challenges to be faced when setting up an 'e-lending' service can be seen as a microcosm of those faced by public librarians more generally over the past 20 years or so, particularly those who have struggled to cater for demand for what is essentially the same content but which is presented in different formats; for example, should films be purchased on VHS (video home system) or Betamax; on DVD or Blu-ray? And should recorded sound be purchased on vinyl or on cassette; on CD (compact disc) or on MP3?

For most of these decisions, the principal question raised is: will the service pay its way? For most library authorities in England and Wales it has been possible to introduce new services like these because they are permitted to make a financial charge for them under the Public Libraries and Museums Act 1964. Consequently, the justification for provision of a particular service or format is very straightforward: there has been a demand for the service, and it can be used to raise additional income to support the traditional book-based lending service. This scenario has formed the basis for the introduction of most new services offered by UK public libraries over the past few years, and explains how they have managed to remain innovative and contemporary despite constant budgetary constraints.

However, the position regarding e-books has been less clear, as they simply provide a different form of access to print-based content (as opposed to recorded sound or film), and so appear not to be a service that can be charged for. This is explored further in the section 'Budgeting and finance' later in this chapter.

Against this background, why would any library service want to consider introducing e-books? Limited resources, a potential legal ban on charging, and a confusing array of unresolved technological questions would seem to make the decision *not* to do so the logical path to follow. Even these pale into insignificance if a library service is based in an area with limited broadband provision, as slow downloads are likely to be a serious deterrent for most people.

However, this negative stance fails to recognize two key elements:

1 *The audience, actual or potential, for the service.* Are there groups in the community whose needs (whether expressed or implicit) can be met only by use of this material? If so, what evidence is there to support this, who and where are these people, and what do they want?
2 *The technology.* Does it offer a more cost-effective way of providing content? Will the investment in e-books make it easier and more affordable to provide the material to a larger number of people?

These are crucial questions for any library service, but particularly in the case of public libraries. First, for many people, reading for pleasure on a computer screen is a completely alien concept, particularly for those who spend much of their week reading in this way at work; 'Reading a paperback is my way of knowing I'm not at work' is a typical comment. Meanwhile Alberto Manguel, perhaps one of the most influential commentators on reading and its effects on both the individual and society, encapsulated the thoughts of many in a radio interview when he said that he had nothing against e-books, but they were not his preferred medium for reading, providing the following analogy: 'You know . . . some people like virtual sex; I still prefer the real thing' (Manguel, 2010). Many who share this point of view will, therefore, be surprised to find that their public library is diverting money that perhaps could have been spent on more paperbacks towards something they have no plans to use. It should also be noted that the enthusiasm shown by public library managers for abandoning traditional information provision in favour of computer-based approaches as described above has not always been shared by their customers.

Second, the fact that some kind of device is required to read this material can be a further disincentive to any reader who is even slightly technophobic, and for whom the traditional printed book is the perfect, self-contained, solution to their reading needs.

So, if many library users feel ill-disposed towards the use of electronic formats even where the benefits seem to be self-explanatory, what is the justification for introducing them where the advantages are less evident at first sight? There are many ways of approaching this question, but the reality for most public libraries is that it relates to a much broader debate than simply one of e-books versus print books; it is much more about how the public library serves those parts of the community that are often described as 'hard to reach', a term that disguises the fact that it is usually the library itself that is hard to reach. While the 'traditional' service provided by public libraries may well meet the needs of their mainstream audience, it often fails to address the requirements of a significant number of other sections of the community, many of whom may well be entirely dependent on the library for their reading.

There are, then, two main justifications for the use of e-books in a public library: they may provide at least a partial solution for people unable to use traditional public library formats; and they may be a more efficient and effective way of providing simultaneous access to material for a large number of people. Ideally, an e-book service will meet both of these requirements, but this may not always be possible.

The audience

The potential audience for an e-service can be very diverse. Some people, for example, may have a disability that prevents them from using the traditional service because they cannot leave the house; others may have commitments that prevent them from visiting the library, even where opening hours have been extended to include Sundays and late evenings.

Some people may have no computer of their own, but may discover that public terminals or other devices provided by the library service offer access to material that can support their studies, search for employment or recreational reading. Meanwhile, for people with a visual impairment, e-books can offer an immediate extension of the material available to them when the range of titles produced commercially in an appropriate format (whether large print or audio) is otherwise limited to 5% or less of the total available to everyone else. The RNIB (Royal National Institute of Blind People) has produced some useful guidelines on e-book accessibility that appear in Part 6 of this book.

At first sight, these groups may seem to have little in common apart from the fact that their needs are ill-met by the traditional public library service, but it can be useful to look at them in terms of the way they might use e-services. Using this approach, it is possible to identify three main categories of user:

1 *Remote users*: people who primarily need access to content from home or work.
2 *Mobile users*: people who want to be able to read while travelling, such as commuters or those whose work regularly takes them away from home.
3 *People with no other access to technology*: people who may wish to come to the library and use public computers or other devices to make use of e-material, whether for reference/study use or for recreational reading.

Such an approach can be useful in a number of ways, not least of which is to evaluate the benefits and disadvantages of the services provided by different suppliers, and how they might best be marketed and promoted to different groups of potential users.

The technology

However, alongside these questions of audience needs and demands, public librarians also need to address another fundamental question, this time relating to the technology – what, in public library terms, exactly *is* an e-book?

As far as the majority of the public are concerned, an e-book is simply a device – something that can be held in the hand, having a screen and possibly some kind of keyboard, which enables them to carry around a number of 'books', which can be read for as long as the battery lasts. Such a perception is hardly surprising since almost all of the marketing for e-books aimed at the general public has been undertaken by the manufacturers of such devices, and is designed to encourage the consumer to spend money on an item of proprietary hardware that usually performs no other role.

However, the audience for a service based on hardware provision would seem to be very limited; why would a library user want to borrow such a device? It does offer the facility to carry around the equivalent of hundreds of print books in one convenient package, but this is countered by a number of disadvantages, particularly for those not technologically inclined. These range from the very simple, such as the need to charge batteries, to the complex procedures required to control some of the more sophisticated e-readers. Additionally, some readers may simply not want the responsibility of being in possession of a piece of equipment that may cost hundreds of pounds to replace or repair.

The experience of one of the early adopters in UK public library e-book provision certainly suggests that a service based on the lending of e-book readers may not be of great interest to the public. Market Harborough piloted such a service in 2000-1, in a project observed by James Dearnley and Cliff McKnight of nearby Loughborough University (Dearnley and McKnight, 2001), and which was based on lending pre-loaded Rocket Book readers. While some users found the service interesting and thought it had potential, the majority were 'underwhelmed' by it and the project was comparatively short-lived.

Subsequently, the direction taken by three projects which began in the UK from 2003–4 moved away from the idea of basing a service on a specific e-reader. Instead, they explored the possibilities of services using more generic, multi-purpose devices. Blackburn with Darwen used personal digital assistants (PDAs) as the basis for their project, while the London Borough of Richmond explored the use of collections that were accessible via personal computers (PCs) and laptops. A further project – again involving Loughborough University, and hosted for Co-East by Essex County Council's Library Department – investigated similar approaches, using both PDAs and remote access to services requiring only a PC, laptop or other generic device.

Consequently, by 2005, those e-book services that were being provided by UK public libraries, albeit few in number, were based firmly on the idea of the e-book simply as content or software, and independent of any single proprietary device. In 2010, this continues to be the case, mainly reflecting the fact that until recently there has been a lack of reliable and affordable devices on which to base an e-service. However, the introduction since 2008 of a new generation of devices (Kindle, Sony Reader, IRex Iliad, Cybook and more), which for the most part use e-ink to provide a more reader-friendly experience than previous hardware such as the Rocket Book, has led some public libraries (mainly in the USA) to base a proportion of their electronic services on the loan of e-readers. Some have been lending Amazon's Kindle devices (Oder, 2009) despite confusion as to whether this falls within Amazon's terms and conditions of use, as well as Sony Readers.

Regardless of whether or not libraries offer such devices themselves, publicity about them has further reinforced the public perception of the e-book as a piece of hardware rather than as software or independent content. Sales are also accelerating. Waterstone's reported selling 30,000 Sony Readers in the three months following its launch in September 2008, and although Amazon does not reveal its sales figures, it is estimated that up to 500,000 Kindles were sold up to the end of 2009 (Johnson, 2009).

For public libraries, this emphasis on the idea of the e-book as a device has resulted in a further complication: in addition to a lack of interoperability, some of these e-readers are predicated on a business model designed purely to meet the needs of a retail service rather than those of a library environment. This is explored further in the section 'Formats and DRM' on the next page, but the overall effect is not only confusing for libraries and their customers, but also seriously fragments the library market.

In most similar circumstances, library managers would look to standards to offer a solution. Unfortunately, there has been little aid from this quarter for most early adopters. This is also explored further later in this chapter but, even though the position is beginning to change at the time of writing, there is still much more to be done in this area.

Matching the audience to the technology

There are two main types of e-book provision available to public library services: those where users download files and keep them for a specific period; and those where the content is accessed and read online, via a web browser or proprietary software. The decision regarding which of these options to choose will be influenced primarily by the needs of the intended audience:

1 *Who are the users?*: Will they be in the library? Will they be on the move or at a desk? Or a combination of all of these?
2 *What type of content will be offered?*: Will it be mainstream, bestselling 'reading for pleasure'? Or more academic titles, aimed at students or other users of more specialist non-fiction?

Downloads

Download services are perhaps the closest to most public library users' perceptions of what an e-book service should be; they use an operating model very similar to that of the traditional lending library and the typical e-reader device. In public libraries in the UK and USA, OverDrive (www.overdrive.com) is the largest supplier of this type of service, where an item is 'borrowed' for the agreed loan period, after which it becomes available for another reader. The only difference from the loan of a printed book is that the borrower has no need to 'return' the item – the downloaded file becomes inactive at the end of the period, and so needs only to be deleted from the host device. One benefit from the point of view of the 'borrower' is that the item cannot become overdue, and so there are no charges for late return. Another is that, once downloaded, the file can usually be transferred to another device, such as an e-reader, a PDA or a smartphone – a very attractive facility for people wishing to use the material while out of the house or office.

Although download services are very popular, and represent by far the largest growth area for e-book provision in public libraries – being described as 'geometric' in the USA by one observer (Genco, 2009, 17) – some users can find the process required to obtain the title they want confusing and difficult.

Formats and DRM

These difficulties are not, however, through any fault of the suppliers, whose systems are generally very user-friendly, but rather a reflection of the nature of the e-book market. At the heart of this is the wide range of formats still in general use – Adobe PDF, Microsoft Reader, Mobipocket, to name a few. The EPUB format has recently been introduced and offers some possibility of providing a standard format for all publishers to use – a hope that has been further strengthened by Apple's decision to use it as the basis for its iPad and accompanying iBooks service, rather than introducing another proprietary Apple format. Nevertheless, the EPUB format still requires further development in some aspects of its design before its use can become standardized.

In the meantime there is much confusion over which formats are useable by which devices: a brief look at a very useful Wikipedia page devoted to this – see 'Useful links' later in this chapter (*Comparison of E-book Readers*) – demonstrates just how arcane a subject this is. This is further complicated by the use of DRM software, which is designed to protect the rights of the copyright holder by controlling the way in which the material can be used; however, its use is controversial in many areas, and its effects are often confusing to the end-user.

For example, some devices may be able to read Mobipocket files, but not Mobipocket files that have DRM. As the download services available to public libraries all make use of DRM, owners of devices that clearly state that they can read a particular format understandably become unhappy when they discover that they cannot use the public library download service, despite appearing to own a compatible reader. This is also currently a source of confusion for iPad users, whose device is clearly designed to work with EPUB as its format of choice but which is unable to read the EPUB material that their public library offers because it is 'wrapped' in DRM software.

Even if such questions of matching format to device do not arise, the process for downloading titles can be off-putting for some potential borrowers, and confusing even for people with a relatively good track record of technology use. For example, OverDrive's support notes describing how to download Adobe titles are admirably clear and very helpful, but nevertheless still quite involved for the lay person to put into practice.

Online access

Conversely, services based on online access to material are generally much easier to use, needing only a web browser (or at worst a one-off download of a piece of reader software) to use. They do, however, require access to the internet and so are immediately limited to use in situations where this is available. Originally, e-book services using this model tended to be aimed primarily at the more academic end of the spectrum, at audiences more likely to be static and using a PC, and rather less so at recreational readers; however, as mobile web access becomes increasingly widespread via smartphones and other devices, this is beginning to change.

Ebrary (www.ebrary.com) is one of the longest established suppliers of online access e-books. More recently, Bloomsbury has also adopted this approach, providing 'electronic bookshelves' of specially selected titles to public libraries (www.publiclibraryonline.com). Interestingly, they are also one of the few publishers to date that provides its material directly rather than via an intermediary/aggregator such as OverDrive or ebrary.

Although there are benefits for users of this type of operating model, including a less complex mode of access, one of the disadvantages of online services is that they are often not perceived as e-books by the public – particularly those who have bought an e-book reader. With the notable exception of Amazon's Kindle, most e-book reading devices do not currently have internet access, and so are unable to make use of services provided in this way.

The other disadvantage from the public librarian's point of view is that payment for online access services may be a subscription based on the size of the population or active membership being served. As a consequence, this may require something of a leap of faith on the part of the librarian, being required to commit what may well be a significant sum of money without any guarantee that the product itself will prove popular with users.

Platform

Common to both download and online access approaches is the need for a platform on which to deliver the service. There is a growing demand among librarians for the provision of a common platform for e-services, to enable content to be purchased independently of the method of delivery. At present, even where material is bought on a one-off basis rather than through a subscription, continued access to it often remains dependent on the supplier's delivery platform and the payment of an ongoing hosting fee.

At the time of writing, some suppliers are beginning to offer services based on a free platform, avoiding the need for long-term financial commitment to ensure continued access to the material, although even this type of arrangement is unable to guarantee the existence of a platform in perpetuity. This remains relatively unexplored territory for public libraries, but will clearly be of growing importance as the market develops. In the meantime, library managers need to be aware that what they are buying is usually a licence to use e-material, not the material itself. This has obvious implications for collection development, and is a point explored further later in this chapter.

Authentication

Both download and online services require some means of establishing the right of access to the material. Again, public libraries differ from their counterparts in other sectors in this context. Academic and health service libraries, for example, often use the Athens service to provide a simple and easy method of recognizing users and their rights. Academic libraries have also moved towards federated access management (Shibboleth) in recent years. However, public libraries have looked elsewhere for authentication and access management.

In some cases, suppliers will provide their own way of doing this, but for the most part the library service itself will need to source a solution. It is likely that many services will already have some experience of this from providing electronic reference material, and the methods used may often be the same. For example, possible options, depending on which service is being accessed and from where, may include IP address recognition, a secure referring URL, or use of a proxy server.

However, the most effective method will often be to use the LMS, using the Standard Interchange Protocol (SIP) from 3M Library Systems or some similar link between the LMS and the e-book supplier's platform. Many libraries will already be using such an approach to provide links to self-service or other third-party applications. This method will be easier and cheaper to put into practice for some LMS than for others, but it does offer some advantages. The most obvious of these is that it provides a direct link to the membership database. This in turn provides the ability to differentiate easily between adult and child users – and so to limit access to what may be perceived as unsuitable material – as well as offering the facility to carry out more detailed statistical analysis of user behaviour, fully exploiting all of the information stored on the LMS database.

Security

Other areas of concern are likely to be expressed by the Information Technology Department of the local council, through which most public libraries will be obliged to work. Despite many years' experience of providing public access to council services, many IT departments still find the library service's desire to expose their resources to the widest possible audience a fundamental challenge to what they perceive as their main role – to protect the security of the council's network and systems. Most suppliers should be able to provide reassurance about this, but early liaison and co-operation is nevertheless vital in helping to avoid delays and problems later in the process.

Promotion and marketing

The experience of early public library adopters of e-books suggests that promotion and marketing of these services can be particularly difficult, as they do not lend themselves easily to displays in the library or similar physical approaches. However, linking to the LMS will, in addition to managing access, provide one of the most effective vehicles for the promotion of the service – the library catalogue. One of the main problems in promoting e-material is its invisibility, so direct access to the catalogue entry for an e-book will often provide a user's first experience of e-services.

Traditional bookmark, leaflet and poster campaigns may be of value, but again it is important to keep in mind the intended audience. If the service is aimed mainly at people using the library remotely, then advertising and other promotions that are restricted to the library building are unlikely to have much impact. Instead, many public libraries have begun to introduce e-newsletters, which have proved to be very useful in increasing awareness of e-services, particularly since people who elect to receive this kind of update are typically already well disposed to the technology-based delivery of services.

However, the range of e-services and the differences between them also complicate the promotion of e-books in a public library context. The fact that there is more than one type of e-book service and more than one type of e-book audience means that different approaches will probably be required for each. To promote both a download service and an online access service generically as 'e-books' is potentially confusing for all, and so it is likely to be more helpful to tailor the marketing of each type of service to the relevant audience rather than trying a one-size-fits-all approach.

Experience to date suggests that personal recommendation may be the most effective way of increasing awareness of e-book provision, with many users finding their way to the service via Google or e-book-related blogs. Some suppliers have recognized this; OverDrive, for example, offers links from its service to Twitter, MySpace and other social networking facilities, which allows users to recommend its content to others.

Collection development in the public library

As noted above, the dependence of e-content on a platform for its delivery means that collection development of public library e-material is fundamentally different from that for printed material. Instead of being free to choose whatever titles they feel are likely to meet the needs of their communities, librarians are able to select only the material available from the provider(s) with whom they have engaged. Collection development is, therefore, currently as much about the selection of a supplier as it is about selection of individual titles, although choice of supplier will be partly dictated by the material it has to offer. This situation is continually evolving as more and more suppliers enter the market, with different content and software to offer. However, there will usually be a choice between two main approaches: buying individual titles or buying complete packages.

Individual titles versus packages

Subscription to, or purchase of, a package offers a number of benefits, many of which have been described in Chapter 2 'An Introduction to E-book Business Models and Suppliers':

- The task of selection is transferred from the librarian to the supplier, saving a great deal of time and effort.
- New titles may be added to the collection at no further cost.
- A critical mass of material will be immediately available.
- It is usually possible to search across titles simultaneously and to access other support such as electronic dictionaries.
- Simultaneous access to all users is available, meaning that there is no need to choose the number of copies to purchase.

There are also some disadvantages:

- There may be titles in the collection that are not relevant to the audience.
- There may be limitations in coverage of particular subjects, or an emphasis on material more suitable for one country than another.

■ Titles may occasionally be removed because of a change in the publisher's permissions.

Conversely, choosing individual titles will usually require all of the skills associated with traditional stock selection; finding material that reflects the needs of the community being served and in sufficient numbers to satisfy demand. There is also a further question to be considered – whether demand for particular genres or subjects differs substantially between e-books and printed books.

The experience of early adopters suggests that there is clearly some overlap: material that is popular in print is likely to also be so as an e-book – bestsellers remain bestsellers regardless of format. However, there do appear to be some topics that are more popular in libraries as e-books than their paper cousins. These are often subjects that users prefer not to be seen to be borrowing, such as titles on self-help, sexual health, divorce and similarly 'private' topics.

High levels of demand for some other subjects may be less surprising. For example, titles on information technology and related topics tend to be very popular, and there is considerable interest in many categories of fiction, contrary to the popular belief that it is unsuited to the e-book format.

File formats also need to be considered when selecting material for some download services. A wide variety is available, and suppliers often offer individual titles in a range of them. Early adopters often had to choose whether to buy titles in Adobe PDF rather than Mobipocket – or perhaps both. Some services made it a basic rule of thumb to buy non-fiction in PDF, and fiction in Mobipocket. The reason for this was that PDF was able to include photographs and charts more easily than Mobipocket, which often omitted them altogether. On the other hand, the downloading process for Mobipocket was generally much more straightforward, and thus if a title was simply text, it would probably be preferable to buy the title in that format.

However, this has changed with the advent of the EPUB format. This is rapidly being adopted as a *de facto* standard by many publishers, and is compatible with a number of popular devices, including some e-readers (such as those produced by Sony) and multifunctional notebooks and tablets, such as the iPad – although this is problematic for libraries as the iPad does not recognize DRM at present. E-books produced in the EPUB format also cope well with photographs and charts, and so it seems likely that buying titles in this format will offer the best approach for public libraries looking to maximize their audience. Indeed, an increasing number of publishers are making their material available in EPUB format only.

E-audio

For many public libraries and their users e-audio is often a more attractive use of online technology than e-books, and may well be their main reason for moving into the e-services arena. It not only extends the audience for the service to those unable to use text for any reason, but also helps to mitigate the problems commonly experienced by stock managers in providing audiobooks in more traditional formats, such as audiocassette or CD. These range from the multi-part nature of the product (particularly with unabridged versions) and the possibility of loss or damage to individual discs or cassettes, to the question of cost, where audiobooks in CD or cassette format may often be the most expensive items that a lending library will buy.

However, while e-audio editions of audiobooks may often be cheaper than the CD/cassette equivalent and be easier to manage in terms of storage and product integrity, there are some disadvantages. Questions of format and compatibility between different types of player (particularly between Apple, via iTunes, and Microsoft, via Windows Media Player devices) can create confusion among users, as well as requiring librarians to purchase the same content in multiple formats to satisfy demand. This situation is evolving, with many suppliers now providing files that can be converted to provide compatibility across different devices. There are several commercial library suppliers in the e-audio market, such as UK-based company W. F. Howe with its ClipperDL service, as well as free online audiobooks from Project Gutenberg, available worldwide through the Librivox service.

Suppliers

There are numerous suppliers in the e-books market, ranging from traditional library suppliers such as Dawson and Askews, to aggregators such as NetLibrary and ebrary, and publishers such as Taylor & Francis. A selected list is available in Part 6 'Useful information' at the end of this book. However, two of the main players in the public library e-books market, OverDrive and Public Library Online, are described in more detail below.

OverDrive (www.overdrive.com)

OverDrive has become the dominant supplier of downloadable material in recent years, serving 9000 library services worldwide. Based in Cleveland, Ohio, and with almost half of its customers coming from the USA, its 100,000+ title content reflects this, but much material from the UK is included. Providing e-books in EPUB, PDF and Mobipocket, and e-audio in WMA (Windows Media Audio) and Apple-compatible formats, all protected by DRM and readable on PCs, Macs and laptops and transferable to a variety of mobile devices, OverDrive also supplies a website to act as the supply platform, which in turn is accessible via the library website and catalogue. Content is mainly from the publishing mainstream, with the emphasis on recreational rather than academic material. Both adult and children's titles are included, although the latter tend to be more US-orientated than the former. Access is usually provided remotely, although OverDrive also offers download stations for use within libraries.

Public Library Online (www.exacteditions.com)

Originally launched as Bloomsbury Online, this service is provided on the Exact Editions platform and has expanded to provide coverage of a wider range of publishers such as Faber and Quercus, as well as magazines and Wisden. Access is provided online, both from within the library and remotely, and material is collected and offered as 'bookshelves' rather than as individual titles, which libraries purchase on subscription based on the size of the population served.

Staffing and workflow considerations

Service delivery

As with all other aspects of public library provision, the quality of library staff input will be crucial to the success of e-book provision. However, the level and nature of staff involvement required will vary considerably, depending on the type of the service being provided.

For example, a service based on the lending of devices will be very intensive in terms of the staff time required. Apart from the physical processes involved, which may include loading, lending, returning and checking devices, there will be a significant training requirement to ensure that staff are able to support users satisfactorily, whether answering enquiries about content or undertaking basic troubleshooting. Provision of access via in-library computers may be less demanding of staff time, but will also require familiarity with content and an awareness of how the material being made available electronically complements the print items held by the library, and the relative merits of each.

In contrast, for remote access services it may be possible to centralize provision of support and so limit the number of staff that need to be trained. The experience of some early adopters suggests that most users of this type of service rarely come to a library building and communicate instead by telephone or e-mail, making provision of a single point of contact the logical approach to take. However, with remote access services there is a danger that front-line staff will be unaware of the e-material that is being made available by their library service, which is highly undesirable for both the staff concerned and the user. Reminders through staff newsletters, e-mail or more traditional training and awareness sessions will usually be needed to help maintain staff familiarity with what is on offer.

Stock selection, acquisition and management

The amount of staff time involved in these processes will vary according to the type of service. As noted previously, the purchase of packages will – after the initial decision about which collection to purchase – not require much staff involvement, other than to monitor levels of take-up, and so inform the decision about whether to renew or not at a later date.

Conversely, services based on the purchase of individual titles are likely to be as staff intensive as the methods used by the library to select print material, requiring a similar balance to be achieved between front- and back-list titles, for example, as well as waiting list maintenance and all of the other traditional stock management techniques.

However, once selected, the workflow for the acquisition of all e-books is usually much simpler than that for printed material. As there is no physical product, and therefore no parcels to transport, unpack and check, staff involvement is minimal. In addition, most suppliers now make full MARC records available for download, while invoices can also be dealt with electronically, either by EDI or e-mail.

Budgeting and finance

As mentioned earlier in this chapter, although the existing legislation can be interpreted in different ways, the Department of Culture, Media and Sport's (DCMS's) review of the public library service states that for English public libraries:

> Government expects e-books to be loaned for free. Government will under section 8(2)(b) of the Public Libraries and Museums Act 1964 make an (affirmative) Order preventing libraries from charging for e-book lending of any sort including remotely.
>
> (DCMS, 2010, Proposal 34)

This aspect of the review proved to be controversial, with the Booksellers Association describing the provision of free online books by libraries as likely to lead to the undermining of revenue for both authors and booksellers (Gallagher, 2010). The Publishers Association, however, supported the proposal, but the public library community's views were mixed; some welcomed the recognition that e-book use is simply reading – albeit using electronics rather than print – and so therefore should not be chargeable, while others made it clear that without the ability to raise income from e-books, they would not be able to provide them in the absence of extra funding.

It is not currently clear whether this order will be put into effect – in fact in light of the current Coalition Government's views about the public finances, it might seem a highly unlikely outcome, although at the time of writing the new Minister for Culture, Communications and Creative Industries Ed Vaizey has indicated only that he 'would like to understand more about the different views of stakeholders before making any decisions about the question of e-books in libraries' (Bintliff, 2010).

Nevertheless, the DCMS review recommendation currently remains the context for any English library service that is preparing a business case for e-book provision. This uncertainty over the law seems likely to cause a hiatus in take-up by English services, although – while clearly important – the legal situation is also slightly academic when viewed against the reality of existing e-book provision in the UK, where none of the public library services providing e-books at the time of the review's publication does actually charge for them.

The reasons for this vary, including the fact that some were originally set up as pilot projects to assess the early viability of e-book provision and so did not charge in case it adversely affected the project; but one of the main contributory factors is that most supplier platforms in the public library arena do not yet support financial transactions by end-users.

Consequently, the rationale for e-book provision for most services will usually need to be based on something other than income generation. It may still have a financial basis such as the saving of money that might have had to be spent if electronic provision were not to be made. An example of this might be the purchase of a subscription providing simultaneous multi-user access to complete collections, which can be shown to remove the need for the purchase of multiple copies of individual print titles.

Such an argument clearly will not be sustainable for other types of e-book (or e-audio) provision, particularly for download services. Indeed, in some cases, such as e-audio and its effect on use of charged-for CD/cassette audiobooks, there is a danger of adversely affecting existing income streams. Also, while there may be benefits to be had from a consortial approach to purchase, these may be less evident than they are with print material, and are likely to accrue from the sharing of costs and stock rather than volume-based discounts.

Therefore, it will probably be necessary to return to the original rationale for providing such services. If, as suggested, this relates to meeting currently unmet needs or unserved segments of the community then the decision must be made either to find ways of doing so from within existing resources, or to seek additional funding from elsewhere.

Conclusion

It is clear that – in whatever form – e-books are being seen by more and more public libraries as a valuable addition to the range of material they offer, and by a growing proportion of the public as something they should be able to access from their local library as a matter of course. As the technology matures and becomes more stable, the provision of e-books seems set to become an accepted, and expected, part of the mainstream service of the 21st-century public library.

Useful links

Comparison of E-book Readers (Wikipedia)
    http://en.wikipedia.org/wiki/Ebook_readers
E-books Service Development for Public Libraries
    www.communities.idea.gov.uk/comm/landing-home.do?id=3643455

References

Bintliff, E. (2010) Libraries Turn Up Volume in E-books Debate, *Financial Times*, 23 July, www.ft.com.

Dearnley J. et al. (2002) *The People's Network, Public Libraries and E-books: specification for baseline intelligence-gathering work*, Department of Information Science, Loughborough University.

Dearnley, J. and McKnight, C. (2001) The Revolution Starts Next Week: the findings of two studies considering electronic books, *Information Services & Use*, **21** (2), 65–78.

Department of Culture Media and Sport (2010) *The Modernisation Review of Public Libraries: a policy statement.*

Gallagher, V. (2010) BA Uneasy over Library e-book Proposals, *The Bookseller*, 25 March, www.thebookseller.com/news/114971-ba-uneasy-over-library-e-book-proposals.html.rss.

Genco, B. (2009) It's Been Geometric! Documenting the growth and acceptance of ebooks in America's urban public libraries, *World Library and Information Congress: 75th IFLA general conference and council, 23-27 August*, www.ifla.org/files/hq/papers/ifla75/212-genco-en.pdf.

Johnson, B. (2009) Amazon Keeps Market Guessing as Secrecy Shrouds Kindle Sales, *The Guardian*, 24 December, 15.

Manguel, A. (2010) Interviewed on Open Book, BBC Radio 4, 18 April.

Oder, N. (2009) Mixed Answers to 'Is it OK for a Library to Lend a Kindle?', *Library Journal*, 7 April, www.libraryjournal.com/article/CA6649814.html.

6

E-books for further education

Karen Foster and Emma Ransley

Introduction

In this chapter, we consider the background to the development of an e-book collection within the FE sector. The themes of the chapter include how e-books fit in with a growing emphasis on using technology to enhance learning across the sector, the ways in which an e-book collection can be developed and managed, budgeting for e-books and finally the potential impact on staffing.

Throughout, we will be using examples from Yeovil College, a tertiary college providing post-compulsory FE opportunities to around 7000 learners from South Somerset and North Dorset in the UK. The college has two main campuses situated in Yeovil, the Further Education campus and University Centre Yeovil (UCY), which focuses on HE. There are also two off-site locations, North Dorset Skills Centre and Lufton Construction Centre. The college offers academic qualifications ranging from diplomas aimed at 14–16 year olds up to first degree level, as well as vocational courses, apprenticeships and courses aimed at adults in the workplace.

Using technology to enhance learning

In 2005 the UK Government produced *Harnessing Technology: transforming learning and children's services*, a report highlighting the ways in which technology can enhance the work of the education sector (Department for Education and Skills, 2005). It fostered an expectation that colleges would embrace many types of digital technology and ensure that all learners have the opportunity to access e-resources as part of their educational experience, particularly in order to direct and manage aspects of their own learning.

More recently, the strategy was reviewed and revised by Becta, the government agency responsible for promoting innovative use of technology in learning, resulting in two reports: *Harnessing Technology: next generation learning 2008-14* (Becta, 2008) and *Harnessing Technology Review 2009: the role of technology in further education and skills* (Becta, 2010). These reports conclude that the need to use technology in education remains, although some issues have been identified with the transition of young learners from a school setting to a FE setting where technology is more central to independent study.

Gunter et al. (2009) identify differences in attitude towards technology between the Google Generation, which was born after 1994 and has therefore been brought up in the internet era, Generation Y (born between 1978 and 1993) and Generation X (born prior to 1978). Both Becta and Gunter show that learners expect to use technology in their daily lives, but their actual ability to use e-resources effectively for independent research and study varies by age and experience. JISC's report *In Their Own Words* also examines the ways in which students interact with internet technology and touches on how libraries and learning resource centres (LRCs) need to develop their practice to take account of this, noting:

> Search engines, in particular Google, and collaborative websites, such as Wikipedia, are the mainstay of learners' research activities. While some digital learners have developed sophisticated techniques for verifying what they find against approved sources of information, the convenience and low cost of internet-based research – compared to purchasing text books or travelling into a library – mean that less-skilled learners also rely on this practice. Academic, library and learning centre staff, and learners, would benefit from evaluations of how best to conduct and support research activities in an age in which unprecedented levels of information are freely available.
>
> (JISC, 2009a, 28)

This emphasis on easy access and lack of awareness of search techniques is supported by the results of the JISC NeBO project (JISC, 2009b), which concluded that learners found e-books useful mainly because they were online and therefore more accessible. Of the survey respondents, 52.4% noted 'availability online' as the major advantage of e-books, whereas only 13.2% identified ease of searching for text within them as an advantage.

Hence, the strategic case for using e-books in education is clearly supported at the national level by research from national bodies such as Becta and JISC. The increasing use of e-books in FE also follows the trend in HE, with the launch of the e-Books for FE Project in 2009, led by JISC and sponsored by the Learning and Skills Council. This built on the results of the NeBO project, which was focused on HE. The NeBO project reported that 65% of students use e-books for their studies and that over 50% of these were provided by the university, indicating to college LRCs that they may also have a role in developing e-book collections for lower level courses.

In the FE environment the strategic advantages of e-books are clear; they allow learners to make choices about when and where they study, which are not tied to library opening times or the numbers of resources that can be borrowed. They can also be used as a tool to promote independence and create an environment where students can increasingly manage their own learning.

Introducing e-books to support college strategies

The college LRC manager should examine their institution's ICT and learning strategies and then model the LRC strategy and development plan in order to meet the college's strategic aims. This approach will give the LRC a sense of direction and purpose when looking at the medium- and long-term plans for both staffing and service. It is also crucial to explain the strategic need for new developments in order to secure financial and personal backing from both senior managers and teaching staff.

At Yeovil College there has been a focused effort to develop e-learning across the whole organization, through the use of the VLE Moodle. For example, *Yeovil College IT/E-Learning Strategy 2008* notes, 'Content and curriculum delivery will be developed to ensure that technology is used to enable the delivery of personalised learning that meets the needs of every learner' (Yeovil College, 2008). Also, *Yeovil College Strategic Plan 2009-10* includes aims such as ensuring that 'clients, learners and stakeholders have access to high quality human, physical and virtual resources . . . through . . . continued development of Moodle as the sole source of curriculum information' (Yeovil College, 2009).

These aims have provided the LRC management team with a framework for developing its own learning resources strategy, which also now bases critical functions on the VLE, particularly as a gateway to curriculum-based resources such as e-books.

The development of both online electronic resources and e-books has been part of the learning centre strategy for five years. As Kern Vickers, Librarian and Systems Manager, says:

> We have always been keen advocates of using e-resources for learning at Yeovil College. We have tried to complement our physical stock collection with a selection of e-resources that give learners the opportunity to undertake independent research without having to rely heavily on the open internet. We feel that at FE level it is better for learners to get into the habit of using subscription based e-resources as this is what they will be expected to go on to use at university.   (Vickers, 2010)

When considering a strategy for introducing e-books, it should be remembered that there are significant differences between students in FE and those in HE. The most fundamental is the relevance of the material and the readership level at which it is aimed. The learner at FE level is often directed to read material from just one or two core textbooks, and only a few will look at additional texts. FE also encompasses courses from pre-entry to level 3 (A level) standard and above, so the variety and breadth of academic ability is wide. Furthermore, some learners feel that having a physical book in front of them indicates to others that they are working, and offers a sense of comfort in a LRC setting, so they may be reluctant to move to a more computer-based mode of accessing texts.

However, although there are differences between FE students and those in HE, there are some similarities, for example:

1   A large number of learners will be using resources off-campus, for example those who are following work-based learning programmes or placements, or are engaged in distance learning. It is essential to provide relevant resources that are fully accessible for these modes of study.

2   E-books offer learners with disabilities the opportunity to enhance the text to suit their requirements, including the ability to mark key text and save selections for future reference.

3   E-books are not a 'fit-all' solution. Many learners comment on their unwillingness to read large amounts of text from a screen and therefore often wish to print out sections of books.

Another strategic consideration is that of space. LRCs have become a hub of college learning activity, with demand for increasing numbers of computers and flexible working spaces, incorporating movable IT equipment, presentation facilities and furniture. This puts pressure on book and journal space, the backbone of the traditional library service. However, there should be a vision of fluidity within a LRC to ensure that learner demands and needs are constantly addressed. The JISC publication *Designing Space for Effective Learning* (JISC, 2006), promotes a multifunctional approach to the modern LRC, but more importantly highlights the need to develop areas where virtual learning can occur as part of normal academic activity.

The integration of e-books into the collection of resources offered at FE level provides an opportunity to reduce the physical collection of text and therefore free up valuable space for other purposes. E-books can supplement current texts; for example where traditionally four copies of an edition might be purchased in hard copy, this could be reduced to two copies – one for loan and one for reference – plus one e-copy, cutting the required shelf space by half. Thus, e-books are an ideal way to provide relevant resources in a limited space without compromising the amount of academic material available to learners, so long as appropriate texts can be acquired.

Developing and managing an e-book collection

Collection development and management remains an essential element of the work of LRCs, which often have policies and procedures in place that have evolved over a period of time and which are based on the management of traditional materials. The introduction of information in electronic formats has complicated the task and introduced many new factors into the collection management equation, several of which are examined below, before we go on to consider Yeovil College's stock management policy.

Currently, the primary factor is the availability of appropriate texts. Most courses offered at FE level have accompanying textbooks, which are the staple resource of those studying a particular course. However, there are currently very few e-books available to support FE courses specifically, particularly those focused on vocational subjects. Therefore sourcing the right e-books, which would then encourage staff and learners to embrace them and appreciate their relevance, is a major challenge.

Another factor is that learners often have a preference for the physical experience of working with the print copy, which is a known quantity and a familiar part of the learning process. Approaching the shelves and scanning for textbooks is seen by many learners as the only option to locate and access books. This wariness could also be attributed on the part of some learners to a lack of confidence in the use of IT, which they feel may be unpredictable, or to a lack of understanding of the processes connected with accessing online resources. Colleges should consider how they will effectively overcome technical barriers, making sure that consideration is given to the provision of adequate hardware, appropriate software, and sufficient user education and instruction.

Further factors that may have an impact on the development of an e-book collection are the issues of copyright and licensing. Many learners and staff lack knowledge and understanding regarding what they are allowed to do with electronic resources and can perceive these as a reason to avoid the use of e-books and continue instead with their reliance on physical copies.

Developing a stock management policy

A revised stock management policy has been developed at Yeovil College, which specifically refers to e-books, in order to raise awareness both with the LRC staff who select resources, and among the teaching staff. The principal aim of the policy is to ensure that e-books are given as much consideration as print copies, so that they are seen as an acceptable way of providing copies of texts to learners, and also to assist in the establishment of a budget to develop the e-book collection.

Selection policy

LRC staff are asked to consider the following factors when deciding whether to purchase the electronic version of a text:

- *Audience.* Who will be using the text, for example does the intended audience work off-site?
- *Demand.* Is the text likely to be used by high numbers of learners, with possibly more than one course or cohort wanting access?
- *Cost.* Would it be cheaper to purchase one e-book rather than multiple print copies?

A key point in the policy is the identification of texts for which there is likely to be high demand. As most libraries have discovered, it is difficult to provide enough physical copies of such books, as many learners on a particular course or module may often require simultaneous access. An electronic version can be one solution to this problem, and thus LRC staff should be aware of existing print copies that are heavily borrowed, as well as new texts that may be added to reading lists, recommended by tutors in class or adopted as textbooks for specific courses, so that an e-book version can be purchased where possible.

Budget policy

Careful consideration has been given to the benefits of investing in e-books. E-books can potentially provide solutions to a number of pressing issues facing the LRC at Yeovil College, and FE in general, as noted above. Having identified the benefits, the decision has been made to assign a budget specifically for the purchase of e-books. It has also been decided that once the collection of e-books was developed, and the principle that the purchase of e-books would be given equal priority to print books established, the funds would be devolved back into the standard book budget.

It was made clear to academic staff and learners that the e-book format was acceptable, and that the college supported the development of a collection of e-books. Teaching staff were informed that it was the intention to purchase texts in the new format, and all users were made aware that the number of e-books was likely to increase.

At this point key areas of the curriculum were identified where developing the e-book collection was deemed a priority. It was decided that working with these groups and investing in the provision of e-books in specific areas would eventually help to encourage the wider acceptance of e-books. The key areas were courses taught off-site, specifically those delivered for the Ministry of Defence (MoD) in countries such as Afghanistan, and for HE courses taught within the FE setting.

Reading lists

It was decided that an effective means of developing the e-book collection would be to aim whenever possible to purchase items from reading lists as e-books. This would provide greater access to key material, as well as encouraging the wider use of e-books generally as the resources required most were provided in this new format.

Management and maintenance

Many of the primary concerns for those managing physical collections relate to organizing the space to house the full range of resources, and updating the collection to ensure that it is current and relevant to the needs of the curriculum. This is a time-consuming and repetitive task, as the curriculum and qualification framework changes frequently. In addition, in the FE environment most purchasing decisions are driven by the requests of academic staff, who do not always have a good working knowledge of the resources available, and may need advice from LRC staff.

Physical collection management also involves setting limits on opening times and loan periods in order to maximize circulation within the budget and staffing resources available. These limits are felt more acutely by certain groups, for example off-site and non-traditional learners. Access to collections can also be difficult at peak periods of demand, when there is a need for multiple copies. E-books can potentially provide solutions to these problems.

However, as well as solving some of the issues, e-books present new challenges for those responsible for collection management. For example, it is critical to decide where best to place the e-book links. Options include individual links from the library catalogue, full text made available in a learning objects repository (if this is allowed under the terms of the licence), links to a large subscription collection from the LRC's website, and links within a VLE.

Consideration should also be given to the ways in which learners will view the items, for example whether it is possible to download e-books to be read later, or whether a live internet connection will be required at all times in order to access the full text. This may depend on the IT infrastructure available at the institution, as well as on the policies and systems of the e-book supplier, some aspects of which are explored by Anna Grigson in Chapter 2.

Further consideration should be given to the means by which the e-book collection will expand and develop, beyond the purchase of the initial titles. There are a number of factors that will facilitate further development, for example changing the way that budgets are organized, as well as encouraging learners and staff to use e-books through effective and sustained promotional activity. Technical factors, such as easier access and the increased use of mobile devices, are also likely to encourage growth. Additionally liaison with suppliers of e-books to request that they make more items available will encourage the use and development of e-book collections across the FE sector.

Finally, consideration should be given to arrangements for weeding the e-book collection, that is removing items which are no longer required or not required to the same extent as they once were. Many of the prompts that exist in the physical world for this process, for example the condition of items being returned to the LRC, do not exist in the virtual library, so new methods must be found, for example through the collection and analysis of usage statistics. Reading lists should be checked and revised annually to ensure that they include the latest editions of e-texts, and links to old editions should be removed from the library catalogue, the VLE and any interactive reading list documents if they have been superseded and are no longer available. This is a time-consuming process, perhaps more so than with physical books, and this needs to be taken into account when producing collection management policies.

Using e-book usage statistics for collection management

Usage statistics are important for a number of reasons: they can be used to assess value for money (by comparing the cost of the resource to the number of times it has been used over a certain time period); they can be used to identify titles where a limited usage licence is about to expire and therefore an additional payment is required; and they can be used to identify titles that are not being used and therefore should either be removed from public access or promoted to raise awareness. Statistics can also be used to assess activities such as training and promotion, which are addressed in the section 'Staffing and workflow considerations' below.

Many e-book suppliers provide access to an administration area which allows LRC staff to download title-by-title or collection-level usage data. Often this data is presented as a monthly breakdown, but some suppliers allow staff to request data for a customized time period, which is particularly useful in measuring activity after training events or after introducing e-books to learners during an induction session. Again, collating usage statistics can be very time-consuming, particularly if undertaken on a title-by-title level, so care should be taken to ensure that the data is used productively.

Finance and budget considerations

One of the roles of the LRC manager is to ensure an adequate spread of monetary resources to accommodate the variety of preferred learning styles amongst the student population. The advent of e-books has led to a dilemma over whether these should be considered in the same category as e-resources (such as bibliographic databases), or as part of what would be considered traditional bookstock, and if so whether one of these budgets should be reduced in order to accommodate the new format.

The decision on how to budget for e-books may depend on how they are purchased. For example, large subscription-based collections will almost certainly fall into the category of databases. However, if purchasing individual titles these could be treated as a separate entity requiring a completely new budget or, alternatively, they could be paid for out of the same budget as the physical book collection.

No matter how the budgets are arranged, e-books can appear expensive in comparison with their hard copy counterparts, and a careful cost analysis should be carried out before purchasing any new resources for a collection. The decision to spend what is likely to be an already tight budget on e-books should not be taken lightly, as sound financial management requires that both the benefits and the risks are taken into account.

Since colleges are generally expected to buy materials through purchasing consortia, it is important that the LRC manager involves either the procurement office or finance department in large-scale purchasing decisions. As well as advising on consortium purchasing, members of the finance team often have the ability to negotiate with reputable suppliers in order to get the best value for money. This might not necessarily mean a reduction in overall cost, but could involve extending a subscription by additional months, or gaining access to additional collections available from the same supplier.

Advantages for multiple-site campuses

In some FE colleges the campus is split over multiple sites, which creates additional challenges for LRC staff. For example, transporting physical books from one campus to another in response to learner requests has a cost in terms of postage or fuel, as well as in administration time. The e-book format requires no transport and has the potential to significantly reduce costs, particularly in staff time.

Equally, multiple-site campuses often find it difficult to split stock and decide which items fit best with the specific curriculum being taught at each site. In some cases it is common practice to purchase a copy for each site, so having a single e-book allows cost savings, not just in purchasing the book itself, but also in making the most of valuable space.

Perhaps one of the more obvious cost benefits of e-books is that they cannot get lost in the physical sense. Missing books are a particular issue for multiple-site campuses, but also affect single sites. LRC managers are well aware that replacing missing and long overdue items can be a significant expense to the annual budget, particularly in FE.

Budget management at Yeovil College

The Yeovil College Learning Centre, as with those at most FE colleges, has a devolved budget, which is used to purchase appropriate learning resources to meet the needs of the curriculum. This budget covers the cost of physical resources such as books, journals, DVDs and also virtual resources such as subscriptions to databases and e-books. In addition the budget covers the materials needed to process the resources so they are fit for use by learners, such as adding book covers. The college has two main sites: the Further Education site has a large physical learning resources collection, but the HE site has no physical collection. These facts have influenced decisions about how best to manage and develop an e-book collection.

When beginning to introduce e-books, the college initially decided to subscribe to a package from Taylor & Francis, which provided access to a large number of books through a searchable interface. However, analysis of the monthly usage statistics showed that learners were not accessing the resources as much as was first hoped. After investigating the popularity of individual titles, it was clear that those at a slightly lower level and also those that related closely to the FE curriculum were the most frequently accessed. (Although Yeovil College does have a population of 'HE in FE' learners – those studying on a degree course within the college environment – they have access to relevant e-book collections via their partner university's portal.)

The development of a reasonably large e-book collection by the Learning Centre's preferred physical book supplier (Dawson Books) during 2008–9 provided an opportunity to begin purchasing individual e-books as and when requested by the curriculum librarian. In order to find out whether this was a preferable method of acquiring e-books than subscribing to a large collection, the cost per book title in the large package was compared with the cost per title for individual purchases.

Initially, the package appeared better value, as individual titles were cheaper. However, so few of the books in the package were relevant to the FE curriculum that it was considered to be better value for money to buy individual titles. The Dawson*era* platform also offered other benefits: the interface was thought to be easy for learners to interact with; links to the texts could be simply added to the VLE; usage statistics would be easy to gather; and access would be based on a credit system, which would offer simultaneous access to many learners, an important requirement for our service. Additionally Shibboleth authentication was available, which was compatible with college systems already in place.

Therefore the package was cancelled and the budget used instead to pilot the purchasing of individual titles for one year. In the longer term it has been decided that the e-books will be purchased as part of the main book collection budget, and also that physical and virtual books will be managed as one coherent collection.

E-book costs
Subscribing to collections of e-books

The cost of a large collection of e-books is usually set by the supplier, who may be open to negotiation, particularly later on in the academic year. It can be worthwhile contacting colleagues at university and college libraries in the local area to discover what their costs have been for the same resource, in order to inform negotiations. One possibility is a discount on the annual cost in return for a commitment to purchase over the next two or three years, but this should only be considered if the resource has already been proven to be valuable to learners in the institution.

The main financial advantages of subscribing to a large collection are the ability to budget up front and the large volume of e-books that are immediately available to learners. The cost per title is likely to be small, and this can appear to be excellent value for money. However, it is important to remember that in FE there are very few courses that require extensive additional reading, and learners often require only the core textbooks. It would therefore be a useful exercise to base the cost per copy not on the total number of titles in the collection, but on the cost per *relevant* title, and then compare this to the total cost of purchasing the same titles on an individual basis. If the cost of the collection is the same or lower than that of the core texts purchased individually, then any additional titles in the collection can be considered a bonus to the LRC's stock of background reading, even if they are only used occasionally.

Purchasing individual e-books

In contrast to the costs for collections of e-books, the cost of purchasing an individual title is usually set by the publisher. In most cases the cost of an e-book will be more than that for purchasing an individual physical copy, especially when hosting fees and VAT are taken into account. It should be noted that in some cases the e-book licence is purchased with a limit to the number of downloads that are allowed; for example, there may be the stipulation that the title may only be accessed or downloaded up to 500 times within a single year. Once the download limit has been reached, the e-book will cease to be accessible to learners until an additional licence (or 'copy') has been purchased.

The elevated cost of individual e-books can be discouraging and one might question why the e-book version should cost more than the print copy, especially when considering that there are no physical manufacturing costs and costs for distribution are relatively low. However, it should be remembered that one e-book may potentially be accessed by a great many more users than a print copy within the same time period, thus justifying the higher cost.

In contrast, for e-books with limited licences the download limit may quickly be reached for very heavily used texts, requiring more purchases than might have been made with a physical text, simply to retain access to it. If a text is in high demand, the purchase of a mixture of long loan and short loan print text with a supplementary e-book copy could be suitable and may ultimately work out to be more cost effective. On the other hand, where LRC staff are aware that the syllabus and/or course structure changes frequently, they might consider that investing in physical copies that may only be relevant to learners for one or two years may not be best value for money, whereas buying an e-book version and topping up the licences as and when required could be a more cost-effective approach. Since there are many factors to take into account,

LRC staff need to find out as much as possible from both suppliers and teachers before making final decisions.

Economic pressures on students, libraries and publishers

LRCs may also feel pressure to provide access to electronic texts on behalf of learners who cannot afford to buy physical copies. The JISC NeBO project noted that nationally the purchase of student textbooks dropped by around one-fifth between 2004–5 and 2007–8, suggesting that this might be because of pressures at this time on the disposable income of learners. However, while the college LRC could possibly purchase access to texts and make them available to multiple users online, thus saving money for learners, publishers fear that this would lead to a reduction in the sales of popular textbooks, and there is a danger that publishers would subsequently increase the cost of e-books to colleges so as to make them beyond the reach of the FE sector.

The project report concludes with a stakeholder statement (JISC, 2009b, 43) that states the need for libraries and publishers to find prices for e-textbooks that are affordable on limited education budgets, mentioning that by embracing e-books publishers could benefit from increased sales across the formats in the long term. It also highlights the issue of the lack of critical core textbooks to support courses in HE, a situation that is even more acute in FE.

The JISC E-Books for FE Project

A follow-up project to examine the suitability of a variety of business models for e-textbooks in the HE environment was carried out by JISC during 2009–10, with the final report of Phase 2 still pending at the time of writing (see www.jiscebooksproject.org/business-models). In the meantime, the E-Books for FE Project was initiated by JISC in 2009 with the aim of sourcing a critical mass of titles appropriate for this sector, as well as to promote the use of e-books within FE in general (see http://fe.jiscebooksproject.org).

Almost 3000 e-books were purchased by JISC following a consultation process with colleges, and made freely available to FE learners via the ebrary platform from May 2009. The project also aims to provide a licensing structure and appropriate support so that colleges can incorporate e-books successfully into their teaching and learning activities, for example by embedding links into VLEs. The titles have been licensed until August 2014, after which a hosting fee may be payable. However, the fact that a large number of titles have been made available at no initial cost has been welcomed by colleges. As Kern Vickers (Librarian and Systems Manager) says:

> We have signed up to the JISC e-book collection for further education as this is an excellent free resource. There are a wide range of titles for all areas of the curriculum, and we hope that in time the JISC collection will grow and develop into a resource that will support all of our key teaching areas with up-to-date copies of core texts. There has been an added benefit to this free collection in terms of the promotion and development of our 'paid for' collection. We are also investing in e-books from our book supplier, mostly in preference to hard copy text. The fact that we now have these titles as well as the books from the JISC e-book project has meant a huge leap forward in the number of resources learners can access from home or the workplace during this academic year. We have been able to heavily promote the two together, and the learners have started to recognise that there is a wealth of information available to them, at a suitable FE level, beyond just using the open internet.
>
> (Vickers, 2010)

Staffing and workflow considerations

Staff in LRCs are used to adapting to new ways of working, and have enthusiastically embraced the changes resulting from technical developments in the past. While the technology of e-books and the methods for accessing them are now commonplace, e-books continue to bring new challenges to the staff involved in the development and promotion of these new resources. There may be increased workloads, and the variety of the tasks that staff are asked to undertake may be broader. Meanwhile, the presence of the new collection may call on a mixture of the traditional skills that information professionals already possess and new skills that may only be applicable when working with e-books. Therefore, in the early stages of developing an e-book collection it is essential to consider the impact and cost of the additional staffing requirements, and to ensure that staff with the correct skills and knowledge are in place.

Bringing users and e-books together

The primary role played by LRC staff in developing the use of e-books within the FE sector is to act as a link, ultimately bringing users and e-books together. They must be involved in all stages of this process, from liaising with teaching staff to raise awareness, through selecting and purchasing e-books, to the final stage of giving instructions on how to access and use e-books. The liaison role in particular is crucial, as potential users (both teaching staff and learners) are not always aware that they have access to these resources and may simply miss out altogether, particularly if their first port of call for online research is typically Google. The JISC NeBO project found that learners discover e-books in a variety of ways, but most are led or influenced by LRC staff. The main means of uncovering e-books were through:

- information skills sessions
- promotional activity by the library or LRC
- independent discovery, via the library catalogue or web pages that list e-books
- recommendations from a tutor or friend
- specific references found via a VLE module, reading list or course guide.

The project also found that once users had discovered e-resources (including e-books) they often encountered various difficulties in:

- identifying the benefits of accessing e-resources provided by their home institution in preference to information freely available on the web
- finding out about e-resources relevant to their study
- discovering which e-resources they have full access to
- dealing with the restrictions on using e-resources imposed by DRM software

- dealing with the complex and/or time-consuming procedures required to gain access to e-resources
- dealing with authenticating to, and navigating through, e-resources.

If these issues are not addressed and appropriate solutions developed there will ultimately be a lack of uptake amongst learners. Therefore, to make the e-book collection a success it is essential to make available a user education or information skills programme to both staff and learners and to offer the programme in as flexible a way as possible. Our experience has shown that the design and delivery of such a programme can become one of the biggest tasks for staff to manage. At Yeovil College training in using e-books has become part of a programme of information skills sessions, and is offered on a one-to-one, small group, class and workshop basis. The team of learning resource advisors deliver the session and design the content. Each session is broken down into approximately 20 minutes demonstration, 20 minutes hands-on practice and 10 minutes for feedback and evaluation. The following topics are covered:

- accessing and logging on to the resource
- ways to customize the resource
- effective searching, navigation and annotation of the text
- ethical use of the resource.

Promotion

Staff at Yeovil College have invested a significant amount of time in the promotion of e-books, including raising awareness with senior college managers, department heads, academic staff and learners. A wide range of promotional activities have been undertaken in relation to e-books and the time and staffing requirement involved should be acknowledged from the beginning, as the success or otherwise of the e-book collection may rest upon the ability of the team to undertake promotional tasks.

Collection development and management tasks

A significant amount of staff time is spent in the investigation, negotiation and administration of arrangements with suppliers of e-books in order to complete the initial purchase or subscription, as each supplier offers differing licence arrangements, varying costs, different interfaces and access arrangements. This task can be very intensive in the initial stages of establishing an e-book collection, and our expertise has increased as we have explored several providers and methods of acquiring e-books, with each change of direction requiring an additional input of staff time in terms of research and administration. Each new system also requires an investment of time in terms of training and familiarization for staff.

As e-book provision is still evolving it is also necessary to spend time providing feedback to publishers and suppliers to assist in the development of resources at the correct level for FE.

Similarly, introducing e-books has added a new element to the task of managing collection development funds. Guidance has been given to staff explaining how and why the e-book collection is being built and which subject areas are priorities for e-book purchase (see the section 'Developing a stock management policy' above) and this has enabled individuals to make decisions on which formats to purchase.

We have also identified that the maintenance requirements of the e-book collection will be an additional demand on staff time; for example ensuring that all links added to the library catalogue and VLE are working, giving smooth access to the collection and undertaking quality assurance within the collection by reviewing the relevant metadata and catalogue records.

The final additional task is the analysis of the data relating to the e-book collection. Usage statistics are important as a way of monitoring the take-up of e-books, checking whether promotional activity has been successful, and potentially deciding to remove unused items. The information that is gathered can also inform decisions relating to how the collection should develop and which titles or business models should be selected in the future. Feedback from information skills sessions can also be collated and reviewed alongside usage data, to find out whether learners have followed up on the session by accessing the resources that have been highlighted. Information from these different sources can then be discussed within the appropriate institutional forums, in order to inform future policies and strategies.

Skills and attributes

As well as recognizing the tasks and additional workflow that an e-book collection will bring, it is important to consider the skills and attributes staff require in order to make a success of the collection. For example, at Yeovil College Learning Centre the following have been identified: traditional information management skills; IT skills; enthusiasm; teaching skills; and skills in analysis and reflection.

Traditional information management skills

These include identifying and selecting appropriate resources, managing a budget, liaising and negotiating with suppliers, and managing access to the collection. Methods for the identification and retrieval of resources can be applicable to e-books as much as to traditional resources, therefore cataloguing and classification skills are still relevant.

IT skills

IT skills are essential for information professionals and this requirement continues to grow alongside the increase in digital content and online resources. Staff may need to be familiar with new technology such as e-readers, be competent using a variety of platforms, have an understanding of systems of authentication, and develop confidence in searching and using e-books online.

Enthusiasm

Our experience at Yeovil College has demonstrated that the successful development of e-books within an institution can often be reliant on the enthusiasm of a small number of individuals. To successfully promote e-books and convince others of the benefits, staff need a passion for e-books and must be able to make the most of every opportunity to encourage users (especially teaching staff) to access them.

Teaching skills

Staff must be confident and competent in effectively demonstrating to users how to access, navigate and use the functions of e-books. Teaching sessions should be well designed and well delivered to make learners feel comfortable using the resources and clearly understand how to get the best from them. Sessions should be imaginative and use relevant examples in order to 'hook' users onto using e-books.

Analysis and reflection

Staff should be encouraged to reflect on the tasks that they have undertaken, identifying what has been successful and what has not worked so well, with a view towards continuously improving processes and practices. For example, examining usage data and feedback could generate ideas on how to improve information skills sessions, choose more relevant texts, or target promotional activity more successfully.

Conclusion

E-books have clear benefits to learners in the FE setting, and can be integrated into college strategies which aim to enhance learning through the full use of technologies such as virtual learning environments. To make the most of e-books there are many challenges, from finding relevant texts at the right level, to procuring the funds to pay for them. However, with a well thought out collection management policy, good promotion and skills training for users, and careful consideration of the staffing implications, a collection of e-books can help to raise the profile of LRCs while ensuring that learners are able to access appropriate learning materials at the right time and place for them.

Bibliography

Abdullah, N. and Gibbs, F. (2006) A Survey of E-book Awareness and Usage amongst Students in an Academic Library. In *Proceedings of International Conference of Multidisciplinary Information Sciences and Technologies*, 25–28 Oct 2006, Merida, Spain,
http://strathprints.strath.ac.uk/2280/1/strathprints002280.pdf.

Abdullah, N. and Gibbs, F. (2009) Students' Attitudes Towards E-books in
    Scottish Higher Education Institute, *Library Review*, **58** (1), 17–27.
Appleton, L. (2005) Using Electronic Textbooks: promoting, placing and
    embedding, *The Electronic Library*, **23** (1), 54–63.
Armstrong, C. and Lonsdale, R. (2003) *The E-book Mapping Exercise: draft report on
    phase 1*,
    www.jisc.ac.uk//uploaded_documents/eBook_mapping_exercise_
    FinalReport_0403.pdf.
Becta (2008) *Harnessing Technology: next generation learning 2008-14*,
    http://publications.becta.org.uk/download.cfm?resID=37348.
Becta (2010). *Harnessing Technology Review 2009: the role of technology in further
    education and skills*,
    http://feandskills.becta.org.uk/display.cfm?resID=41523&page=
    1886&catID=1868.
Bennett, L. (2005) E-books in the Academic Libraries, *The Electronic Library*,
    23 (1).
Briddon, J. et al. (2009) 'E-books are Good if There are No Copies Left': a survey
    of e-book usage at UWE library services, *Library and Information Research*,
    33 (104).
Department for Education and Skills (2005) *Harnessing Technology: transforming
    learning and children's services*,
    http://publications.education.gov.uk/eOrderingDownload/
    1296-2005PDF-EN-01.pdf.
Gunter, B. (2005) Electronic Books: a survey of users in the UK, *ASLIB
    Proceedings*, **57** (6), 513–22.
Gunter, B. et al. (2009) *The Google Generation: are ICT innovations changing
    information-seeking behaviour?*, Chandos Publishing.
Herther, N. (2005) The E-book Industry Today: a bumpy road becomes an
    evolutionary path to market maturity, *The Electronic Library*, **23** (1), 45–53.
JISC (2006) *Designing Spaces for Effective Learning*,
    www.jisc.ac.uk/uploaded_documents/JISClearningspaces.pdf.
JISC (2009a) *In Their Own Words*,
    www.jisc.ac.uk/intheirownwords.
JISC (2009b) *National E-book Observatory Project*,
    www.jiscebooksproject.org.
JISC (2009c) *E-books for FE Project*,
    http://fe.jiscebooksproject.org.

JISC (2009d) *Libraries of the Future: a vision for the academic library and information services of the future*,
www.jisc.ac.uk/news/stories/2010/01/lotf.aspx.

Learning and Skills Council (2007) *Guidance for Colleges on the Management of Floor Space*,
http://readingroom.lsc.gov.uk/lsc/National/Floorspace_Guidance_-_02_05_07_doc_v2__2_.pdf.

Siriginidi, S. R. (2005) Electronic Books: their integration into library and information centers, *The Electronic Library*, **23** (1), 116-40.

Vickers, K. (2010) Personal interview, 29 March.

Yeovil College (2008) *Yeovil College IT/E-Learning Strategy 2008*, unpublished.

Yeovil College (2009) *Yeovil College Strategic Plan 2009-10*, unpublished.

7
E-books for higher education

Jim Dooley

Introduction

This chapter will describe the decisions made, and the methods used, by the University of California (UC), Merced Library, to acquire e-books. As used here, 'e-books' include monographs and reference works but not textbooks, since the Library does not collect textbooks in any format. The Library collection is intended to support the teaching and research activities of the University, in conjunction with the combined collections of the University of California as a whole. Up to this point, the Library has not acquired e-books specifically for use on portable e-book readers, nor does it make such readers available to users. It is working to optimize the delivery of all electronic content on mobile devices such as smartphones.

Background

The University of California, Merced, opened in September 2005 as the tenth campus in the UC system. Although the Office of the President provides many central administrative functions, each campus has its own administration and manages its own library. Strategic directions for the libraries as a whole are determined by the ten University Librarians acting as a group. The California Digital Library (CDL) licenses electronic resources on behalf of the UC Libraries while also providing technology services to the libraries.

While the campus is projected to eventually grow to accommodate

25,000 students, it began with 850 students and one academic building on the outskirts of Merced, a city of approximately 80,000 residents. The Library began in a building on an abandoned air force base ten miles from the permanent campus site. Books, computers and staff were moved to the campus in the summer of 2005, barely in time for the September opening. Because the Library building was the only academic building ready for occupancy, all first semester classes were held there. The next two academic buildings opened in January 2006. The University graduated its first four-year class in spring 2009 and will enroll approximately 4200 students in the autumn of 2010.

The growth of the Library has paralleled the growth of the campus. Because the Library is a UC library, it immediately had access to the 36 million print volumes in the University of California system, collectively the largest research library collection in the world. The University supports an intracampus ILL (interlibrary loan) operation with a dedicated courier service, so books from other UC libraries are normally available to UC Merced patrons within 24 to 36 hours. Print journal articles are scanned and delivered electronically to the user's computer. Materials not available from within the UC system can be accessed through OCLC ILL systems. The Library also immediately had access to the centrally licensed electronic resources available to all UC campuses, including over 34,000 electronic journals, over 300 databases and several thousand e-books in collections such as Institute of Electrical and Electronics Engineers (IEEE) Conference Proceedings, Safari Tech Books and SourceOECD (Organisation for Economic Co-operation and Development).

Currently the UC Merced Library catalogue contains almost 800,000 bibliographic records, approximately 88% of which represent some type of electronic resource, including monographs, serials, monographic sets such as EEBO (Early English Books Online) and federal and state government documents. Although the intent was never to build an all-electronic library, both publication trends and user preferences, especially in science, technology and engineering, have clearly moved the Library in this direction. While the Library continues to purchase and lend print books, print has become an increasingly small part of the collection.

Most, if not all, academic libraries have been experiencing this shift in recent years at varying rates. The ratio of electronic to print is even higher for the UC Merced Library because of the Library's very small print collection. The consensus appears to be that academic libraries will continue to collect print monographs, probably at decreasing rates, for the foreseeable future. According to a recent study from Springer, 'print and electronic can exist together and will complement each other's strengths' (van der Velde and Ernst, 2009, 570). In a recent survey of faculty attitudes, 31% of the respondents believed that e-books 'would be important in their professional lives in five years' (Schonfeld and Housewright, 2010). Many librarians would argue that a much greater percentage of faculty will find e-books relevant in five years.

The ten UC libraries have recently articulated a vision of a single University of California Library Collection comprising 'all print and digital resources, archival collections, and shared purchases of the UC Libraries' (University of California Libraries, 2009b). The UC Collection is further described as 'an integrated, shareable, user-centric collection that supports and enhances the mission of the University of California'. Extensive work is also currently under way to greatly increase co-operation among the libraries. Under the name Next-Generation Technical Services, this initiative will redesign 'technical services workflows across the full range of library formats in order to take advantage of new systemwide capabilities and tools, minimize redundant activities, improve efficiency, and foster innovation in collection development and management for the benefit of UC library users' (University of California Libraries, 2009a). It is expected that the implementation of specific recommendations to achieve these goals will begin in late 2010.

Strategic decisions

Any collection development decision needs to proceed from the vision of the library. For the UC Merced Library, the vision has always been to support access to, and the use of, information, not to build collections for their own sake. The basic principle is access rather than local ownership. As described above, the UC Libraries are working to implement a vision of a single University of California collection. In this environment it makes no sense for the UC Merced Library to have the goal of building a local collection as an indication of value. At one time building a multimillion volume local collection was a meaningful aim, but not in the current University of California, regional, national and international context. The UC Merced Library is also fortunate in that it does not belong to any organization that ranks members by collection size. This shift in thinking from building collections to providing services is articulated in a recent article by Paula Kaufman, University Librarian and Dean of Libraries, University of Illinois at Urbana Champaign. In it, Kaufman (2009) states: 'The library of the 21st century will be distinguished not by the content of its collections, but by the scope and quality of its services.'

In this context, the decision to build local e-book collections was first of all a service decision rather than a collections decision. Whether library users want e-books, and, if so, how should the library provide them, are fundamentally different questions from how e-books should be catalogued, managed and counted. These are important questions, but the Library proceeded to acquire e-books before they were answered with the expectation that they would be addressed in time. Similarly, the question of the preservation of e-book content was understood to be very important, but the decision was made not to wait until it was fully resolved.

The decision to acquire substantial numbers of e-books was made easier by the fact that the Library was part of a new organization. There was a very small staff that was accustomed to working in a start-up environment without an existing set of expectations. Decisions could be made quickly, both to start new initiatives and to end them without recriminations if they did not work. In a more established library, a decision to acquire e-books would probably require the formation of a committee representing multiple constituencies that would need to reach a consensus on all possible aspects of the plan before moving forward. The UC Merced Library simply did not have these constraints.

It is important to remember that the Library was founded as the shift from physical to digital resources was accelerating. As Kaufman (2009) notes: 'Access to digital content has transformed our approach to collection development and management, and it will continue to do so; more importantly it has transformed our users' approach to information seeking and use.' The acquisition of e-books needs to be understood in the context of this transformation in user expectations.

In contrast to the situation on many more established campuses, the academic members of faculty were also willing participants in this shift to digital resources. The founding faculty members were all senior scholars from large research universities, yet they did not insist that the Library replicate the collections of their former libraries. Perhaps this was because most of them were working in the disciplines of science and engineering. Perhaps they saw themselves as part of a new institution that could do things differently. Whatever the reason, they supported the Library's decision to emphasize electronic resources. Younger faculty members, even in the humanities, are engaged in digital scholarship, such as the creation of databases, alongside traditional print publication. If a faculty member wants a print book, the Library will try to acquire it, but on the whole UC Merced academic staff have demonstrated a high comfort level with digital resources.

Two decisions that were made before the campus opened in response to changing user expectations have influenced the Library's approach to e-books. First was the decision to acquire journals in electronic form unless the journal was only available in print. If the publisher requires a subscription to print as a condition for online access, the print version is not added to the collection. This decision stemmed from a conclusion that journal publishing had reached a 'tipping point' such that increasing numbers of journals would be available electronically in a short time. Events during the past five years have confirmed the correctness of this decision. According to one recent faculty survey, 75% of the respondents agreed that it would be 'fine' with them if their libraries only subscribed to current journal issues in electronic form (Schonfeld and Housewright, 2010). Currently the UC Merced Library subscribes to a total of 13 print serials.

The second decision involved the acquisition of US federal government documents. Since the Government Printing Office (GPO) had announced that it was moving towards exclusively electronic publication, the Library subscribed to the 'Documents without Shelves' service from Marcive, a library service company located in San Antonio, Texas. This service provides a bibliographic record with a URL for each federal document available electronically. At this point the Library has over 125,000 bibliographic records in its catalogue for US federal documents. Normally, libraries in the USA provide access to federal documents through membership in the Federal Depository Library Program. This enables libraries to acquire federal documents, traditionally in print, microform and CD-ROM formats, and make them available to the public. Because the documents remain the property of the US Government, the libraries must agree to accounting and inventory management requirements that many consider onerous. Since the UC Merced Library already had electronic access to so many federal documents, it was able to become the first all-electronic Federal Depository Library in 2006.

Collection development for e-books

Because the Library was at the same time part of a new institution and part of a major library system, the environment was different in many ways from that of a more established library. Despite this, many of the considerations regarding the implementation of a significant e-book initiative were the same. When collection planning began at UC Merced in 2003, the Library was comfortable providing scholarly journals and federal government information almost completely online, but was not comfortable with a similar decision to prefer e-books over print books, as evidenced by the establishment of a print book approval plan. The e-book market simply did not appear to be mature enough at that time to justify such a decision. Much has changed during the past seven years.

Through the 1990s various vendors promoted a vision of huge libraries of e-books available to everyone, everywhere, all the time; most of these vendors disappeared in the dot.com crash (Coyle, 2003). Those that were left confronted libraries with a bewildering range of choices. Each vendor had its own, often proprietary, platform and interface. Each restricted to a greater or lesser extent what users could do with the books through the use of DRM software. Some allowed printing of only one page at a time, others allowed printing more; some allowed downloading, others did not; some allowed e-mailing, others did not. Business and pricing models were immature, as most publishers appeared to see e-books as a threat to print sales rather than as an opportunity to expand their business. Licensing restrictions often prevented libraries from using e-books for interlibrary loans, course packs or reserves. Many vendors did not understand the importance of MARC records for libraries and so provided no records at all or else records of poor quality. All of these issues created multiple problems for public and technical services in libraries and so tended to relegate e-books to the status of experiments or projects. One writer referred to the situation in 2000 as a 'muddle' in the title of an article in *American Libraries* (Crawford, 2000). The landscape had not improved significantly in 2003.

One response to this largely chaotic environment would have been to wait until things sorted themselves out. For example, the market ultimately provided a winner in the contest between VHS and Beta. A similar process could be expected to work over time to determine preferred access, business and licensing terms. Another response would be to recognize the chaotic nature of the e-book environment but to proceed to enter it carefully, recognizing that initial decisions may need to be revisited. The UC Merced Library chose the latter course.

What follows is a largely chronological description of the decisions made by the UC Merced Library to acquire e-books and the various vendors with whom the Library has worked. Descriptions of vendor services are taken from the vendors' websites which are listed in 'Useful links' at the end of this chapter.

E-book collections

The Library's first acquisition of e-books was a subscription to the ACLS (American Council of Learned Societies) Humanities E-Book Project (HEB). According to its website:

> Humanities E-Book Project is a digital collection of 2,200 full-text titles offered by the ACLS in collaboration with nineteen learned societies, nearly 100 contributing publishers, and librarians at the University of Michigan's Scholarly Publishing Office. The result is an online, fully-searchable collection of high-quality books in the Humanities, recommended and reviewed by scholars and featuring unlimited multi-user access and free, downloadable MARC records.
>
> (American Council of Learned Societies, 2009)

The collection is planned to grow by approximately 500 titles per year; as of March 2010 it contained 2700 titles. While most of the HEB collection consists of scanned page images of previously published titles, there are now 75 new titles available in XML format containing hyperlinks, enlargeable images and sound and video files.

The Library chose to subscribe to this collection for several reasons. They are:

- unlimited simultaneous access
- a growing collection
- a very reasonable subscription price
- a non-commercial scholarly publisher
- a vetted collection
- an association with the University of Michigan.

Since these titles are largely classics in the field, the Library would probably have had to retrospectively acquire them in print if not for the availability of HEB.

The next acquisition of e-books was also through a subscription model, this time to Academic Complete from ebrary. This is a growing collection of over 50,000 academic titles from a variety of university and commercial publishers available through the ebrary platform. The advantages of this collection to the Library are:

- simultaneous multi-user access
- affordable full-time equivalent (FTE) based pricing
- an interface that is popular with users
- a growing collection
- free MARC records.

In addition to Academic Complete, ebrary also has over 160,000 e-books available for purchase individually with perpetual access. These titles may be purchased directly from ebrary or through library suppliers with either single-user or multi-user access. Recently ebrary has announced that it is piloting a patron selection model for e-book acquisition.

Because the Library did not intend to have a print reference collection, it subscribed to the online equivalent offered by Credo Reference, formerly known as Xrefer. This aggregator currently provides access to more than 475 reference works, such as dictionaries and specialized encyclopedias, from over 70 publishers.

As stated, HEB, Academic Complete and Credo Reference are subscription e-book collections. Libraries do not select the titles and they retain access only while the subscription is active; there are no post-cancellation rights to the content. Such a model provides access to a large number of titles at a low unit cost. Libraries will need to evaluate whether this advantage outweighs the lack of perpetual access to these titles and how this issue can be mitigated.

Individual titles

One mitigation strategy is to purchase e-books with perpetual access either directly from publishers or through aggregators or library suppliers. At about the time the Library subscribed to Academic Complete, it acquired approximately 8000 titles through NetLibrary. This aggregator began as an independent corporation, but was acquired by OCLC in 2002. Its inventory currently includes over 200,000 trade, reference and science, technology and medicine (STM) titles available through direct library purchase as well as patron selection. In March 2010 OCLC announced that it had sold NetLibrary to EBSCO Publishing.

The UC Merced librarians worked directly with a librarian at NetLibrary to individually select titles by LC (Library of Congress) classification in support of specific academic programmes. MARC records were provided by OCLC. While the selection experience was positive and mirrored traditional print book selection methods, the Library has not purchased additional titles from NetLibrary because of dissatisfaction with the access model. NetLibrary titles are not available with multiple simultaneous user access. The NetLibrary access model is patterned after traditional print book circulation in that each book can only be accessed by one user at a time. The only way to provide access to multiple users simultaneously is to purchase additional copies of the e-book.

The Library next made another purchase of e-books with perpetual access from Baker & Taylor. This company had recently purchased the Library's print book vendor, so the sales staff were interested in customers acquiring e-books as well. The librarians selected approximately 500 titles, again in support of specific academic programmes. Unfortunately, not long thereafter, Baker & Taylor decided that the e-book business was not sufficiently profitable and so transferred all e-books to NetLibrary. All of the Baker & Taylor e-books purchased by the UC Merced Library remain available as NetLibrary titles, so the Library has not suffered any loss in this sale. It is a cautionary tale, however, in that it demonstrates how access, business and licensing terms for e-books could well be affected by commercial transactions. As stated above, NetLibrary itself has now been sold to EBSCO Publishing.

Up to this point, the Library had acquired e-books by one of two traditional methods – subscription or individual purchase. In 2004, as a result of a presentation at the American Library Association (ALA) Midwinter Meeting, the Library began to employ a new method of e-book acquisition – patron selection.

Patron selection

The basic model of patron selection for e-books is that a library places a large number of bibliographic records in its catalogue which point to e-books available from a particular vendor. The library purchases an individual title after it has been accessed an agreed-upon number of times. Users are unaware that they may have caused the library to purchase any particular title; they have simply accessed an e-book available from the library. From the library's perspective, patron selection ensures that purchased titles are actually used, rather than being purchased simply in the hope or expectation that they will be used. A recent study of print approval plans revealed that 40% of the books purchased on approval by the University of Illinois at Urbana Champaign did not circulate within one to two years of availability and that 38% of the total approval budget was spent on unused books (Alan et al., 2010). The same study showed that 31% of approval receipts at the largest Pennsylvania State University campus at University Park did not circulate within one to two years of availability. This and similar studies, along with the current financial environment, are causing many libraries to re-evaluate how they acquire monographs. Patron selection represents a shift from a 'just-in-case' model to a 'just-in-time' model. It is particularly suitable for e-books because the user has immediate access to the title through the bibliographic record.

Some have objected that patron-selected e-books will be used less often than library-selected e-books, that they have a narrower audience and that such collections are less balanced. In a paper presented at the 2009

Charleston Conference, Jason Price and John McDonald (2009) examined e-book collections in five libraries that contained both patron-selected and library-selected titles. Their statistical analysis showed that patron-selected e-books are used on average twice as often per year as library-selected titles, are accessed by twice as many individual users per year and that both acquisition methods resulted in similar subject profiles as evidenced by Library of Congress classification.

Financial management of a patron-selection plan is very important. An amount of money will need to be set aside up front to cover anticipated costs. Of necessity, the initial amount will be based largely on professional judgement. As time proceeds, the budgeted amount will need to be monitored to anticipate usage trends, particularly as these trends are likely to be upward. If necessary, the number of publishers or subjects covered can be reduced to limit expenditure.

In 2004, aside from NetLibrary, the one major aggregator offering a patron-selection e-book plan was EBL. This supplier offers over 100,000 titles, chiefly in science, technology and medicine, for sale through both library-selection and patron-selection models. EBL offers multiple concurrent access and titles can be accessed online through a PDF-based reader or offline by downloading Adobe Acrobat e-books. A pay-per-use model called Short Term Loan is also available.

The UC Merced Library has loaded all of the available MARC records from EBL and receives a monthly file of new records. There is nothing in the record that indicates to the user that any particular title is part of a patron-selection plan. Users can browse any book for ten minutes before they are required to take some action in order to continue accessing the title. If a book has not already been purchased, users are asked if they want a one-day, one-week or two-week Short Term Loan. After three Short Term Loans of any length, the book is automatically purchased on the fourth access. Thus the library is only purchasing titles that have been accessed a minimum of four times. The number of purchased titles can be expected to increase as more titles are accessed for the fourth time.

The Library also has a much smaller patron-selection plan with Coutts/MyiLibrary with about 9000 academic titles published from 2008 onward. E-books may be purchased with either single-user or multi-user access; the UC Merced Library purchases all titles with single-user access.

This plan works somewhat differently from EBL in that the Library purchases the title on the third access.

A relatively new development is the ability of traditional library suppliers to include e-books along with print books in approval plans. Both YBP (originally Yankee Book Peddler) and Coutts Information Services, for example, now offer integrated print and e-book approval plans with e-books available from both aggregators and publishers. This allows libraries to use vendor services to manage format duplication as well as to integrate e-books into established selection and acquisitions workflows. A further development would be the integration of patron-selection e-book plans with print approval plans to control unwanted print duplication.

Collaborative purchasing

Various other UC libraries have been slowly acquiring e-books locally. At this point four campuses have subscribed to ebrary Academic Complete. Two campuses are investigating pilot patron-selection e-book plans. As mentioned above, the California Digital Library provides access to e-books through various publisher packages that also include journals, conference proceedings and so on. Until recently, there has not been a system-wide purely e-book contract with any publisher or aggregator. This situation has had negative implications for public services in that bibliographic records for local library e-book acquisitions are in the UC union catalogue, but access is only available on the individual subscribing campus.

In 2008 the UC Libraries Collection Development Committee published the report *Guiding Principles for Collecting Books in Electronic Format* (University of California Libraries, 2008), which contained preferred access, business and licensing terms for a UC-wide e-book agreement. This facilitated negotiations between the CDL and Springer, which resulted in an agreement in 2009. The UC Libraries already had access to Springer journals on SpringerLink; the e-books are also now available on the same platform. This is but one example of an increasing trend, particularly for STM publishers, to make both journal and e-book content available through the same website (STM, 2009). Under this agreement the UC Libraries have obtained perpetual access to nearly every Springer e-book published in English and German from 2005 to 2010. The collection currently includes over 24,000 e-books in every scientific discipline and many social sciences.

The UC Libraries selected Springer for the first major system-wide e-book contract primarily because of Springer's favourable licensing and business terms. The licensing terms are in line with the recommendations in the report *Guiding Principles* including broad academic use rights, favourable interlibrary loan provisions (including the use of electronic ILL), perpetual ownership, unlimited concurrent users and no use of DRM. A print copy of each book published from 2009 forward has been included in the package to allow comparison between print and electronic usage and to reduce duplicate acquisitions across the UC campuses. Users can also choose the print-on-demand purchase option on the Springer website, called *MyCopy,* to order a printed copy. This is a soft-cover black and white edition that is intended only for personal use. The agreement with Springer is officially a pilot and needs to be renewed on a year-by-year basis. A task force has been appointed to conduct a systematic assessment of the pilot programme in 2010. Contingent upon the outcome of this assessment, negotiations to continue the programme for 2011 will occur in late 2010.

Business models and licensing terms

While libraries are still faced with many choices in acquiring e-books, the situation is much clearer today than it was in 2003. Libraries need to examine available options and make decisions in several areas: business and access terms, licensing terms and the user experience.

There are multiple options for e-book purchase and subscription, and Chapter 2 of this book, 'An Introduction to E-book Business Models and Suppliers' can be referred to for some detail on these. Libraries need to evaluate which combination of options will best meet the needs of their users.

Continuing access and digital preservation

An important aspect of collection development is the implementation of contingency plans for accessing e-books should they become unavailable from the original supplier for any reason. Catastrophic system failure is always a possibility, but bankruptcy or the sale of the business is more likely. Suppliers will often agree in the licence to provide the library with a copy of the digital files for hosting on the library's servers in the event that the vendor ceases business. The library will need to determine if it has the technical capacity and staff expertise to make this viable.

Another option would be for the library to join an organization such as Portico or to utilize technologies such as LOCKSS or CLOCKSS to archive purchased e-books. Portico originally focused on the preservation of e-journals, but currently holds over 33,000 e-books in its archive. The California Digital Library uses Portico for preservation of licensed e-journals and e-books and continues to encourage additional publishers to deposit content in Portico.

Multiple concurrent access

This discussion of access terms has already touched on one aspect of the user experience – whether concurrent access is limited or unlimited. For academic libraries this question becomes important if lecturers assign e-books as course readings. The e-books may well not be intended or marketed as textbooks, but students will become frustrated if access is limited to one or a few people at one time. Often the library will not know that an e-book is being used in a course until students complain about lack of access, by which point it may be too late to solve the problem for that particular course. Therefore it may be necessary to explain to the faculty member and students that these books can only be accessed by a limited number of users at a time. User expectations are different in a digital world from those in an analogue world and libraries need to do what they can to meet or at least manage these expectations.

Acceptable use

Another very important aspect of the overall user experience with e-books is what can be done with them: print, copy-and-paste, download, e-mail and so on. Publishers and aggregators are rightly fearful of large-scale illegal downloading of copyrighted content, but students want to be able to use e-books in ways that make sense to them in a digital environment. Aggregators, because they deal with many publishers, tend to apply the user controls of the most restrictive publisher to all the available content. This 'lowest common denominator' approach means that a library can often get better user permissions directly from the publisher than through an aggregator. This is certainly the case with the Springer content licensed directly by the University of California. The same content is available through aggregators with much more restrictive user permissions.

The user experience is related to licensing terms, but licensing also governs what libraries can do with e-book content, specifically use in interlibrary loans, course packs and e-reserves. The CDL has published a model licence that describes the library permissions the University of California desires in any system-wide agreement for electronic information resources (California Digital Library, 2009). Publishers will often refuse to accept some of these permissions, but the model licence does set forth the expectations of the UC Libraries. Ultimately, each library will have to decide which user and library permissions it believes that it must have in a licence agreement.

User attitudes towards e-books

An important aspect of collection development is understanding user preferences. In the past five years there have been a small number of published surveys documenting user attitudes towards e-books. Gregory (2008) conducted a survey of undergraduates at the College of Mount Saint Joseph in Cincinnati, Ohio, in 2004. Of those surveyed, 66% preferred print books and 34% preferred e-books, yet 89% said that they would use e-books if that was the only format available. In a survey of undergraduate and graduate students at the University of Strathclyde in 2005–6, 67% preferred e-books for reference purposes, but only 6% preferred e-books for extended reading (Noorhidawati and Gibb, 2008). In 2008 a survey of faculty, graduate and undergraduate students at the University of Illinois was conducted in which 57% of the respondents had used e-books and 86% of graduate and undergraduate students found e-books useful. These results led to the conclusion that 'acceptance of e-books has reached a level where they have become an important library service' (Shelburne, 2009, 59). Other recent articles (STM, 2009;

van der Velde and Ernst, 2009; HighWire Press, 2010) have documented the increasing acceptance of e-books in academic libraries.

Usage statistics

Since UC Merced had few students and faculty when the Library opened and the surveys noted above had not yet been published, it was necessary to proceed on professional judgement rather than on quantitative evidence. The librarians believed that a tipping point had been reached by 2005 in the transition from print to electronic journals, and that a similar tipping point for monographs would be reached in the foreseeable future. The question at this point is whether there are now usage statistics that validate this hypothesis.

At the end of 2009 the UC Merced Library had a print collection of approximately 90,000 volumes. In calendar year 2009, 10,900 volumes or 12% of the collection circulated. For a research university library, this is a relatively high circulation rate. In comparison, according to statistics provided to the CDL by Springer, during 2009 there were 8350 full-text chapter downloads at UC Merced just from Springer e-books. So usage of Springer e-books at UC Merced was equal to 80% of the total print book circulation during 2009. Within the total UC system, there were 647,000 chapter downloads from Springer e-books in 2009. Also during 2009, according to COUNTER reports from ebrary, there were 44,460 accesses of ebrary titles at UC Merced or over three times the total print book circulation. Granted, an e-book 'access' does not necessarily equal a print book loan, but the comparative numbers are nonetheless useful in evaluating user preferences.

Because the UC Merced academic year ends in early May, April 2010 is the latest month for which meaningful statistics can be obtained. In April 2010, 1639 print books circulated at UC Merced. During the same month there were 3123 accesses of ebrary e-books or slightly more than 190% of print book circulation.

Obviously, these numbers must be used with some caution. Both availability and adoption of e-books are still greater in the sciences than in the humanities, for example. This parallels the situation in journal publishing. Usage statistics certainly do not prove that the Library should no longer acquire print books. They do point to a general acceptance of e-books at UC Merced and give a strong indication that, at least at UC Merced, the tipping point for e-books has been reached.

Staffing and workflow considerations

Workflow for e-books can be broken down into a series of steps similar to those for the acquisition of databases and e-journals. These are:

- choose appropriate subject categories and mode of access
- choose a business model
- choose a supplier
- negotiate with the supplier
- obtain MARC records from the supplier
- load the records
- process record updates
- solve access issues
- pay invoices.

The first three steps are normally carried out in collection development and/or acquisitions. The library first needs to decide how and in which subjects it wishes to acquire e-books. It then needs to evaluate possible suppliers in terms of its preferred business model and minimum usability and licensing terms. In this context 'supplier' includes both publishers and aggregators. At this point it is also good practice to invite public service staff to evaluate the interface.

Once the licence is signed, technical services staff need to begin to work with the supplier to acquire MARC records. An effort should be made to get the supplier to provide any necessary customization of the records in order to eliminate local editing. Examples of record customization are changes to the text of the public note accompanying the URL and the addition of fields to track payment information. Once these issues have been resolved, the records can be downloaded from the supplier's site, holdings can be set in OCLC WorldCat if required, and library patrons will have access to the e-books.

The last three steps are part of ongoing maintenance. The supplier will normally provide a file of new, updated and deleted records monthly. Libraries have no control over the business relationships between aggregators and publishers, so occasionally aggregators will lose access to some or all of the titles from a particular publisher. When this happens, the aggregator should send a file of records to be deleted from the local system and staff need to delete these records promptly. If the library sets its holdings in OCLC, then holdings for titles that are no longer available will need to be removed.

As with other electronic resources, some time will need to be spent resolving patron access problems. Some of these problems may be technical, for example the wrong URL may be in a record or the supplier may have lost access to a title and not sent a delete record. Other technical problems may involve computer hardware or software, browsers or network issues. It will also be necessary to communicate with users and library staff as to what they can and cannot do with particular e-books under the applicable licence.

Procedures for paying invoices should be the same for all types of electronic information resources. Since in an electronic environment the supplier can instantly cut off access in the event of non-payment, it is good practice to pay invoices promptly.

The size of the library will tend to determine the degree of staff specialization. At UC Merced one person handles collection development and licensing, another handles cataloguing and a third deals with financial services. This is probably as simple as it can get in a research university library. In spite of having such a small staff, the Library has been able to build a collection of 800,000 titles in five years by making the most of vendor and consortial services.

Budgetary considerations

The cost of e-books will depend first of all on whether the library implements a subscription or purchase acquisition model. Subscription prices are often based on the size of the student body. At times publishers will offer a significant discount for the purchase of a package of titles. While subscription and package acquisition are cheaper, they do have some disadvantages such as the possibility of acquiring material that is inappropriate for the library's users.

To this point, publishers have usually linked e-book prices to print prices, with the e-book priced at some level of premium over the cost of the print. This makes sense from the publisher perspective if the e-book includes multiple concurrent access since presumably fewer books need to be purchased to meet the same level of demand. From the library perspective, a premium of 10% to perhaps 15% over the print price for multiple concurrent access would appear reasonable. It is harder to make a case for a premium over print price when the e-book access model is single user. Ultimately, the library is concerned with the price of the e-books and whether that price appears reasonable, rather than with the specific model used by the publisher. As e-books become more accepted and as they move beyond the digitization of existing print versions, such as the Humanities E-Book XML titles described previously, it is likely that new pricing models will emerge that are not based on print. Another possibility, particularly for STM titles, would be to price by the chapter since that is the item of most relevance to the user. Bibliographic control in a world of discrete information items will be challenging (Carpenter, 2010).

Aggregator prices seem to vary widely from print prices. In a recent small-scale survey of UC Merced titles, the e-book version cost from 97% to 133% of the print version. It appears that most aggregators are currently charging 1.5 times the single user cost for multi-user access. If a library is considering working with a single e-book supplier, it would be a good idea to compare prices over a wide range of useful titles among several suppliers. It is also important to remember that a higher price may be justified by additional services, a better interface or superior user tools.

When considering the total cost of e-books, it is also important to consider cost savings from not acquiring print. The first significant cost saving is in shelf space. Many academic libraries have to weed print collections or move significant amounts of print to off-site storage in order to free space for new uses such as collaborative work rooms, computer labs, information commons and increased study space. If e-books are acquired instead of, rather than in addition to, print, this will help reduce the growth of the physical collection and ease space pressures.

The second significant cost saving is in physical processing, shelving and circulation staff. E-books do not need to have property stamps or spine labels attached; they do not need to be re-shelved or kept in class number order on the shelves; they do not need to be checked out or checked in. All of these activities require staff and so incur staff costs. Again, if e-books are acquired instead of print, staff could be reassigned or overall staff costs could be reduced.

Of course, the general shift of library collections from print to digital, not just e-books, will have implications for staff training. As part of this transition, the library will need to develop licensing expertise. Cataloguing staff will need to work with vendors to edit MARC records to meet library requirements and become proficient in the importing, exporting and manipulation of large files of records. Staff will also have to stop individual editing of bibliographic records. If the library chooses to implement a patron-selection e-book plan, the greatest impact is likely to be on bibliographers and subject specialists who may be concerned with the transfer of book selection from librarians to users.

Conclusion

The UC Merced Library has made a significant commitment to e-books over the past five years with the result that today the Library has an e-book collection several times the size of its print book collection. Usage statistics and other measures of user preference continue to validate this approach. E-books have been fully integrated into monographic collection development and acquisitions. Patron selection has emerged as the principal means of local e-book acquisition, while the licensing of publisher packages such as Springer seems to be gaining support at the system-wide level. This all seemed quite radical five years ago, but increasing numbers of research libraries, including very large ones, have begun moving in this direction. During the past ten years the adoption of e-books by academic libraries has trailed that of e-journals. At the current rate, it is not unreasonable to predict that the market penetration of e-books will equal that of e-journals within five years. This will not signal the end of print, but it will require libraries to embrace a transformative change in publishing and user preferences.

Useful links

ACLS Humanities E-book www.humanitiesebook.org

CLOCKSS www.clockss.org
Coutts Information Services www.couttsinfo.com
Credo Reference http://corp.credoreference.com
Ebook Library www.eblib.com
ebrary www.ebrary.com
LOCKSS http://lockss.stanford.edu
NetLibrary http://company.netlibrary.com
Portico www.portico.org
Springer www.springer.com
YBP www.ybp.com

References

Alan, R. et al. (2010) Approval Plan Profile Assessment in Two Large ARL Libraries, *Library Resources & Technical Services*, **54** (2), 64–76.
American Council of Learned Societies (2009) *ACLS Humanities E-book - general information*, www.humanitiesebook.org/intro.html.
California Digital Library (2009) *Standard License Agreement*, www.cdlib.org/gateways/vendors/docs/Model_License_LATEST_Revised_10-09.rtf.
Carpenter, T. (2010) Moving to Collections of Items, *Against the Grain*, **22** (1), 82.
Coyle, K. (2003) E-books: it's about evolution, not revolution, *Library Journal Net Connect*, Fall, 8–12.
Crawford, W. (2000) Nine Models, One Name: untangling the e-book muddle, *American Libraries*, **31** (8), 56–9.
Gregory, C. (2008) 'But I Want a Real Book': an investigation of undergraduates' usage and attitudes toward electronic books, *Reference & User Services Quarterly*, **47** (3), 266–73.
HighWire Press (2010) *2009 Librarian eBook Survey*, http://highwire.stanford.edu/PR/HighWireEBookSurvey2010.pdf.
Kaufman, P. (2009) *Carpe Diem: transforming services in academic libraries*, https://www.ideals.illinois.edu/handle/2142/12032.
Noorhidawati, A. and Gibb, F. (2008) How Students Use E-Books - reading or referring?, *Malaysian Journal of Library & Information Science*, **13** (2), 1–14.
Price, J. and McDonald, J. (2009) *Beguiled by Bananas: a retrospective study of the usage & breadth of patron vs. librarian acquired ebook collections*,

http://blog.eblib.com/?attachment_id=2416.

Schonfeld, R. and Housewright, R. (2010) *Ithaka S+R Faculty Survey 2009: key strategic insights for libraries, publishers, and societies,*
www.ithaka.org/ithaka-s-r/research/faculty-surveys-2000-2009/Faculty%20Study%202009.pdf.

Shelburne, W. A. (2009) E-book Usage in an Academic Library: user attitudes and behaviors, *Library Collections, Acquisitions & Technical Services,* **33** (2/3), 59–72.

STM (2009) International Association of Scientific, Technical and Medical Publishers, *The STM Report: an overview of scientific and scholarly journal publishing,*
www.stm-assoc.org/news.php?id=255.

University of California Libraries (2008) *Guiding Principles for Collecting Books in Electronic Format: report of the collection development committee task force on E-books,*
http://libraries.universityofcalifornia.edu/cdc/taskforces/ebooks_final_report.pdf.

University of California Libraries (2009a) *Next Generation Technical Services (NGTS),*
http://libraries.universityofcalifornia.edu/about/uls/ngts.

University of California Libraries (2009b) *The University of California Library Collection: content for the 21st century and beyond,*
http://libraries.universityofcalifornia.edu/cdc/uc_collection_concept_paper_endorsed_ULs_2009.08.13.pdf.

van der Velde, W. and Ernst, O. (2009) The Future of eBooks? Will Print Disappear? An end-user perspective, *Library Hi Tech,* **27** (4), 570–83.

Part 3

Delivering e-books to library users

Overview

Once decisions have been made regarding the procurement of e-books and a strategic plan is in place to establish them as an important part of the library's collection, the next major challenge is to ensure that library users are able to access them! In this section, the authors discuss some of the practical aspects of connecting readers with e-books in the library setting.

Anna Grigson (Chapter 8) of Royal Holloway, University of London, provides a practical overview of the steps that need to be taken to establish the visibility of e-books within the library catalogue, as well as within other systems. Grigson considers cataloguing policy and workflows as well as the challenges of ongoing records management, and establishes clear guidelines for good practice.

Karen Gravett (Chapter 9) of the University of Surrey provides an insight into the diverse ways that the institution has supported user interaction with e-books, from formal information skills training to informal one-to-one support, as well as by facilitating self-help through online guidance. Gravett also reflects on the ways that e-book provision could be further developed in order to improve the experience of readers.

Finally, James Clay (Chapter 10) of Gloucestershire College considers some of the technical challenges that can face users in their interaction with e-books, from authentication and authorization to DRM. Clay also provides an examination of the exciting opportunities offered by e-books in a mobile learning environment.

8
Making e-book collections visible to readers

Anna Grigson

Introduction

It has always been a challenge to make virtual library collections visible. Options for physical signposts to e-books are limited – users cannot browse the shelves to see what is available, look at a new book display, or discover a book on the reshelving trolley – all of which puts more emphasis on the effectiveness of the library catalogue as a means to highlight the availability of library e-books. However, the cataloguing of e-books presents some significant challenges, and a recent report found that many libraries struggle to catalogue all of their e-book holdings (Research Information Network, 2009).

Conversely, the visibility of e-books in the wider world has increased significantly in recent years. The increasing popularity of e-book readers and now the iPad has raised the profile of books in e-formats, and, with their facilities for full-text searching, sites such as Amazon and Google Book Search make e-books for consumers easy to find and purchase. For those trying to make *library* e-books visible, however, this creates another challenge. If libraries are to be effective in connecting users with their e-books, they need to consider additional options that could offer more effective and efficient ways to increase the exposure of library e-books, alongside the traditional library catalogue.

E-books on the web

Studies show that a decreasing number of library users start their search with the library catalogue, and are instead beginning with Google and other search engines (CIBER, 2008). For users, these offer two major advantages over the library catalogue: they can search in more detail, and they can cover more content. As Anderson (2010) points out, a catalogue listing the contents of a local collection was an acceptable discovery tool in the past, where the average user only had access to whatever was available in the library. But in a world where search engines make it easy to both identify and gain access to full-text content outside the library collection, users wish to search beyond the limits of the local catalogue.

So if users are not coming directly to the library catalogue, is it possible to make library content discoverable via search engines? In theory, link resolver services or widgets such as LibX can provide links from search engines to library content, so that when a user discovers a book in (for example) Google Scholar they are presented with a link to the library's copy of the e-book. In practice, however, discovery of library collections from search engines does not match the standards of accuracy and reliability that would be expected from a library catalogue. The quality of metadata is variable, which affects not only the quality of search results but also the accuracy and reliability of the links. Nevertheless, embedding links to library content into search engines is a useful complement to the catalogue and despite these limitations represents a good opportunity to increase the visibility of library e-books.

In the longer term, is it possible that web search could replace the library catalogue? As well as offering a more effective search, it would also be a more efficient way to make library content discoverable. As Anderson (2010) points out, creating a local catalogue is inherently inefficient since much of it duplicates metadata that is already available elsewhere. If reliable links to library holdings could be attached to the metadata already available on the web, there would no longer be a need to create a catalogue of local metadata.

This goal is not likely to be achieved in the short term. Improving the reliability of linking from search engines raises significant technical challenges, including issues surrounding metadata quality and standards, and the interoperability of search engines with library management and linking systems. Moreover, it is not just technical issues that need to be addressed. As the Research Information Network report (2009) notes, it is not clear how supporting the discoverability of library content would fit with the current business models of search engine providers. But there is no doubt that the focus of resource discovery is moving away from the local catalogue and towards web-scale discovery.

E-books in shared catalogues

Another option for increasing both the effectiveness and the efficiency of resource discovery is to move towards a greater use of shared catalogues. Many libraries are already using consortia catalogues on a local or regional scale, but the trend now is to develop shared catalogues on a larger scale – either nationally, for example the current project on the feasibility of a national catalogue for UK academic libraries (SCONUL, 2009), or internationally, for example increasing use of OCLC WorldCat Local. Large-scale shared catalogues offer a more efficient way for libraries to catalogue their local collections, and they also significantly broaden the range of content covered, thus coming closer to competing with web search engines.

E-books in other systems

More immediately achievable options for increasing the visibility of library e-books are also available. Creating browseable A–Z lists of titles, or highlighting collections by subject or genre on library web pages, offer simple ways to introduce relevant e-books to users. In the academic context, e-books can also be embedded into online resource list systems such as Talis Aspire (see www.talis.com/aspire), and virtual learning environments, an option that is discussed elsewhere in this book (see, for example, Chapter 12).

There are also other resource discovery systems that can improve the search offered by the library by increasing both the range of content and the level of detail which can be explored. Federated search systems such as MetaLib (ExLibris), 360 Search (Serials Solutions), SwetsWise Searcher and EBSCOhost Integrated Search offer the potential to complement the title-level search offered by the library catalogue with full-text searching of the library's e-book collections. 'Pre-harvested' search services such as EBSCO Discovery Service, Primo (ExLibris) and

Summon (Serials Solutions) can extend the range of the library catalogue by querying a centralized database of metadata taken directly from vendors and publishers, and integrating the results with those from the library catalogue. Both systems can potentially reduce the amount of metadata that has to be added directly to the library catalogue.

There are limitations to what these systems can deliver, and neither is yet an ideal solution. Not all e-book websites are compatible with federated search systems, and not all e-book packages are indexed by pre-harvested systems. Moreover, neither system can entirely replace the local library catalogue, so they must be maintained as additional systems, at additional cost (for more detail see Stone, 2010; Walker, n.d.). However, they do provide a way to extend search facilities beyond the title level offered by the library catalogue and therefore have the potential to significantly improve the discovery of e-books.

E-books in the library catalogue

In the longer term, search engines and shared catalogues may replace the local library catalogue, and in the short term, options such as federated search and pre-harvested search offer valuable complementary data and search services. But despite its limitations, the humble catalogue can still make an effective contribution, a point confirmed by both the SuperBook study (Rowlands et al., 2007) and the JISC National e-Books Observatory Project (2009), which found that usage of e-books increased if they were listed in the catalogue. Therefore, adding e-books to the local library catalogue is still a worthwhile enterprise, and the rest of this chapter looks at how to achieve this effectively.

Creating a cataloguing policy

When cataloguing e-books, the aim is to offer the best possible search experience, with each book catalogued with rich, accurate metadata, which can be found via multiple discovery points. But the extent to which these aims are achievable will be constrained by costs, including both direct costs such as paying for imported records, and the indirect cost of staff time spent creating, editing and updating records.

The tasks involved in cataloguing e-books are similar to those for print books: adding records for new books, making changes to new records to bring them up to required standards, and deleting records for items withdrawn from collections. However, although the tasks are the same, the workload for e-books is likely to be on a much larger scale. Instead of adding and deleting individual records, libraries acquiring packages of e-books may find they have to work with hundreds or even thousands of new books at a time. E-book collections can also be more dynamic than print collections, with frequent changes to titles included in packages, so as well as adding records for new e-book packages it may also be necessary to add records for books that are newly included in existing packages, and to make changes to keep existing records up to date, for example if URLs change.

As with print cataloguing, it is essential to maximize efficiency by outsourcing and automating processes where possible, and by minimizing the need for in-house editing of records. But even the most efficient cataloguing processes may struggle to cope with the scale of work involved in cataloguing e-books. So it is necessary to make a realistic assessment of what can be achieved with the resources available, to evaluate the costs and benefits of each option, and to formulate a cataloguing policy that sets priorities as to which books to catalogue, and the quality required for each record.

Choosing which books to catalogue

Many libraries will purchase individual e-books to meet the needs of specific users. Although the cost per book of cataloguing individual titles can be relatively high in terms of staff time, making these books discoverable is likely to be the highest priority. However, for e-book packages, especially for very large packages, a more selective approach may be required.

First, it is necessary to establish whether it is actually possible to catalogue the titles in a package. For some packages, especially 'mixed-content' databases including e-books, e-journals and other items, it may be difficult to find out which e-book titles are included. If there is no easy way to find out which books are in the package, and to keep up to date with any changes, then it may not be possible to catalogue the titles at all.

Second, for those packages where it is possible to catalogue the individual titles, it is necessary to consider the costs and benefits of cataloguing on a case-by-case basis. The cost per book may be relatively low as packages can often be catalogued in bulk. But given that e-book collections may range in size from fewer than 100 to over 100,000 titles, the overall cost to catalogue an entire package could be substantial. There may also be other less obvious costs of adding such a large number of records to the catalogue database. A LMS vendor's fees may be related to the size of the catalogue database, so adding a large number of records could result in higher software maintenance fees, and hardware costs may also rise if additional servers are needed to support a much larger bibliographic database.

Furthermore, the benefits of cataloguing some packages may not justify the costs involved. Packages can sometimes be highly specialized in nature, for example Eighteenth Century Collections Online (ECCO). The value of these collections to users often lies more in the full-text content in totality, rather than the specific titles they contain, and if users are searching by subject rather than seeking particular books, basic title-level records may be of limited use. It is therefore worth considering whether adding title-level records is likely to benefit users sufficiently to justify the costs. Instead of listing the individual books, a more cost-effective solution may be to create a collection level catalogue record and use this to direct users to the website where the books are hosted so that they can search the full text on the supplier's platform.

As well as cataloguing e-books which the library purchases, there may be demand to catalogue selected free titles of particular interest to the library's users. But although the content may be free, the staff time needed to catalogue the e-books is not, and careful consideration needs to be given to the feasibility and costs of obtaining metadata, keeping records of the titles added to the catalogue, and keeping these records up to date if the book changes, moves, or disappears entirely.

Setting quality standards

As well as assessing the number of e-books to be catalogued, it is also necessary to consider the quality of cataloguing that can be achieved, both in terms of the level of detail in each record, and the accuracy of the data.

Ideally all e-book records should include an appropriate level of detail, and should be checked and edited to ensure that they are completely accurate. But more detail usually results in higher costs, both for the records themselves and for the time spent checking and editing them. So it may be necessary to accept a lower level of detail, especially for large packages where obtaining or creating full MARC records could be very expensive, or for free e-books, where the value of the resource may not merit cataloguing in as much detail as paid-for titles. Similarly, rather than aiming for complete accuracy, it may be necessary to adopt a more pragmatic approach and accept that some records may be missing, some may have a less than ideal level of detail, and some may contain errors.

As with print books, the minimum acceptable level of detail will depend on the type of collection and the needs of its users. A collection of research monographs in an academic or national library may require more detailed records, including subject headings where possible, whereas for a collection of fiction it may be sufficient to provide a more basic record giving just author, title, publication details and ISBN. Developing a specification document listing the fields required in MARC records for e-books can be a useful tool for clarifying requirements, and for use as a benchmark in assessing the quality of supplied records.

Managing workflows

As well as creating a policy on what to catalogue, it is important to make best use of staff resources by developing efficient workflows to streamline the processes of creating and maintaining the catalogue. To a large extent it is possible to align e-book workflows with those for print, especially for individually purchased titles. But there are some differences to workflows for e-books that may require adjustments to ensure that the workload is managed efficiently.

In particular, it can be more difficult to track the progress of e-books through cataloguing. New processes therefore need to be developed to monitor the 'arrival' of new books, and ensure that all newly acquired books are catalogued and linked. It is also necessary to develop procedures to track changes to e-book holdings. When managing print collections, changes are usually initiated by the library, for example, staff decide which books to withdraw from the collections, or which books need to be relocated and reclassified. Co-ordinating any necessary changes to the library catalogue is therefore a straightforward issue of internal communications. But when dealing with e-books hosted on remote websites it may be the vendor who initiates changes to the content or location of an e-book package, and they may or may not send notification to the library. So procedures need to be put in place to ensure that any notifications of changes sent by the vendor are received and acted upon as appropriate, or, if no notifications are provided, that library staff proactively check for changes.

Managing MARC records

Having defined a cataloguing policy, the next step is to put it into practice. The next section outlines some of the solutions available for obtaining and managing the MARC records that will show users what is available, and looks at how to add the links needed to direct users from the catalogue to the e-books.

Using supplied MARC records

As with print books, sourcing MARC records from external suppliers is usually the most cost-effective way to provide title level metadata for e-books. In many cases e-book vendors may provide MARC records, either included in the purchase price of the book, or for an additional charge. In some cases a basic record may be provided for free, with a higher quality record available for an additional fee.

When purchasing individual e-books, the records may be automatically loaded into the catalogue as part of the ordering process. For large packages of e-books, the records are likely to be provided as a single MARC file, which can be downloaded from the supplier's website or FTP server.

In each case it is necessary to assess the records, preferably by obtaining samples from the supplier, and then to decide whether or not they are of sufficient quality to add to the catalogue:

1   Are the records from a bibliographic supplier (such as Library of Congress, OCLC, British Library), or are they created by the e-book supplier?

2   Are the records compliant with cataloguing standards? Are the records in your preferred MARC format? If standards change, will the supplier provide replacement records that match the new standards? For example, will they offer records that meet any new requirements introduced with the Resource Description and Access (RDA) guidelines?

3   Is the data accurate? Is the level of detail sufficient for the library's needs? For example, do the records contain subject headings and additional author entries, or just basic author, title and publication details?

4   Are the records specific to the e-book format, or are they actually records for the print equivalent? Do the records correctly identify whether the e-book is a reproduction of a print work, or a 'born digital' work?

5   If the library has a local specification for e-book MARC records, can the vendor supply records that meet the library's requirements, such as adding local fields, customizing link fields, or deleting fields not required? If so, would they charge for any amendments or enhancements required? If they cannot supply records in the desired form, would it be possible to use the functionality of the library management system to automatically make any necessary amendments when uploading new records?

Adding records

If new titles or new editions are added to e-book packages, it is necessary to establish if, how and when MARC records will be updated:

1   If books are added to the package are new MARC records provided by the vendor? If so, is there an additional charge for the new records?

2   Will notification be sent when new records are available, or is it necessary check the vendor's website regularly?

3   How are the updated files made available for download? Is there a

single file of all updated records, and if so is there a list of which books are included? Is there an option to obtain selected updates? Can individual records be downloaded, or is it possible to obtain a batch file that includes any records added since the previous file was retrieved?

4   If titles are added to the package in batches, for example as quarterly updates, are new MARC records made available at the same time? If titles are added on a rolling basis are MARC records supplied individually as new titles are added, or as a batch file some time after the new content has been made available? If there is a delay between books being added to the collection and MARC records becoming available, how long is that delay and is it acceptable?

If MARC records for updated titles are not supplied or are supplied late, then some of the content the library has paid for will effectively be invisible to users. This may reduce the value of the e-books, particularly in subject areas where the usefulness of the content lies principally in its currency, for example computing and law.

Deleting records

Records may also need to be deleted, either for individual books that the vendor has withdrawn from a package or for whole packages if a subscription is cancelled by the library. If only a few titles are withdrawn, it may be simplest to obtain a list of the titles and delete the records manually. If large numbers of titles are removed, the vendor may supply a 'delete' file, which can be uploaded to the catalogue. If all the records for a package need to be taken out of the catalogue, the bulk update functions of the LMS could be used to delete a whole set of records.

Updating records

When managing large numbers of additions and deletions, it can be difficult to keep up to date with the changes. If the vendor offers a single file containing all the MARC records in the current package, it may be simpler to delete all the existing records from the catalogue and reload the new set. However, regularly adding and deleting large sets of records may have an adverse affect on the indexing of the catalogue, so caution is required before making bulk changes.

As well as adding and deleting records, it may also be necessary to make amendments to whole sets of records, especially if links change. Once again, the simplest option may be to delete and reload new records. Alternatively, if new records are not available or are too expensive, it may be possible to use the bulk update functionality of the LMS to make the changes locally.

Creating MARC records in-house

There may be cases where using the vendor's records is not a cost-effective option, for example if the quality is such that they would need substantial manual editing, if the supply process is unworkable, if the delay in providing the records is unacceptable, or if the cost of the records is prohibitive. In some cases, particularly for aggregated databases that include both book and journal content, the vendor may not supply records at all. In these cases it may be possible to obtain records from an alternative supplier, for example OCLC or SkyRiver. If not, it may be necessary to create records in-house.

For small, static e-book collections, it may be feasible to catalogue individual e-books manually, using templates to minimize the amount of information entered in each record and to ensure that all records meet minimum standards. However, for large packages containing hundreds or thousands of titles, a more efficient and scalable solution is required. One option is to use an open-source MARC conversion tool such as MarcEdit or MARCConvert from OCLC. Conversion tools can import data in a standard format, for example a list of titles in a spreadsheet, and convert it to basic MARC records. Alternatively, if programming expertise is available in-house, it may be possible to create a custom MARC conversion programme.

Whichever option is used, a source of bibliographic data listing the titles to be catalogued will be required. There are several potential sources:

- The vendor may supply a list of sources, or it may be possible to download one from their website.
- If the vendor provides usage statistics at title level, then a usage

report may also function as a title list, although it may be necessary to establish whether the report includes all titles in the collection or only those that have registered some usage.

■ If the library uses a link resolver service it may be possible to obtain a list of titles from the knowledge base, subject to permission to reuse the data.

As with any title list for a large e-resource collection, the quality of information in the list may vary:

■ Some titles may be missing from the list, or the list may not have been updated to reflect changes to the content of the package.
■ The information about each title may be limited; for example, it may not include the author, the date of publication or the edition.
■ The accuracy of the data may be poor; for example, the list may not distinguish between authors and editors.
■ The format of the list may be unmanageable; for example, it may list author and title in the same column.

In some cases it may be possible to improve the list. For example, if lists are available from two or more different sources and each contains different information about the books, it may be possible to combine the lists to capture more detail about each title. However, if improvement is impossible or unreasonably time-consuming, then it will be necessary to decide whether the metadata is worth using at all. In some cases the accuracy may be so poor that it would be better to leave the books uncatalogued than to fill the library catalogue with poor quality records. If the accuracy is acceptable but the level of detail is low, it may still be worth using the metadata because even a record simply giving the title of an e-book may be better than no record at all.

Managing links

A signpost is of no use if it tells users where they can go, but does not show them how to get there. So as well as showing users which e-books are available, the catalogue should also provide links to the e-books themselves.

Users will expect these links to be reliable, direct and seamless, but creating and maintaining such links presents a number of challenges:

1 Most library e-book collections are hosted across a range of different websites, so there will be a number of different sites to link to, some of which may be more difficult to manage than others. For example, some sites may not support direct links to specific e-books, while others may require a complicated log-in process.
2 As well as supporting links *to* a number of different sites, it may also be necessary to support links *from* multiple sites. For example it may be necessary to support links not only from the library catalogue but also from an A–Z list, a VLE, a federated search engine, or a reading list system.
3 As both the contents of e-book collections and the websites on which they are hosted may be subject to frequent changes, it is essential to find an efficient method of keeping links up to date.

There are various options for providing links from the catalogue, each of which has advantages and disadvantages.

Embedding URL links

The simplest option is to embed the URL for the e-book in a field within the MARC record, and then configure the catalogue to display the field as a hyperlink. Vendor-supplied MARC records will almost always include a URL link, which can be customized to suit local requirements if necessary. For example, the URL can be amended to direct users to the library's chosen log-in point. Alternatively, the URL can point to a web page giving additional information and help for the user, or terms and conditions of use. The link becomes active as soon as the record is uploaded to the catalogue, so the initial set-up is relatively quick and the costs are low.

However, MARC record links have the major disadvantage that they may require ongoing maintenance. Because they point to a specific URL, the links will need to be amended if the publisher changes its platform or if the library moves its log-in point. If the URL for an entire e-book package changes, updating all of the affected records could create a significant volume of work. If MARC records are provided by the vendor, they may be able to resupply the records with the updated URL, but in many cases it will be necessary to make the changes in-house.

Using DOI links

Alternatively, links based on digital object identifiers (DOIs) can minimize the need for local maintenance. DOI-based links can automatically redirect the user to the current URL for the e-book, so even if the e-book moves there is no need to make changes to the link embedded in the catalogue record. However, because they use redirects, DOI links may restrict the librarian's control over exactly where the user is directed. For example, if an e-book is available from multiple websites, the DOI may not necessarily direct the user to the site to which the library has access. So although DOI links may reduce the workload of link maintenance, this may be at the expense of usability.

Using link resolvers

A more flexible but more complex option is to subscribe to a link resolver service such as 360 Link (SerialsSolutions) or SFX (ExLibris). Like DOIs, link resolvers can automatically redirect users to the current URL, minimizing the need to make changes to catalogue records. But, unlike DOIs, where a book is available from more than one website, a link resolver allows the librarian to retain control over which website the user is directed to. Link resolvers therefore have the potential to strike a balance between the efficiencies gained by outsourcing maintenance and the effectiveness of providing links customized to local requirements.

Links supported by resolvers also offer potentially greater flexibility than either direct or DOI-based links. Resolvers create links 'on the fly' by picking up metadata from the catalogue records and matching it to a URL recorded in a central database, so that they can be configured to work with any compatible system containing bibliographic metadata. This gives the potential to add links to library e-books from multiple discovery points, including VLEs, reading list systems and even external search engines, all with very little additional maintenance input from the library. They therefore represent a highly efficient way to extend the visibility of library e-books beyond the library catalogue.

However link resolvers do have some drawbacks. Some e-books in the library's collection may not be covered by the service, in which case it may be necessary to wait for the link resolver's database to be updated, or to add a manual link to the MARC record. Also, although link resolvers may allow savings on maintenance, they are not cost free. In addition to the cost of subscribing to the service itself, they also require staff time and expertise to configure.

Of the various options available for creating links, no single solution is ideal. It may be necessary to take a mixed approach, using a link resolver where possible with embedded MARC record links as a back-up. Whichever solution is used, managing links requires a significant investment of both time and money. As a relatively new aspect of the cataloguing workload it may be more difficult to find the resources required to support it adequately. But providing reliable links is an essential element of an effective catalogue search – there is little point investing time and resources in acquiring high quality MARC records to make e-books visible in the catalogue if poor quality links mean that users cannot access the books once they have discovered them.

Moreover, investing in a versatile solution, which can support links from other systems, can make library e-books discoverable beyond the catalogue, something that even the best quality catalogue record cannot achieve. As the ability to support multiple discovery points is increasing in importance, investing in link management arguably makes a greater contribution to the provision of an effective search than managing catalogue records. Finding the resources to support linking is therefore an investment well worth making.

Presenting e-books

Making e-books visible is not just about providing metadata and links. It also involves considering how e-books are presented within the catalogue, which search options to provide and how to highlight e-books in search results.

Users looking for a particular item may want to carry out a single search, which returns a results list of all matching items including both print and e-book titles. Where both formats are available they should be grouped together in the results list, and ideally it should be possible for a user viewing the print record to link directly to the equivalent e-book, although this may not be achievable with limited staffing resources.

Where e-books are presented alongside print books, it is useful to provide a clear means of differentiating between the two in search results, for example by adding appropriate icons to the records, and by using clear wording to show which books are located 'in the library' and which books are 'available online' (Figure 8.1). Not only does this make it easier for users who prefer e-books to spot them in the results list, but it also highlights the availability of e-books to users who may not be aware of the library's collection.

Figure 8.1 *Distinguishing e-books in the search results lists*

It is also important to ensure that the links to online e-books are prominently displayed, so that users can navigate quickly and easily from the catalogue to the book itself. If there are other links in the catalogue that do not lead to the full text, but, for example, to a table of contents, then it is important to differentiate these from e-book links.

As well as providing options to search all books, it may be useful to provide a search that is limited to just e-books. Placing an e-book search option on the catalogue front page also serves as a useful way to market the existence of the library's e-book collection. Browse indexes can also be added to draw attention to e-books, offering users the chance to explore the library's collections to find out what is available (Figure 8.2).

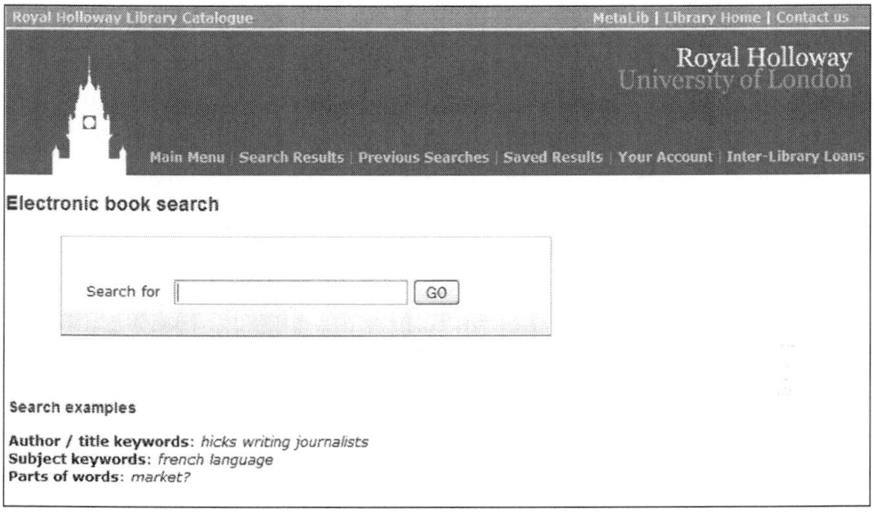

Figure 8.2 *A dedicated e-book search can be a useful option*

Case study: Cataloguing in practice at Royal Holloway, University of London

The following section provides a case study of e-book cataloguing policy and practice at Royal Holloway, University of London. RHUL is a research-focused university with around 8800 students. The Library's e-book collections are growing rapidly, and currently include hundreds of individually purchased items as well as a number of large packages, which altogether include well over half-a-million titles. Staff resources to carry out cataloguing are modest (two part-time Cataloguers, with contributions from a Library Systems Officer and an E-resources Manager), and workflows for cataloguing have recently been reviewed to increase efficiency by integrating workflows for individual e-book purchases with print procedures. Cataloguing processes for e-book packages do not fit the same workflow, so are managed separately by the E-resources Manager.

The Library Catalogue remains a key search tool, and the policy is to catalogue individually purchased books as the top priority, to catalogue packages wherever possible, and to catalogue selected free e-books if there is evidence of user demand. Vendor-supplied MARC records are used where possible, and are available for almost all individually purchased e-books and some packages. However, records are not available for several of the largest packages, so other options are currently being investigated for making these e-books more visible. A local specification for e-book MARC records serves both as a benchmark for evaluating the quality of vendor-supplied records, and as a template for the small number of records created in-house using MarcEdit. Links are provided by a link resolver service (SFX), but several e-book collections are not covered by this, so MARC record links are used as an alternative.

Alongside the catalogue, full-text searching is provided by a federated search system (MetaLib), although not all packages are compatible. A new pre-harvested search system (Summon) has recently been implemented. As well as improving the quality of search, it is hoped that this will provide a source of metadata for packages for which MARC records are not currently available, which will both increase the visibility of e-books and reduce the cataloguing workload by replacing the need to load MARC records for other packages.

A number of other discovery options are also supported. There is a web-based A–Z listing of e-book packages, which are also listed on the relevant subject resource pages (Figure 8.3).

Links to library e-books are embedded into online teaching materials in the VLE, and beyond the library links to the collections are embedded into Google Scholar. The Library also has a customized LibX toolbar, which users can install in their web browser as another way to link to library e-books from search engines.

Supporting this broad range of discovery points helps to raise the visibility of the Library's e-books but it also takes significant resources. Cataloguing solutions are therefore reviewed regularly to identify which are the most effective, and to focus resources on those that deliver the most impact.

Conclusion

There are plenty of opportunities to draw attention to library e-books in different places – including the library catalogue, federated search tools

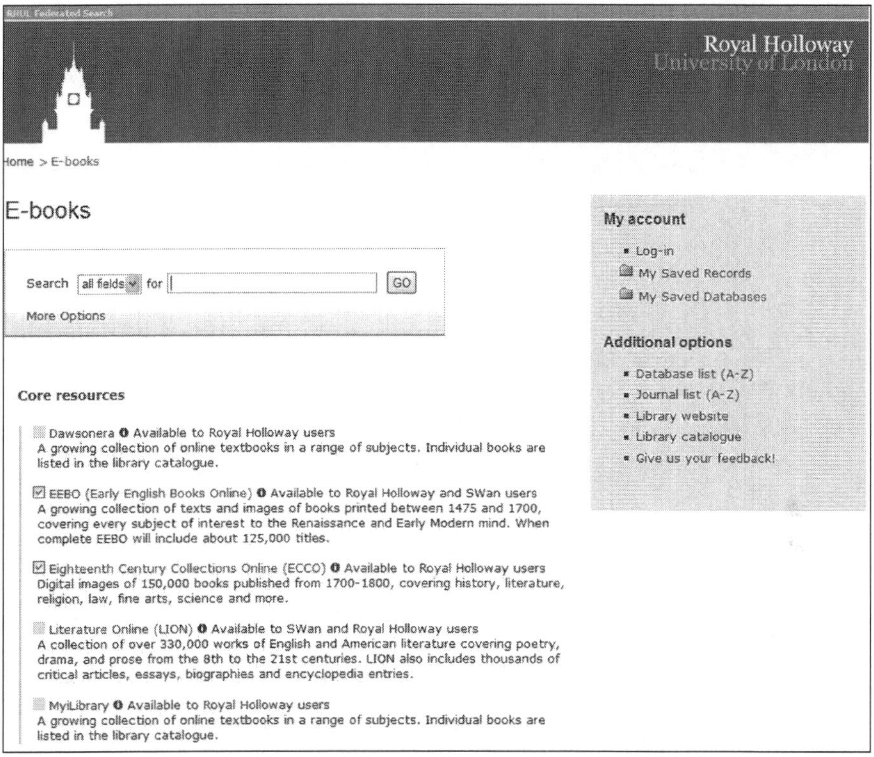

Figure 8.3 *E-book collections A–Z list*

and remote search engines. Making e-books visible involves choosing options that will best suit the needs of the library and its users, based on the size and nature of the collections, the discovery systems in place and the resources available to support e-formats. It also involves the challenge of managing scale, providing access to large numbers of books, possibly across multiple discovery points.

With the solutions currently available it is difficult to catalogue every book in every discovery system, and with limited resources the cataloguing of e-books also inevitably involves compromises on the quality and number of records that can be created. Finally, making e-books visible means keeping pace with rapid change, not only by updating the catalogue, but also by responding to wider changes in resource discovery and in the nature of e-books themselves. This evolution demands continual reassessment of the efficiency of procedures and the relevance of specific objectives.

Above all, the decisions made by the library to improve the visibility of its e-book collection should be informed by the needs of the users. Whether they choose to search the library catalogue or the wider internet, the user should find clear signposts with direct and reliable links to the content they require, making access as quick and intuitive as finding a book on a shelf and opening it.

Useful links

LibX http://libx.org
MarcConvert www.worldcat.org/devnet/wiki/MARCView
MarcEdit http://people.oregonstate.edu/~reeset/marcedit/html/index.php
OCLC www.oclc.org
Royal Holloway, University of London www.rhul.ac.uk/library
SkyRiver http://theskyriver.com

Bibliography

Anderson, R. (2010) Scholarly Communications: the view from the library. In Woodward, H. and Estelle, L. (eds), *Digital Information: order or anarchy?*, Facet Publishing, 35–56.

CIBER (2008) *Information Behaviour of the Researcher of the Future: a CIBER briefing paper*,
www.ucl.ac.uk/infostudies/research/ciber/downloads.

JISC (2009) *JISC National E-books Observatory Project: key findings and recommendations*,
www.jiscebooksproject.org/reports/finalreport.

Research Information Network (2009) *Creating Catalogues: bibliographic records in a networked world*,
www.rin.ac.uk/system/files/attachments/Creating-catalogues-report.pdf.

Rossmann, D., Foster, A. and Babbitt, E. P. (2009) E-book MARC Records: do they make the mark?, *Serials*, **22** (3), supplement.

Rowlands, I., Nicholas, D., Jamali, H. R. and Huntington, P. (2007) What do Faculty and Students Really Think about E-books?, *Aslib Proceedings*, **59** (6), 489–511.

SCONUL (2009) *HEFCE Shared Services Study: business case*,

http://helibtech.com/Shared+Services.

Stone, G. (2010) Resource Discovery. In Woodward, H. and Estelle, L. (eds), *Digital Information: order or anarchy?*, Facet Publishing, 133-56.

Walker, J. (n.d.) New resource discovery mechanisms (2), *The E-Resources Management Handbook*, UKSG, http://uksg.metapress.com/link.asp?id=0387n6738v23j305.

9
Providing guidance, training and support for readers using e-books

Karen Gravett

Introduction

Information professionals have a long history of providing guidance, training and support to their users. In recent years, the growth of electronic resources such as online databases and electronic journals has meant that this support has become even more valuable, particularly as the users of these resources often expect simplicity of access and possess a limited awareness of how to search effectively.

The way that e-books should fit into library training and support strategies is an interesting area for discussion, although little has been written on this topic. Whether we view e-books as an extension of our printed collections or as unique and more complex electronic resources that can only be partly understood from within the constraints of the print legacy will inevitably impact on the way that we present them to readers. As Cox suggests:

> Another point to consider is the positioning of e-books among other e-resources offered by libraries. Do we, and should we, market them distinctively to users, or are they simply another source of content which happened to originate as printed books?
> (Cox, 2004)

This chapter will discuss how, at the University of Surrey, experience has shown that the present delivery and design of e-books mean that accessing them bears little relationship to reading the printed text.

As a result, support strategies are required to ensure that users understand how and when to access e-books. Interestingly, in their study *Promoting the Uptake of E-books in Higher and Further Education* JISC advises information professionals to 'demand time' for a dedicated range of training and support activities in order to effectively 'promote and communicate [e-books] to users and patrons' (JISC, 2003, 160).

This chapter will discuss the wide range of training and support activities in place at Surrey to promote e-books to users and to guide them through this learning process. Further, this chapter will analyse the role of effective liaison with academic staff, and consider how this can be another important means of providing guidance to both staff and students alike.

The means by which e-books are delivered, read and used are also developing and changing rapidly, and, as a result, this discussion will suggest some potential new strategies for training and guidance. Lastly, it will detail some wishes for improvements in the business models and technologies that underlie e-book provision.

Background: e-books at the University of Surrey

The University of Surrey is an international, research-intensive university based in Guildford. Currently, the University has more than 30 research groupings and over 14,400 students. The University's core strengths are in science and engineering, but its focus is broadening and there are now also successful divisions of business and law, health and social care, human sciences and performing arts, and over 50 subjects are now taught at undergraduate level. Within the University Library, e-books have become a key component of the electronic resources collection. In the early 2000s library staff began to evaluate e-books as a potential new resource in which to invest (Green, 2003), and as a result of positive feedback e-books became part of the Library's collections across a range of subject areas. Currently, the Library holds around 90,000 e-books (plus another 100,000 if the Early English Books Online package is included) and 650 new e-book titles were purchased individually during academic year 2009–10.

This investment in e-books reflects the Library's commitment to 'maximising the benefits of current and future technological developments in order to deliver high quality information services' as well as to 'leading the academic community in exploiting and managing information resources' (University of Surrey Library, 2010). E-book collections are built in two ways. First, individual titles are purchased from the suppliers MyiLibrary and NetLibrary, or directly from publishers for some reference works such as dictionaries, encyclopedias and clinical manuals. Second, the Library subscribes to several large packages of e-books such as ebrary's Academic Complete, Knovel Interactive Library and several CRC NetBASEs in different subject areas. E-books are selected by one of seven designated academic liaison librarians, who work in close conjunction with academic staff to develop and manage collections. In addition, the Library has been a participant in the UK JISC National e-Books Observatory Project, which examined how e-books are used, exploring impacts and observing behaviours. The results of the project will be referred to in more detail throughout this chapter.

Guidance – why and for whom?

At Surrey, the provision of support for the use of e-books is an important part of the work of the Academic Liaison Librarian team. In order to deliver high quality information services, and to effectively support teaching, learning and research, it is crucial that effective use is made of our resources, and the first step is to ensure that users are aware of what is available. In Springer's 2008 user survey, it was noted that respondents found the 'primary obstacle to e-book usage [was] a lack of awareness of e-book resources available through their libraries' (Springer, 2008, 3). Promotion is therefore the first impetus for delivering training. However, complex delivery methods and multiple e-book platforms mean that use of these resources is not straightforward, another reason why support for users is necessary.

Furthermore, for many students e-books are still an entirely new resource. Questions such as, 'So is that the same as the printed book?', 'Can I actually read it online?' and 'How much of the book is included?' are frequently heard during training sessions. These questions reveal the lack of experience and understanding that users have of the format, and the fact that they often do not know why and on what occasions e-books should be used. Finally, training is also important to ensure that readers do not fall foul of plagiarism guidelines or copyright legislation.

This guidance is largely being delivered to students, who are the most frequent users of our collections. However, guidance for academic staff is an area that should not be overlooked; e-books are typically as much of an unknown or unfamiliar resource for them as they are for students. Promoting e-books to academics is important to increase their understanding of the resources the Library has to offer, and to assist them in advising their students appropriately, directing them to useful resources and encouraging them to make use of new or alternative sources of information. Experience at the University of Surrey has shown that positive promotion of e-books by academic staff can have a significant impact on usage, and therefore encouraging them to become familiar with and positive about e-books can be as worthwhile as providing training for students.

Main issues to address

Resource discovery

The first, and perhaps most frustrating, issue to address when supporting staff and students in the use of e-books is that of resource discovery. Unfortunately, for many users, finding e-books is not straightforward. The 2008 student survey sponsored by ebrary discovered that the primary reason given for not using e-books was that students could not find them (ebrary, 2008, 37). As at many institutions, the University of Surrey's e-books are delivered through a range of different publisher interfaces: MyiLibrary, ebrary, Science Direct, NetLibrary and many others. These differently packaged e-books are then displayed in a number of different places: a list of packages on the Library's 'Electronic Books' web page, links from online Subject Guides, links on the Library Catalogue, links from reading lists, and links from the University's VLE. It is unsurprising then that comments such as 'I find the e-books difficult to get to' were a prevalent feature of the JISC National e-Books Observatory findings (JISC, 2009a). This issue of multiple access points is compounded by the fact that each platform has a different interface, requiring the user to become familiar with a different viewing tool for each one. In their recent survey, ebrary found that users are frustrated by this need to learn multiple interfaces:

Users 'come upon' the vendor interfaces through the online catalog. Some are in the last minutes of getting a paper completed and the digression into learning the interface is most unwelcome.   (ebrary, 2008, 38)

The experience at Surrey also suggests that multiple interfaces can lead to an unhelpful confusion among users between content and technology. Comments such as 'MyiLibrary is a good resource for me to use' are commonly heard and reveal that users are being distracted by the different database platforms and aggregators and away from the content of the resource itself. The confusion caused by this multiplicity of platforms and access points is something that guidance can certainly help to overcome. Showing staff and students some simple ways to find e-books is therefore the very first key element of the training process.

Coverage in different subject areas

Informing users about the coverage in their subject area is another important issue. When introducing e-books to students during training sessions, a question that commonly arises is, 'Are the books on my reading list available as e-books?' and, similarly, 'What percentage of the books in my subject are available as e-books?' Even at Surrey where the e-book collections are considerable, the lack of availability of core texts from publishers means that it is simply not possible to acquire an e-copy. For the user it is unclear why core reading may be absent from e-book collections, and library staff have to explain to users which texts are available, and importantly that limitations on collections are driven by a lack of supply rather than a lack of willingness on the part of the library to invest in e-resources. These limitations are one of the main frustrations about current e-book provision, and an important aspect of delivering training is often to encourage users to search by topic across packages to find related books rather than focusing solely on their core reading list texts.

Practical aspects of using e-books

A further challenge that arises with current e-book models is the practical aspect of using the book online. Navigation between pages on e-book platforms is not intuitive and this problem is further exacerbated by the differences between the interfaces of various packages. Once the book is successfully displayed, the discomfort of reading from the screen means that the next step for users is often to seek a way of reading it offline, for example by e-mailing, saving or printing the text. The complexity arises because different e-book interfaces allow different user activities. For example, ebrary permits the downloading or printing of up to 40 pages of a text at a time, while MyiLibrary permits only up to ten pages. Academic liaison librarians must therefore give guidance to users as to how the e-book can be read, used and downloaded, and how these functions work in different packages. Interestingly, more technologically aware students often wish to know how they can access e-books with an expanding range of hardware options, such as personal digital assistants and e-book readers.

Enabling use by different groups

Another challenge to address is that of enabling different user groups to access e-books. Training will require different strategies according to the ability level of the particular group and according to their familiarity with information technologies and the e-book format. Associated with this is the issue of how students with physical disabilities or learning difficulties may be supported in accessing e-books effectively.

Current practices at the University of Surrey

Face-to-face instruction

At the University of Surrey, the primary method of training readers in the use of e-resources, including e-books, is through face-to-face inform-ation skills teaching sessions. This will usually mean delivering a basic library induction, and then a more detailed, 'electronic resources' or 'literature searching' session, usually later in the semester. Training is deliv-ered by the designated Academic Liaison Librarian for that subject. On occasion, training sessions are arranged that focus specifically on e-books, but usually these are included alongside other electronic resources as part of this wider programme.

The first stage of a training session will be to introduce the role of e-books and to explain what coverage is available, while the next stage will be to enable students to effectively discover the resources, covering the issue of multiple platforms and entry points. At Surrey, the majority of e-books are now available on the library catalogue, which provides an effective way of overcoming this problem. Training will therefore often begin with a catalogue search. Indeed, carrying out a search for a text that has both a print and electronic counterpart is a useful way of emphasizing to students that e-books can complement printed collections and be used as an alternative means of accessing a text, as well as highlighting the fact that they can be discovered while carrying out a standard printed book search. At this point, for more basic information literacy level groups, it is often useful to ask the students to spot the difference between the two records, identifying the 'electronic resource' tag or the 'e-link' on the catalogue record to signify availability of the e-book. It is also worth mentioning that the catalogue can be searched for e-books alone by applying the search subset 'electronic books'. Figure 9.1 shows a demonstration of a search for an e-book and printed book record on the library catalogue, taken from a session for pre-registration nursing students.

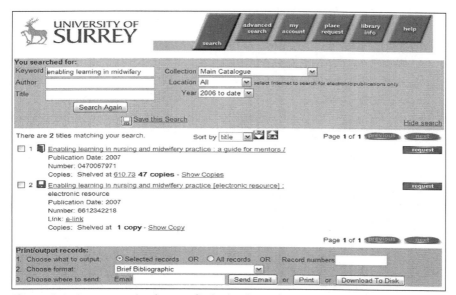

Figure 9.1 *Demonstrating how to find e-books at the same time as print copies*

The next stage of a training session may be to demonstrate an alternative route for searching for e-books within different platforms. For lower level groups, this part of the session will usually include a demonstration of a single key platform, such as ebrary or MyiLibrary. For more advanced groups, the session might aim to cover all or most of the main packages that contain relevant content, for example a postgraduate session for MSc Pharmaceutical Medicine students will cover the CRC NetBases, Science Direct and ebrary platforms. Package searching is useful for subject areas where a large amount of electronic content is available, and where students would be expected to browse for e-books relevant to their topic. For subject areas such as Law, where there is less content available within packages, training may simply focus on finding e-books via the catalogue. Following a demonstration by the Liaison Librarian, there is usually an opportunity for students to have some time at a computer to browse the packages, search for a specific e-book, and learn how to print, download and save e-books.

It is also worthwhile drawing attention to copyright and plagiarism issues. For some users the availability of books online increases the temptation to copy and paste text without appropriate referencing, falling foul of rules on plagiarism. Some academics are so concerned by the ease of copying and pasting from e-books that they would prefer that their students only had access to e-book packages that are covered by the plagiarism detection service Turnitin. It is therefore useful to guide students to sources of further information and advice such as the library's web pages and those of the UK's Copyright Licensing Agency (CLA). Likewise, it is important to raise awareness of copyright issues when explaining the limitations on printing and downloading that students may encounter.

Overall, teaching sessions provide a valuable opportunity to help students and staff with the many issues associated with using e-books. Taking into account feedback gathered through their recent student survey, ebrary emphasizes the importance of such information skills or library instruction sessions:

> Librarians were most often selected as the individuals who introduced students to e-books, 50% (1533). The catalog, 44% (1356), the library website, 44% (1352), instructors, 43% (1316), and Google, 43% (1311), showed up in close

proximity as the second, third, fourth, and fifth selections. . . . Nearly
everybody was introduced through instruction efforts.   (ebrary, 2008, 37)

Comprehensive instruction in the effective discovery and utilization of e-
books in the variety of collections provided by publishers and aggregators as
well as through open source collections would increase student use and
satisfaction with e-books.   (ebrary, 2008, 37)

At Surrey, teaching sessions form a key strand of the support that is
available for library users, and often generate very positive feedback.

Online support

To supplement face-to-face training sessions, online help is available in
a variety of forms. The University Library website is a major source of
information (attracting 196,964 hits within a ten-month period in
2009–10). Each of the Academic Liaison Librarians produce 'My Subject'
web pages, which cover the most significant resources for each
department, and detail relevant e-book packages as well as including links
to individual resources such as online encyclopedias, directories and
dictionaries. These subject guides are now linked directly from the
Library's home page, and are promoted at inductions, as well as being
printed and displayed adjacent to physical collections.

Information about using e-books is also included in an interactive
online tutorial aimed at new library students, the Library Launchpad.
There are plans to develop online help for e-books further, perhaps by
producing animated tutorials similar to those that are already available
for some databases, and a specific area of the website for information
literacy support is also being created.

One-to-one support

A relatively new feature at Surrey is the creation of a dedicated advisory
zone on the third floor of the Library, aimed at providing intensive
support for areas of information literacy such as searching databases and
using e-books effectively. This zone is staffed by academic liaison
librarians from 11a.m. to 3p.m. Monday to Friday during the academic

term. Outside these peak times more basic help is available from an information desk on the ground floor. The advisory zone is run on a drop-in basis, but students may also arrange appointments in advance. Removed from the mainstream of the Library, the advisory zone provides the time and space to answer users' questions in detail and for students and librarians to work together to search resources. However, this service still needs to be marketed more effectively to ensure that students make maximum use of the support it offers.

Support for students with disabilities

Support for students with physical disabilities and specific learning difficulties is delivered by a team of Additional Learning Support (ALS) staff, based in the Library building. Guidance is offered at individual appointments, and training on the use of software within the Assistive Technology Centre (also based in the Library) can be booked. However, there are still many barriers preventing students with disabilities accessing e-books effectively. These include discovery issues, as a member of the team explains: 'Some students find it quite difficult to access e-books from our web pages but are ok if I send them the e-link.' There are also problems with the compatibility of some e-books with specialist software such as JAWS for Windows and TextHelp Read & Write. Indeed, one respondent to the JISC National e-Books Observatory survey mentioned that 'it would be great to have e-books usable with speech recognition software' (JISC, 2009b). These problems are often exacerbated by limits on printing and downloading, as the ALS team explain: 'Problems can occur if [students] need to download to use their own assistive software – e.g. MyLibrary restricts downloading to 10 pages.'

Amongst students with additional learning support needs, attitudes to e-books appear to be divided. As a member of staff comments: 'I've found that students with special needs either love e-books or hate them.' However, staff also feel that e-books potentially have many benefits for these users:

One of the reasons I think [e-books] are useful [for students with special needs] is being able to bookshelf, highlight and make notes and retrieve easily. This is potentially helpful for students who have organisational problems.

(E-mail from ALS Adviser)

As well as providing guidance for students, the ALS team are a useful source of information on accessibility issues as they apply to e-resources, and they particularly recommend the Open University's web pages on the accessibility of e-resources as well as the comprehensive information on the TechDis website.

Promotional activities

A number of avenues for the promotion of e-books have been developed over the years. The Academic Liaison Librarians' blog (http://surreywhatsnew.wordpress.com) is a useful space for marketing new resources and pointing readers in the direction of new e-books, as is the Library's newsletter *The Word*; both have proved popular with library users.

The Library has also carried out promotional activities aimed at raising awareness of e-resources, and e-books in particular. On these occasions, promotional materials were obtained from publishers (pens, mouse mats, sweets, shopping bags and so on) and posters advertising the events were then displayed around the campus advertising the availability of 'free stuff' in the Library. Demonstrations of e-books were carried out using networked laptops, and lists of e-resources by subject were made available. The promotional stands in the Library received many appreciative visitors, who were more than happy to learn about specific e-resources once enticed by the free merchandise.

Open days and evenings offer opportunities for similar promotions. For example, a stand was staffed at a recent Health and Social Care open evening in order to meet new and existing students and promote resources. At this event a new e-book, the *Royal Marsden Manual Online*, was unveiled. A laptop at the stand together with printed copies of the text enabled the resource to be effectively demonstrated to students, who made comments such as: 'That's really great, as this is a key resource and I didn't know that it was available online, and wouldn't have known where to find it.'

Liaison with academic staff

An important aspect of providing guidance and support to readers is to show academic staff the benefits of e-books and enable them to support students in their use of these resources, and effective liaison is a key means of achieving this. Carlock believes that caution is the primary response of academic staff to e-books:

> Faculty are especially cautious about using them as textbooks or for course readings due to a perceived learning curve for their students and believing that the technology is too unreliable, which has been proven by their own experiences. They also feel that trying to use them in class, as well [as] in their own research, is tedious and time-consuming.
>
> (Carlock, 2008, 253)

However, at the University of Surrey the response of academic staff to e-books is a very mixed picture. One member of the Chemistry division commented recently that:

> With regard to e-books, I am rather traditional, and like hard copies. However, many students would be happy with e-versions, so perhaps a mix of both, maintaining availability of hard copies for those who prefer them.
>
> (E-mail from Chemistry tutor, 2010)

Other members of staff are extremely enthusiastic about the benefits of e-books such as off-campus access and multiple use, and present them positively to students. For example, a subscription to the new e-version of the *Royal Marsden Manual Online* (mentioned above) was enthusiastically supported by a member of staff within the Division of Health and Social Care, and as a result this resource gained high numbers of users very quickly.

A number of liaison strategies are in place at the University of Surrey. Academic Liaison Librarians present regularly at course and staff meetings, and also have one-to-one meetings with new staff, and these can be great opportunities to bring e-books to the attention of academics, give guidance on how they can be found and used, and give brief demonstrations where possible.

Wishes for the future

Despite the various support strategies described above, a number of obstacles to the effective use of e-books remain and there are still unnecessary and frustrating barriers to delivering them to readers. However, if information professionals and publishers work together to improve usability, interactivity and accessibility, then the future of e-books may look very different. For example, Carlock explains her belief that:

> In addition to marketing e-books to faculty and students, academic librarians have a responsibility to advocate the needs of their users to e-book vendors to consider when planning future product development. Without the input of libraries, e-book vendors' primary clientele, there is no guarantee that the necessary improvements in usability, accessibility, and interactivity would ever be made. E-books have the potential to serve a very real need, and together e-book vendors, librarians and faculty can create a more positive future.
>
> (Carlock, 2008, 253)

One of the most important goals for the future of e-book provision is the development of a single platform for their delivery to the user. This might mean the arrival of an overarching e-book aggregator. But another means to this end would be the inclusion of all available e-books within the next generation of discovery tools, for example Serials Solutions' Summon, EBSCO's Discovery Service and Ex Libris' Primo. At the moment only a fraction of e-book content is available through these discovery services, but increasingly this is the type of 'one-stop' service that students require, and moreover that information professionals should expect. As this student commented:

> I'd like a central search facility rather than having to try each e-book provider in turn to try and find a title. . . . I find the whole online library system very jumbled and [it is] difficult to find what you want without spending ages skipping from section to section. . . . As I rely on online access as a distance learner, it can be very frustrating. (JISC, 2009b)

And for some users, this frustration means that they simply abandon library resources in favour of freely available information:

The web interface is often too long-winded and/or disparate for finding
proper e-books so web searches are more often used and these 'better'
resources are under-utilised.   (JISC, 2009b)

A related wish is for improvements to e-book navigation and reading
functionality. Until e-books can be navigated and viewed as comfortably
as printed texts, they have a significant weakness when compared to
printed collections. Indeed, many of the comments from the JISC report
show students' dissatisfaction with current functionality:

Course texts still tend to be linear – there has to be a lot more effort to
construct them like web pages, with lots of links.

I prefer 'real' books (i.e. books printed on paper). The technology for e-books
is still imperfect, and it's not possible to use an e-book as flexibly as a print
book.

E-books are NOT a substitute for real books. They are OK to quickly see if
the book is relevant, but not for study. Printing out is usually limited and
reading on screen difficult.

                                                                 (JISC, 2009b)

At the moment it seems that e-books are often used for quick searching
and skim reading, as a supplement to the printed version. In the future,
an ideal situation would be that page-turning is quick and easy, that
searching and downloading are simple and intuitive, and that
developments in hardware mean that e-books can be read with comfort
and without eye strain. If these improvements were made then the
popularity of e-books would certainly increase.

Another key goal for the future is the relaxation of DRM restrictions
in order to allow e-books to be used more flexibly. At the moment
restrictions on printing, downloading and e-mailing of content are
frustrating for both students and staff. With reading long passages on
screen still uncomfortable, these restrictions are a major constraint, as
this student comments: 'I hate reading on screen, so try to print bits of
e-books out, but this is incredibly slow and limited in how much I can
print; this is extremely off-putting' (JISC, 2009b). Similarly, the growth

of mobile technologies means that an increasing number of readers will wish to use e-books on their own handheld device, but at the moment many e-books purchased by the library are not available for download in full onto mobile platforms. Ultimately, publishers need to find a solution to these issues so that in the future e-books can be downloaded, used and interacted with as easily as students expect them to be.

A final key wish for the future is for publishers to make available a much greater number of core textbooks in e-format. If more e-content was available then information professionals could expand collections, and if readers become used to the availability of e-options then they will invest more time on becoming familiar with finding and using them. Then e-books will move from being an additional, complementary, resource to becoming as central as the printed text. At the moment, limited coverage is an unnecessary constraint. This comment from a user demonstrates how students currently work around this issue, as well as how e-books can be hugely valued by students:

> Currently using e-book version of Lodish Molecular Cell Biology. Absolutely LOVE the convenience of accessing online (not having to carry weight between home and work) as well as all the hyperlinks, I am sure this is the direction our students will want to take in textbooks. Sadly it does not cover the material I precisely need as well as other textbooks, still only available in print; but I am confident well done e-books . . . are the future!!
>
> (JISC, 2009b)

Conclusion

Currently, the delivery and presentation of e-books mean that there are a number of barriers to their access and use. Yet institutions are still investing in these resources and e-books are gradually becoming a more valued part of academic library collections. As a result, both academic staff and students need to be well supported by information professionals if they are to make maximum use of e-books.

Potentially, the future may bring less need for instruction as platforms and e-books become simpler and more intuitive to readers, and the availability of core titles increases. This would mean that less time is spent by information professionals on explaining the idiosyncrasies of different packages and helping users to overcome barriers to access, and instead more time could be spent on extending other areas of information literacy training. While resources will always need to be promoted and users will always need to be supported in their use to some extent, improvements in e-book usability would release more time for developing students' evaluative skills and their ability to use information more effectively for learning, a future that would be very much welcomed by all concerned.

Useful links

Databases accessibility issues (Open University)
  http://library.open.ac.uk/help/access/index.cfm?id=7007
JISC TechDis and e-Books www.techdis.ac.uk/index.php?p=9_33
Turnitin http://turnitin.com
University of Surrey Library Launchpad
  www.surrey.ac.uk/library/resources/tutorials/launchpad
What's new in your subject? The Academic Liaison Librarians' blog
  http://surreywhatsnew.wordpress.com

Bibliography

Armstrong, C. (2008) Books in a Virtual World: the evolution of the e-book and its lexicon, *Journal of Librarianship and Information Science*, **40** (3), 193–206, http://lis.sagepub.com/content/40/3/193.full.pdf+html.
Carlock, D. M. (2008) Exploring Faculty Experiences with E-books: a focus group, *Library Hi-Tech*, **26** (2), 244–54, www.emeraldinsight.com/journals.htm?articleid=1729333&show=abstract.
Cox, J. (2004) E-books: challenges and opportunities, *D-Lib Magazine*, **10** (10), www.dlib.org/dlib/october04/cox/10cox.html.
ebrary (2008) *2008 Global Student E-book Survey Sponsored by Ebrary*, www.ebrary.com/corp/collateral/en/Survey/ebrary_student_survey_2008.pdf.
Green, K. (2003) Introducing E-books at the University of Surrey, *SCONUL Newsletter*, **29,** Summer/Autumn, 54–6, www.sconul.ac.uk/publications/newsletter/29.
JISC (2003) *Promoting the Uptake of E-books in Higher and Further Education*, www.jisc.ac.uk/uploaded_documents/PromotingeBooksReportB.pdf.

JISC (2009a) *JISC National E-books Observatory Project: key findings and recommendations*, www.jiscebooksproject.org/wp-content/JISC-e-books-observatory-final-report-Nov-09.pdf.

JISC (2009b) *JISC National E-books Project User Survey January 2009 (local results for University of Surrey)*, unpublished.

Springer (2008) *Ebooks – the end user perspective*, www.springer.com/cda/content/document/cda_downloaddocument/ eBooks.theEnd-userExperience.WhitePaper.pdf?SGWID=0-0-45-877949-0.

University of Surrey Library (2010) *University Library Collection Development Policy*, www.surrey.ac.uk/library/resources/collection.

10
Information technology and e-books: challenges and opportunities

James Clay

Introduction

Printed books do not require batteries or charging, but they do have their issues – readers may not be able to get the most out of a text if they do not possess good eyesight, lack motor abilities, have a specific learning difficulty such as dyslexia, or if the text is not in their first language. This is always assuming that they are able to find a physical copy of the text in the first place: the local library may not hold a copy, or the reader may find it difficult to navigate the shelves in order to locate it.

E-books can offer solutions to issues of accessibility, particularly for remote users, but they can also add an additional layer of complexity for readers, simply because they are inaccessible without the use of information technology, both hardware and software. This chapter explores some of the challenges that this presents, as well as some of the opportunities offered by the availability of books in the virtual world, particularly for mobile learning.

Background

In a traditional library environment, learners can browse books *in situ*, but if they wish to borrow a book to use outside the library, it will need to be issued. This process ensures that the learner has the right to borrow the book, that the library is aware which book has been borrowed, and that the learner is aware of when the book is due back. Most institutions issue students with a card that identifies them as belonging to that institution and using either a number, barcode or chip associates that student with a record in the LMS. The main purpose of this system is to manage stock levels and prevent abuse, for example by users attempting to borrow more titles than is permitted, or keeping those that they have borrowed for too long, and thus maintain the efficiency of the service for all users.

A similar system is required to ensure that an institution only allows authorized users to access its e-book collections. If the library chooses to loan e-book readers pre-loaded with texts, then a similar issuing system to that for printed books can be used. There is always a risk that e-readers may get lost or go missing, but if a robust learner agreement is in place setting down the rights and responsibilities of the student, together with the penalties imposed if the agreement is violated, then this risk is reduced.

The challenge with online collections is that unlike the physical bookstock of the library, e-books can be accessed from a wide variety of locations: elsewhere on campus, at work, at home and at the local coffee shop. Here it is more challenging for a user to present their credentials and prove that they are authorized to access the collection.

The use of usernames and passwords might appear simple, but creates a significant administrative burden. For example, it is critical that the constantly changing list of authorized users is kept up to date and that there is a system for retrieving forgotten passwords. This is further complicated by the fact that most institutions have multiple collections of e-books, e-journals and other online resources, all of which may have their own individual sets of passwords. The solution to this issue is to implement a unified system of access management for e-resources.

Access management

'Access management' is a term used to describe the system or process of ensuring that only authorized users are provided with access to protected resources. It is used to describe both the administrative process of identifying authorized individuals and the processes used to decide whether access should be allowed to a particular resource.

Managing multiple usernames and passwords is confusing and complicated for learners and where possible it makes much more sense, from a learner's perspective, to use a single set of credentials for all online resources, including e-books. A good access management system would allow users secure access to all e-resources using a single authentication system, avoiding the need for multiple passwords or overly complex processes, which can be a major barrier to use.

Remote access to e-books is now much more important to learners who want to use them at a time and place to suit their busy lifestyles and schedules. Therefore it is important that access management processes on and off campus should be identical or similar. There may be valid reasons for different processes on and off campus, for example to maintain system security, and if this is the case, learners need to be made aware of what these are to avoid potential confusion.

IP authentication and proxy solutions

Internet Protocol (IP) authentication is a relatively easy way for the providers of e-book collections to give local access to learners at a particular institution. It restricts access by only allowing connections from those computers with an IP address based at that institution. Responsibility for allowing access then lies with the e-book provider. However, there are several disadvantages to this system:

1   It can be difficult to keep track of all the relevant IP addresses for authorized users, particularly if an institution has many different campuses or venues for learning, or is in the process of a merger or reorganization.
2   It can be difficult to prevent access to some resources for unauthorized users, who may have access to the campus network, but may not be included in the licence for the collection (for example, a start-up company or spin-off business working from a campus location).
3   It can be difficult to identify IP addresses for specific faculties or departments, particularly if a dynamic system of allocating IP addresses to individual computers 'on the fly' is employed at the institution.
4   Hence it can be difficult to negotiate a subscription on any basis other than using a whole institution approach, which can mean

that substantial costs are incurred when only a small minority of staff and students would ever wish to use the resource.

5   Learners who are not on campus are prevented from accessing the resource, a major problem for part-time and distance learners, and for those who are balancing study with other commitments.

One way to address the remote access issue is by implementing a proxy solution, such as EZ Proxy from OCLC. This functions by installing a server to act as an intermediary through which the learner's computer or device can access the resource. The IP address from the requesting computer therefore comes from the proxy server situated on campus, and not the computer or device of the user. The learner authenticates with the proxy server, usually with the credentials that they use to log in to the institutional network.

Athens passwords, PIN numbers and barcodes

Another way to provide access to multiple online resources, both on and off campus, is through the use of an identifier allocated by the library itself, which is then shared with many different service providers. This could be the PIN (personal identification number) and/or barcode that is allocated to a learner so that they can access traditional library resources (in fact the barcode/PIN system is in use by many public libraries). However, the most prevalent system in use in UK educational institutions until recently was the Athens system, provided by Eduserv. This provides a central clearing house through which individual usernames and passwords can be generated by institutions on behalf of students, and an authentication system through which service providers can establish access rights for specific e-resources.

However the principal issue with the original ('classic') Athens system has always been that learners have difficulties understanding that a specific username and password is required for authentication to Athens-protected resources, and they therefore ignore or lose the credentials allocated to them until they are required, at which point library or IT staff are often called upon to assist with resetting the password.

Devolved authentication and federated access management

Devolved authentication avoids both the pitfalls of IP authentication and the administrative overhead of allocating additional usernames and passwords to learners for the purposes of accessing online resources. It functions by devolving the responsibility of identifying the user back to the institution's primary IT systems (for example, Microsoft's Active Directory), on the basis that these are likely to hold the most up-to-date information available about the user's current status, and avoids the duplication of effort involved in creating and managing a separate database of passwords. Devolved authentication also provides privacy for the user, as the publisher or service provider never receives any person-specific information from the institution, merely confirmation that the user is a legitimate member of the organization.

In the UK, devolved authentication is available from Athens, with their OpenAthens LA (local authentication) product, and also through the use of open-source software such as Shibboleth, which enables access management in conjunction with the UK Access Management Federation for Education and Research (UKAMF).

Federated access management

Federated access management is a system that builds a relationship between identity providers (usually educational institutions) and service providers (such as publishers or vendors of e-books). It establishes authorized access through the secure exchange of information, or 'attributes', about both parties. The process of user authentication is thus carried out by the educational institution, while the access rights granted to the user are established by the publisher or service provider.

Different institutions, organizations and companies group together to form a federation with a shared policy regarding the exchange of user information required to allow access to their resources. Federations are usually established at a national level, for example the UKAMF, the Canadian Access Federation, the SURF (Samenwerkende Universitaire Reken Faciliteiten) federation in the Netherlands and UPKI-fed (University Public Key Infrastructure Federation) in Japan.

Benefits of devolved access and federated access management

The use of devolved authentication has advantages for both institutions and the providers of e-book collections. With institutions providing credentials for their own users, publishers do not need to spend time on access issues or administering accounts. Likewise users only need to remember a single username and password for access to multiple resources and services – not just online resources from many different suppliers, but also local resources such as personal files on the institution's computer network, e-mail accounts and the VLE. In addition, security is improved as the username and password used for devolved authentication is also used for access to personal information and resources on the local network, and is therefore unlikely to be disclosed to someone else, a problem that is sometimes encountered with the 'Classic' Athens system and with passwords allocated by service providers.

Because learners can be grouped in different ways using institutional registry data, federated access management has another advantage in that it offers the potential for e-book collections to be personalized by enabling more finely controlled access. For example, chemistry students could be given access to chemistry texts but not necessarily to economics titles. This makes for a more transparent costing structure for institutions in terms of licensing. It also helps remove barriers to learners daunted by being faced with a huge collection of e-books, by targeting specific collections and 'hiding' other e-books that are not (as) relevant.

Issues with federated access management

There is, however, a major issue with federated access management from the user perspective – the discovery problem. Before access can be granted, the service provider needs to know about the user, by 'sending' them to their home institution, the identity provider, who then confirms their identity and passes the right attributes back to the service provider, who then grants access. However, to start this process, the service provider must try to find out or 'discover' which institution the user belongs to, and needs to ask a simple question – or, as it is known, make a 'WAYF request': 'Where Are You From?' The user then chooses from a list provided either by the service provider itself or by a central service such as the UKAMF (see Figure 10.1).

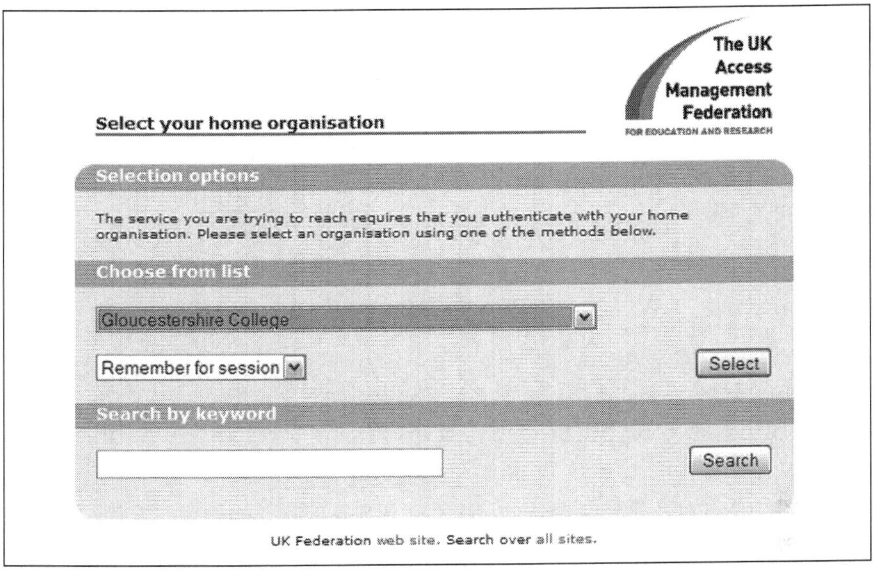

Figure 10.1 *Where Are You From? query from the UK Access Management Federation*

However, there is a problem of scale. As more institutions adopt federated access management around the world, the list of federations and member institutions is quickly becoming much longer. Users may find it difficult to identify which federation is most appropriate, as this is based on the country to which the home institution belongs, rather than the geographical location of the user. Also, users may belong to multiple institutions (for example, they may be a member of staff at one institution whilst studying for further qualifications at another), and may therefore find the WAYF question difficult to answer appropriately. On mobile devices with small screens the process of selecting an institution from a long list can also become problematic.

One option is for the institution to provide learners with carefully crafted links (known as WAYFless URLs) so that their identity is validated *before* being passed to the service provider. Unfortunately, these links tend to be both complex and easy to break, particularly if the service provider makes platform changes. It is also very easy for learners to bypass them entirely, either through a lack of awareness of appropriate access routes, or because they find it more convenient to find relevant e-resources through a Google search rather than their home institution's website.

Client-mediated discovery provides a solution to this problem. The client, perhaps a browser plug-in, 'listens' for the WAYF request generated when the user attempts to access an e-book collection and automatically replies on their behalf. Once configured, client-mediated discovery can provide a good end-user experience, but unfortunately these tools are still uncommon.

Security

Once learners have successfully found a relevant e-book (whether this is through the virtual learning environment, the library catalogue or any of the other search techniques described elsewhere in this book), and negotiated the appropriate access management system, a further issue that can make life difficult for them is the technology employed by the service provider to keep the text secure.

In order to study effectively, learners often want to keep the e-book 'open' as they take notes from it or compose their essay or assignment. They may also want to refer back to it later, whether that is in one hour or in two months' time. However, most platforms employ systems to close open logins after a certain period of time to protect the collection from unauthorized use. This can be a considerable source of frustration to users if accessing that resource again requires a complex set of steps, and may deter them from using it in the future.

Ideally, any authentication process or security protocol that times out access to an e-book platform needs to be intelligent enough to 'remember' which e-book was being used during the previous session and to reinstate that title when the user returns to the platform, preferably regardless of the location or device they were using previously. This intelligence would remove a significant barrier to use, and ensure that learners are able to access e-books at any time, in any place and on any device.

Intelligent security processes should also recognize that not all learners will use the platform in the same way. For example, some platforms interpret a swift 'flicking' from page to page in an e-book (rather than using the table of contents to go directly to a particular chapter) as an attempt to pirate copies, and this can result in lock-outs, not only for the particular reader but potentially for the whole institution, depending on the authentication method in use.

To combat these difficulties, many e-book platforms allow users to create virtual bookshelves that can contain a number of titles. The user is then able to access that bookshelf whenever and wherever they access the platform. Learners can create a personal bookshelf containing the texts they use on a regular basis, while teachers can create bookshelves containing the titles on the reading lists for particular courses or modules, which can then be shared with their students.

Copy protection

Once a learner has found a relevant e-book, they may want to use the content in different ways. Many e-book providers use DRM software to enforce restrictions on printing and copying to prevent users infringing copyright. There is a need to balance these restrictions against the needs of learners who may wish to print parts of the e-book or copy extracts for use in essays or assignment work. When using an e-book platform accessible from the internet, a learner may wish to print sections for future reference when connectivity is poor, unavailable or expensive. The decision to print will often be determined by how much of the e-book is to be used by learners, as they generally prefer to print long extracts for ease of reading, while single pages will be happily viewed on the screen.

Learners may also wish to copy extracts from an e-book to their own USB (Universal Serial Bus) memory stick, laptop or mobile device to provide quotations or references in their essays or assignment work at a later date. Some platforms allow limited copying, and more functional platforms will automatically add a citation or reference to the copied text, which is both helpful to the learner and acts as an additional layer of protection against plagiarism or misuse of the text.

Redistribution of e-book material is another activity that conflicts with security measures; for example learners in a study group may wish to share a text for discussion, and teachers may wish to place a text on an institutional VLE or learning platform in order to share it with their students. One solution is to place a link to the e-book in the VLE rather than uploading the book itself, but even this adds a layer of complexity, which can be a barrier to learners.

E-books for use on e-book readers generally have similar copy protection. Users are often restricted to being able to read a copy on either a single device or a set number of devices. Users may also need to activate the device whilst connected to the internet or a computer before they can access the text. Most e-book readers do not allow text to be electronically copied or printed, and it is therefore important to make learners aware of these limitations before they buy or borrow such a device.

It is important to note that the fair dealing provisions of the UK's Copyright, Designs and Patents Act 1988 allow for the use of printed books in certain ways that are often prevented by DRM restrictions, such as re-formatting the text so that it can be accessed by people with disabilities, and the provision of copies for the purposes of interlibrary loan and preservation. Security measures such as DRM can thus be seen as curtailing some important library functions that are legally permissible in the UK, as well as causing frustration for the end-user.

E-books on the move

Although finding relevant texts, access management and DRM restrictions can all present barriers to their use, e-books do have great potential to improve the experience of those who either need or choose to learn on the move.

The way that students learn changed significantly with the advent of online electronic resources and the provision of desktop computers that allowed them to access information much more easily. Now, with the growth of mobile internet access, through both WiFi (wireless internet) and 3G (third generation mobile phone data transfer) connectivity, it is even easier for learners to access electronic resources at a time and place to suit them. They want access to information on demand, and the availability of e-books online or on e-book readers has the potential to fulfil this need.

Devices

There are many devices that can be used for accessing and reading e-books, each with its own advantages and disadvantages. Some will only work with individual e-books, while others have the capability to be used with online collections of titles.

The following devices do not form an exhaustive list and, as with most consumer electronics, the market, pricing and availability will change rapidly over the next few years. This is one of the challenges faced by learners and institutions as they decide whether to keep pace with technological change or rely on a particular technology or device in which they have already invested. For many there will be no choice as the advances in devices and platforms will mean that new e-books will not work on older devices, and old e-books may not be usable on new devices (i.e. there will be issues of both backwards and forwards compatibility). These advances need to be considered by learners and institutions when choosing particular platforms or devices.

E-book readers

The key technology behind most dedicated e-book readers is electronic paper, or e-ink. This technology involves microcapsules that contain positively charged white particles and negatively charged black particles. When an electrical field is applied, either the white particles or the black particles move to the top layer of the screen, so by applying positive and negative electrical fields in a particular pattern, text can be made to appear on the screen.

The advantage of electronic paper over traditional LCD (liquid crystal display) and other displays is that the image is held without using any power. This has a huge impact on battery life, which is measured in days and weeks for devices using e-ink, compared with laptops and tablet computers, whose battery life is typically measured in hours. Another major advantage of e-ink is that it can be read easily in bright sunlight, unlike an LCD screen.

There are many e-book readers now available, and the market is changing rapidly with new devices and features appearing frequently. Many new e-readers now include a memory card slot, making it easier for users to move content from a computer to the device, and the ability to handle different types of content including PDF, RTF, Word documents, JPEG (Joint Photographic Experts Group) images and MP3 audio files. Some new devices have touch screens rather than buttons, making interaction with the content more flexible.

One of the key challenges with e-book readers is the transfer of content onto the device. Older and cheaper models rely on a USB connection to a desktop computer with an application loaded that facilitates locating and purchasing e-books online, and the subsequent transfer of these onto the portable device. Newer models use WiFi and/or 3G, which allow users to browse and purchase e-books on the reader itself, and download the chosen content whenever and wherever they choose.

A major problem arises when users wish to use their personal e-reader device to access the browser-based e-resources purchased by institutions, which in most cases cannot be downloaded onto e-book readers. Some devices may have a built-in web browser, but these basic browsers either simply do not work or do not have the functionality to allow efficient access to online e-books.

Sony Reader

Sony has been making and selling its Reader range of devices since 2006, and over this time they have been significantly enhanced and upgraded. All now make use of electronic paper for their screens, and one model has a touch interface. In the USA, Sony has made available a model with 3G that allows users to download e-books direct onto the device. As well as viewing e-books, the devices can be used to view PDF and Word documents, using a conversion application on users' desktop computers. The Sony Reader can be used to display JPEG files, although the grey scale screen is not ideal for images, and can also be used to listen to audio MP3 files with headphones. This means that, as well as reading e-books, the device can be used for multimedia-based learning activities such as listening to podcasts.

Amazon Kindle

Amazon, the well known internet retailer, entered the e-book reader market in 2007 with its Kindle device. Initially only available in the USA, the Kindle was different from previous devices in that it had free access to the internet via built in 3G. This allows users to both browse an online e-book store and download the e-books direct to the device wherever they may be. The Kindle also had a simple web browser, allowing users to read RSS (really simple syndication) feeds and web pages on their device. One of the main constraints of the early Kindle was that it could only be used to display titles purchased from Amazon. In 2009 Amazon released the Kindle DX, now with a larger screen and with native PDF support. The concept behind the DX was that it would be suitable for viewing newspaper and academic textbook content. In 2010, Amazon released two slimmer versions of the Kindle, one of which was equipped with 3G as before, as well as a cheaper version with WiFi only, both of which were made available simultaneously in the USA and the UK. These devices sold quickly, showing that although there are other more versatile devices on the market such as the Apple iPad, there is still demand for a dedicated e-book reader.

One of the features of the Kindle is Amazon's 'Whispersync' technology. This allows the same book, once purchased, to be read on multiple devices, whilst the syncing technology ensures that the reader is able to pick up where they left off, even if they are using a different device. Amazon have created software applications for the Windows PC, Mac, iPhone, iPad, Android smartphones and BlackBerry devices so that Kindle e-books purchased from Amazon can be read from virtually all mobile devices. This flexibility, portability and platform neutrality greatly enhances the accessibility of e-books, although not all dedicated e-reader devices are interoperable yet.

Apple iPad and tablet computers

Apple launched the iPad in early 2010 with a colour 9.7 inch LED (Light Emitting Diode) screen and both 3G and WiFi capability. It was immediately obvious that the iPad was viewed by its creators as a platform for e-book access, as the iBook app (application) was released at the same time as the device itself, along with the addition of e-books to the iTunes online store. With its connectivity, built-in browser and support for such formats as PDF and EPUB, the iPad has more in common with a laptop computer than a dedicated e-book reader, and the visual and tactile experience of using the highly interactive touch screen is very attractive to users.

The introduction of the iPad has prompted a resurgence in the market for tablet computers, with other manufacturers developing a range of competing products. These devices will run on Windows, Android and WebOS, all of which are capable of accessing e-book collections through a browser.

Smartphones

There are also e-book applications for smartphones including those running Google's Android operating system, as well the BlackBerry and the iPhone (which is compatible with the iBooks app). The flexibility and portability of a phone for the purposes of reading e-books often outweigh the obvious disadvantage of small screen size. The ability to simply start reading from a phone whilst on the move makes this a highly convenient option for users.

Interoperability is also improving with the introduction of Stanza from Lexcycle, a freeware programme that allows a wide variety of e-book formats to be downloaded and read on Apple devices such as the iPad, the iPhone and the iPod touch. As with the Kindle application, there are versions of Stanza for Windows PCs and Macs.

Laptop and desktop computers

Despite the plethora of new e-book readers now available, one device that should not be forgotten is the familiar laptop or netbook, with which it is possible to carry out multiple tasks ranging from composing essays to accessing e-mail, as well as reading e-books. Failing this, learners will usually have access to an institutional computer either in the library or study centre. The use of laptops and desktop computers offers a certain familiarity and ease of use, whilst software such as Amazon's Kindle application with its syncing ability allows learners to read an e-book on their laptop or home PC and then switch to a portable device if necessary, for example if they are on public transport.

E-books and learning

If learners gain easy access to e-books on the move, through e-readers, smartphones, tablets or laptops, this can change how and where learning can take place. It can enhance and enrich existing learning opportunities and improve the quality of learning outcomes. Access to e-books on the move can also make life easier for learners, ensuring that existing barriers and obstacles to accessing printed books are removed. It can also begin to blur the boundaries between formal, informal and non-formal learning.

E-books for formal learning

Formal learning can be defined as that which takes place within the formal structures and locations prescribed by the institution. As well as taking place in classrooms, lecture theatres and laboratories, formal learning can happen outside the confines of the institution, on field trips or within a VLE.

Within formal learning the role of the book has often been restricted to the core textbook, to which teachers refer during a lesson or lecture. Learners can check their textbook if there is a concept or topic that they feel needs more clarification or explanation. Teachers may also make copies of particularly relevant chapters to give to students as handouts for use during lessons, so long as their institution has the relevant licence in place for photocopying or scanning.

There is a role for e-books within this formal learning context in making it much easier for learners to access core textbooks without the need to carry around a heavy physical text. It is also possible to move beyond a single core textbook, as an e-book reader, for example, can be loaded with hundreds of titles. Students could therefore easily access a number of core texts before, during and after lectures or lessons without there being the usual pressure on the limited number of print books in the library. During seminars, e-books could also allow participants to quickly refer to texts to back up or contextualize an argument or point in a discussion.

In vocational settings it may be preferable to have access to a robust, waterproof or toughened computer or device rather than a paper-based book. Whether the learner is in a workshop, a salon, a kitchen or out in the field, having multiple e-books available rather than a single paper-based textbook could enhance and enrich the vocational experience.

When on field trips, internet connectivity may be non-existent, very limited or costly in some locations and the use of an e-book reader pre-loaded with relevant texts could greatly enhance the learning potential of the trip for students. For example, having access to a range of texts on the relevant historical era could help an archaeology student with the identification and analysis of objects that have been found whilst at a dig in a remote location.

E-books for informal learning

Informal learning can be defined as that which supports the formal process of working towards a qualification, but is outside the direct control of the institution, and takes place at a time and place to suit the learner. It can happen within the institution in social areas or the library, as well as outside the institution at home, at work, or whilst travelling. Examples of informal learning might include a group of business students discussing organizational structure in the college café, a politics student reading a political history book on the train, and employees in a manufacturing company discussing their management course over lunch.

As with formal learning contexts, e-books have a role to play within informal learning. Learners can have easier and more in-depth access to relevant texts without needing to wait until a physical text is available, and can therefore quickly and easily check a book or read a chapter to improve their understanding of a topic. E-books can prompt spontaneous informal learning, as access to relevant and interesting information is possible in those times and places where otherwise no learning would take place, and can provoke immediate discussion and further investigation.

E-books for non-formal learning

Non-formal learning can be defined as that which happens both outside the prescribed confines of the institution and outside the formal framework of qualifications, and in some senses it could be said that we are all engaged in a process of non-formal learning throughout our lives. Examples could include reading a non-fiction book on a holiday for pleasure, using the web to discover how to write an application for a smartphone or following a recipe to learn how to cook a new dish.

As e-books become more commonly used and purchased for leisure and general interest, institutions can expect future learners not only to be already using e-books outside the formal educational environment, but also to wish to use them while studying for a qualification.

Conclusion

Unfortunately, it is often the concerns of service providers with regard to security of access, rights management and copyright protection that prevent users from benefiting fully from the use of e-books. Throughout the process, from searching to access and use of the resource itself, there are areas where the expectations of learners are not met because of technical barriers.

It is essential that libraries make their users aware of these barriers so that they can either avoid them or negotiate them as smoothly as possible, as the opportunity for learners to access e-books at a time and place to suit them can enhance and enrich the learning process, increasing both enjoyment and achievement.

Useful links

Amazon Kindle www.amazon.co.uk/kindleWi-Fi
Apple iPad www.apple.com/uk/ipad
Athens Access and Identity Management www.eduserv.org.uk/aim
Sony Reader www.sony.co.uk/hub/reader-ebook
Stanza E-book Reader App www.lexcycle.com
UK Access Management Federation for Education and Research
    www.ukfederation.org.uk

Bibliography

Ally, M. (ed.) (2009) *Mobile Learning: transforming the delivery of education and training,*

www.aupress.ca/books/120155/ebook/99Z_Mohamed_Ally_
2009-MobileLearning.pdf.
Christodulu, S. (2010) *Generation Y Student Doctors Swap Textbooks for iPhones*,
www.cellular-news.com/story/45657.php.
MoLeNET (2010) *Mobile Learning in Practice*, www.molenet.org.uk/mobilearinprac.
Nie, M. (2006) *The Potential Use of Mobile/Handheld Devices, Audio/Podcasting
Material in Higher Education - a draft review*,
www2.le.ac.uk/projects/impala/documents/resources-and-tools-for-creating-
podcasts/Mobile%20Devices%20in%20Higher%20Education.doc/view.
RNIB College Loughborough (2009) *Visually-impaired Learners Benefit from Audio
and Synchronised Text on their Mobile Phones: an Excellence Gateway case study*,
www.excellencegateway.org.uk/page.aspx?o=245477.
Robinson, J. and Dodd, J. (2005) Case Study: use of handheld computers by
university communications students, *Journal of Online Teaching and Learning*,
http://jolt.merlot.org/05020.htm.
Thomas, R. (2010) Mobilizing The Open University: case studies in strategic
mobile development, *Journal of the Research Center for Educational Technology
(RCET)*, **6** (1),
www.rcetj.org/index.php/rcetj/article/download/80/185.
Wilson, I. (2010) *Literacy Apps*, iPads in Education,
www.ipadineducation.co.uk/iPad_in_Education/Literacy.html.

Part 4
Engaging readers with e-books

Overview

E-books are rapidly becoming established as an important element of information provision across the spectrum of library services, and in this section a range of information and library professionals explore strategies to encourage users to embrace e-books as part of their reading practice.

Martin Palmer (Chapter 11) of Essex Libraries explores this from a public library perspective, considering some of the early barriers to e-book use in the public sector as well as investigating the way that the technology has continued to mature and develop. He goes on to highlight how e-books can benefit certain groups of readers, such as those with disabilities, as well as the potential role of e-books within reader development programmes.

The remaining chapters in this section focus on case studies from two FE colleges and a university in the UK. Sue Caporn and Lee Bryant (Chapter 12) of City of Bristol College describe the findings from a small pilot project conducted with Foundation Degree students and examine the attitudes of both students and teachers towards e-books. Meanwhile, Karen Foster and Emma Ransley (Chapter 12) of Yeovil College discuss the ways in which they have used the VLE to enhance the learner experience and increase the use of their e-book collection.

Finally Anne Worden and Timothy Collinson (Chapter 13) of Portsmouth University examine the ways in which undergraduate students have embraced e-books at the institution and consider the factors that have made this format such a success.

11

Public library users connecting with e-books

Martin Palmer

Introduction

Although public libraries are commonly perceived to be recent arrivals on the e-book scene, some have been involved in providing digital material for recreational reading for almost as long as the technology has been available. Over the same period, there has been a renewed emphasis on the importance of the promotion of reading to the mission of the public library. This chapter explores changing attitudes to both e-books and reader development, and the ways that the two have intersected.

Technology and content

Experience among those public libraries that were early adopters of e-books tends to be fairly consistent in terms of engaging readers: they all found it a very difficult process, at least initially. There were two main reasons for this, each of which is significant enough by itself, but which together can form a cycle from which it is difficult to escape.

First, there is the question of the technology. Five hundred years in the development of the printed book has created a product that is cheap, familiar, easy to use and that does not need to be recharged or connected to the internet. Why then would anyone choose to move to a platform for reading that can appear confusing, has controls that seem to work in a less than intuitive way, has a form of text display that can be tiring and uncomfortable to read and that may also be very expensive?

Second, there is the question of content. In the 1990s, the range of material available to public library users in e-book format was extremely limited. As mainstream publishers struggled to identify sufficient commercial justification for producing their material as e-books (although moving to digitally based processes to produce printed material clearly had a number of benefits, which they quickly took advantage of), most of the titles available at that time were either comparatively specialist reference or other non-fiction titles, or out of copyright material such as that provided by Project Gutenberg.

The possibility of a bestselling novel appearing in such a medium at this time was slim: this was owing not only to a perception on the part of some publishers that there was insufficient demand, but also occasionally to an apparent active hostility on the part of some authors:

> J.K. Rowling has not permitted any of the six Potter books to be released in electronic form. . . . Neil Blair, a lawyer with Rowling's literary agency, would only say that 'this has not been an area that we have sought to license'.
>
> (McHugh, 2005)

Ms Rowling's position on this even became the subject of an April Fool's Day spoof in 2009, which suggested that e-book editions of all seven Harry Potter titles were about to published (Smashwords, 2009). At the time of writing, it seems likely that official Harry Potter e-books are under serious consideration (Page, 2010), but the advice on the official J. K. Rowling website remains unchanged:

> You should NEVER trust any Harry Potter e-books offered for download from the internet or on P2P/file-trading networks. The only genuine copies of Harry Potter remain the authorised traditional book or audio tapes/cassettes/ CDs distributed through my publishers.   (Rowling, 2005)

The combination of these two factors almost inevitably resulted in a situation where many readers were confused by or ill-disposed towards the technology, and even if they could be persuaded to use it, found there was little, if anything, of interest to read.

Consequently, much of the response to early pilot schemes in public libraries was unenthusiastic. The pioneering project conducted in Market Harborough, UK, for example, reported that 'the early excitement had not been reflected in the response from the public' (Collinge, 2002, 18). Similarly, a review by another UK library service (London Borough of Richmond upon Thames, 2003, 3) of the take-up of their e-book services in the three months following their launch in March 2003 showed that although readers had made use of the NetLibrary and Safari services on offer, the levels at which they did so decreased over the period. (However, seven years on, use of NetLibrary at least has been sufficient for Richmond to continue to provide it.)

In light of this indifference on the part of much of the public, and the comparative dearth of suitable material on offer, it is perhaps surprising that any of these early adopters persevered with e-books at all.

Responses of specific types of user

However, by no means all of the feedback received was negative, and some particular sections of the community were very enthusiastic. One element of the Co-East project hosted by Essex County Council's Library Service (Dearnley et al., 2004) was to pilot the use of e-books pre-loaded on personal digital assistant (PDA) devices with specific groups who, it was felt, might welcome the expansion of the range of reading material available to them.

These groups included housebound people and users of the mobile library service, for whom access to the full range of material available from the library was often difficult to achieve, despite the best efforts of the staff or volunteers who served them. For some members of these groups, despite being open to the possibilities that such an approach might offer, the technology proved an obstacle that they were unable to overcome:

> I read quickly, and was irritated by the flicker of moving the small pages on. . . . I found it irritating.

> Just more technology. . . . not as interesting as a book can be.

> The page size is too small. . . . The iPAQ [the Hewlett Packard iPAQ personal digital assistant] imposes its presence on the experience in a way that the paper book does not. (Berube and Palmer, 2004, 10)

For others, however, it was clear that e-book provision could be a major breakthrough in extending the range of reading material available to them. One such group in the Co-East project was people with a visual impairment. The ability to change the font size of any item borrowed, making all material potentially large print, was seen as a step-change in provision, which justified the struggle with unfamiliar devices. In addition, the 'read-aloud' facility provided by Adobe software for some titles – despite being somewhat 'mechanical' in tone and expression – was a further unexpected benefit for many. In fact, for one reader at least:

> The e-book site is wonderful: it's what the internet was invented for. . . . recommending it to all my friends, and a neighbour – who is blind – has just started to use e-books as a result.   (Berube and Palmer, 2004, 10)

Elsewhere, some commentators have suggested that elements of e-book functionality may also be particularly useful for another specific group – gifted children. Although they may find the facility to change font size, for example, just as useful as anybody else, the ability of young gifted readers to appreciate nuances of language in particular is thought by some to benefit from the 'extras' provided by e-books such as bookmarking, links to other support material, and so on:

> Gifted readers in particular can benefit from the added tools and variety afforded by e-books. . . . Whereas e-books can be used as a tool to present text, just as a paper-based book can, they also contain features that can be classified as accommodations or as assistive technology tools for reading . . . including gifted and advanced readers.   (Cavanaugh and Weber, 2006)

However, this suggestion highlights a problem particularly relevant to public libraries in the UK, which is a lack of material for children to read for pleasure. Although this appears to be slightly less of a concern in the USA, much of the children's material provided by US-based suppliers seems either unsuitable or less relevant to British audiences, being either American classics (most of which are available via Project Gutenberg and other free sources) or otherwise very specific to the US market. This is beginning to change as the technology develops but remains a problem whose cause seems to lie right at the start of the e-book creation process.

For example, a major UK children's publisher has been quoted as saying:

> It's not like we haven't tried this market,' says Jason Campbell, marketing director for Harper Media. . . . We've done R. L. Stine and (Meg Cabot's) *The Princess Diaries* and it didn't work. (McHugh, 2005)

One view of the reasons for this, from another publisher, is that:

> There's just not a market for books that don't appeal to adults, because they're the ones with the devices at this time,' says Linda Leonard . . . for Random House Books. 'It is kind of frustrating. Kids are tech savvy, but we can't reach them. (McHugh, 2005)

It seems that this bias towards older users of e-readers has not changed to date, but as other types of device have become available the distinction seems to have developed instead into an age-defined split between users of e-readers and those of other, more generic, devices. A widely cited 'Publisher's Lunch' study, as quoted in *Library Journal*, suggests:

> The Kindle Reader demographic skews upwards, with 70% of users 40 or older. Younger readers prefer smartphones, so the future of the ebook will be 'a common standard' not a 'common device'. (Genco, 2009)

The renaissance of e-readers, and other devices
New growth in the market

With the appearance of a new generation of e-book readers from 2008 onwards, the tide of opinion about public library e-book provision appears to have begun to turn from one of mainly indifference, hostility or surprise that public libraries might be involved in such a service, to an increasing expectation that it should form part of their mainstream provision.

This reflects the changes occurring in the wider world. In the USA, 'sales of e-books overtook those of audiobooks . . . in 2009, with sales rising by more than 170%' (Jones, 2010), while:

> UK publishers saw a 27% increase in digital sales over the two years to 2009.
> . . . Simon Juden, chief executive of the PA [Publishers Association] said, 'The migration of revenues from purely physical to a mixed, increasingly digital ecology has clearly begun, and the launch of new e-readers and platforms will only serve to facilitate the process.'
>
> (Neilan, 2010a)

This wider take-up of e-reader devices has led to increased demand for more and better content. A survey carried out by YouGov in the UK recently found that among 'those who already have an e-reader, the range and quality of books available to download was rated the least satisfying aspect of owning a device' (Neilan, 2009).

To these views of e-reader owners can be added those of the far greater number of people who are reading e-books on other, more generic platforms, such as PCs or smartphones. The iPhone arguably became the most widely used e-book reading device globally as soon as it appeared, despite initially not having a specific e-book 'app'.

The iPhone and dyslexia

One unexpected offshoot of the facility to use smartphones for reading has been the discovery by many people that this technology can help them master a skill which had previously been a closed book to them (quite literally). An article by a 57-year-old man tells how he inadvertently found that, after a lifetime of suffering from a number of the symptoms of dyslexia, the iPhone enabled him to read much more easily. Interestingly, his description of this discovery also shows that the solution resulted from precisely the qualities of the reading experience on the iPhone that more experienced readers dislike:

> So why had I found it easier to read from my iPhone? First, an ordinary page of text is split into about four pages. The spacing seems generous and because of this I don't get lost on the page. Second, the handset's brightness makes it easier to take in words.
>
> (Hill, 2010)

The reason for this is explained in the article as follows:

'Many dyslexics have problems with "crowding", where they're distracted by the words surrounding the word they're trying to read,' says John Stein, Professor of Neuroscience at Oxford University and chair of the Dyslexia Research Trust. 'When reading text on a small phone, you're reducing the crowding effect.'   (Hill, 2010)

As a result of this new-found capacity for reading, and having quickly worked his way through *The Count of Monte Cristo*, this man swiftly went on to read the rest of the classics available on the app that he had downloaded along with all the other products beloved by iPhone users. The effect of this on a middle-aged man is perhaps easily underestimated by those for whom the pleasure of reading is almost taken for granted. He notes that for many dyslexic people, the help with reading provided by the iPhone has improved their sense of self-esteem, and that: 'I share this sense and now see that when I proudly show off my iPhone to others it is not just a new bit of technology, but the centrepoint of my newly ordered life' (Hill, 2010).

Consequently, Apple's more recent development of 'iBooks' for the iPad, and its extension to the iPhone in version 4.0 of the operating system introduced in June 2010, may result not only in the wider availability of e-books themselves but also in making the pleasure of reading available to a still wider audience. For public libraries, unfortunately, the problems of incompatibility between their download e-books and Apple devices arising from the use of DRM currently remain unresolved.

E-books and reader development

Reader development, which is described as 'selling the reading experience, rather than individual writers or books' by Opening the Book, one of the foremost agencies involved in this activity (Opening the Book, n.d.), has become a major focus for public libraries in recent years. Interestingly, the rapid expansion of reader development programmes from the mid-1990s onwards has broadly coincided with the growth of interest in e-books, albeit at a much lower level.

It might be expected, therefore, that there would have been some crossover between the two over the past decade or more. However, this has been comparatively insignificant in reality, with only a handful of projects taking place, with limited success. To some extent, this is not surprising; the underlying reasons for the lack of interest shown by public library readers in early e-book pilots, such as antipathy towards the technology and lack of perceived benefits, are just as applicable to those participating in reader development activities.

Reading groups

In fact, it might be argued that as a large number of participants in reader development activities are particularly enthusiastic advocates of the printed word, they might be even less well disposed towards e-books than other people. This appears to be borne out by a project designed to assess the appetite for using e-books in reading groups, during which 'books of interest' were loaded on to PDAs and given to two reading groups, which then tried the PDAs for a period of three months. The research found that:

> Readers were not too negative about using a new tool/gadget like the PDA, but they did not see any advantage in reading an electronic version of the selected book. . . . readers were so attached to physical books as to feel as if they were betraying them when reading them electronically.
>
> (Landoni and Hanlon, 2007, 612)

The project report goes on to suggest that a different sample of users, one more generally open to this type of approach, might have produced a more sympathetic response. However, it is equally possible that such an outcome was likely regardless of the sample. As with other pilot studies based solely on the loan of devices, it is difficult to see quite what advantages many readers would perceive such a service to have over the provision of printed books.

However, as the technology has developed, it is possible to see how e-books might now form the basis of virtual reading groups and so offer yet another extension to reading group activity. The Public Library Online service from Bloomsbury is set up to do precisely that, offering not only the multiple simultaneous access to content required for groups, but also the kinds of support material that help facilitate the smooth working of reading groups generally, such as author interviews, reader guides and reviews.

Enhanced e-books, interactive fiction, fan fiction and cell phone novels

Reader development has not been slow to exploit the benefits offered by technology: many online library catalogues now feature added-value material such as reviews and ratings, previously the preserve of Amazon and other internet booksellers. Other services include the provision of alternatives to the traditional library catalogue approach of accessing material by author, title or genre; these include whichbook.net, which provides readers with the opportunity to explore books that reflect the way they feel (or want to feel), or by type of character, plot or setting.

Some publishers have also firmly embraced the reader development concept – Penguin, for example, was a pioneer in this area, providing a website to support reading groups with everything from advice on how to make groups work successfully to recommendations, reviews and discounts on books. However, until Bloomsbury's recent entry into this area, most technology-based reader development activity was about providing support and additional book-related material rather than the text of the book itself. The approach offered by Bloomsbury (and now others) in providing simultaneous multiple access to the full text of their books is clearly welcome, but there are still further opportunities which technology offers to move reader development in yet another direction.

Some publishers, for example, are beginning to explore the potential of 'enhanced' e-books, which offer more than simply the text of the book. Again, Penguin is an early example of a publisher using this format to add value to its e-material, adding various features to its e-books classics list: its e-book edition of Jane Austen's *Pride and Prejudice* includes 'a filmography, reviews from the novel's original publication, a chronology of Austen's life and times, recipes, rules of social etiquette and period dancing, and illustrations of fashion, home decor and architecture' (Page, 2008).

For some, unfortunately, this approach is a missed opportunity:

> What makes me want to cry is the monumental inability of a mainstream
> publisher to think beyond paper and the idea that an eBook is only another
> way to represent paper. . . . I am beginning to wonder if it's a plot to kill
> eBooks.   (Ebooks About, 2008)

More recently, however, the additional features being added to e-books
have moved beyond text and illustrations. Hachette's enhanced e-book
of David Baldacci's *Deliver Us from Evil* offers items which will be
familiar to customers now used to finding many hours' worth of special
features on DVD and Blu-ray: 'Audio Q & A, a video of the author's
office, photos of the creative process, and discarded scenes and title'
(Relaxnews, 2010).

It should be noted, however, that many of these features appear to
have been introduced to exploit particular aspects of Apple's iPad, and
will not be accessible to users of dedicated e-book readers. It is possible,
therefore, that this facility may come to be perceived solely as a
marketing device.

Nevertheless, some features do seem to provide genuine benefits. For
example, Walker Books have developed nine of its titles as enhanced e-
books, including Sam McBratney's *Guess How Much I Love You*. Alongside
the less surprising features such as image exploration and jumbo text, the
reader is also offered the opportunity to record their own audio, and
thus a child can hear the voices of their parent(s) reading the book, even
when a mother or father is not around to do so in person (Neilan,
2010b).

Perhaps a more significant innovation is the approach taken by DNL,
which was among the first to develop enhanced e-books that integrate
audiovisual content with their text, so that clicking on a picture may
provide an audio commentary on its subject, or start a related video.

All of these developments, however, begin to raise fundamental
questions about the nature of the product - basically, is it still a 'book'?
This topic is not new, with many of the arguments having been rehearsed
from the 1980s onwards in relation to the development of interactive
fiction in printed form, where the reader is invited to make choices at
critical stages in the narrative to affect the outcome of the story. For
many people, there is little to distinguish most products of this type
from computer games, particularly those that go beyond basic text

provision. However, the existence of groups such as the Electronic Literature Organization, whose aim is 'to facilitate and promote the writing, publishing and reading of literature in electronic media' (Electronic Literature Organization, n.d.), perhaps demonstrates that there is more to the format than some may imagine.

In a similar vein, another e-publishing phenomenon that might be viewed as a limited merging of reader development and literature development is fan fiction. This is a term for stories based on characters or plots of popular or cult fiction, but written by fans rather than the original author, taking the reader development concept of 'creative reading' a step further. Although not widely exploited by public libraries, links to sites devoted to such activity (not all of which is *Star Trek*-related) can provide a further dimension to reader development, which truly is unique to the electronic format, although the extreme content of some sites suggests that care should be taken when selecting sites to feature.

Another area in which the potential role of the public library is difficult to determine is the emergence of new genres of material based on particular delivery platforms, some of which seem to be very culturally or geographically specific. The most well known of these is the cell phone novel, which is both written and read on a mobile phone. 'The cell phone novel first appeared in Japan in around 2003. By 2007, five of the top ten best-selling novels in Japan were cell phone novels' (Peters, 2009).

Harlequin was one of the first English language commercial publishers to appreciate this phenomenon, making its romances available in this way (as well as turning them into Manga – comic-book style – stories to be read on the Nintendo DS). However, although an English language site devoted to this material has appeared (www.textnovel.com), there is little currently to suggest that this particular genre is of much interest to English readers.

However, it does suggest the possibility that e-books may provide a useful way of making material available to users of UK libraries for whom English is not the first language; in fact, for some languages, such as Chinese, e-books may well offer a much more effective way of developing relevant collections than existing print-based services.

The future: engaging with a minority of readers, or most of them?

Currently, problems of compatibility between software and hardware and other obstacles still confuse the public, and so constrain the take-up of e-books: why, for example, is it currently possible to listen to e-audiobooks offered by public libraries on an iPhone, but not to read their e-books on it? Although these technical difficulties remain, it does seem clear that both supply and demand have increased sufficiently to indicate that the original problems of audience apathy and lack of suitable content faced by early public library adopters have now been largely left behind.

Consequently, while the benefits offered by e-books to specific groups remain the fundamental justification for providing them, the point at which e-books become not only demanded but also expected by the majority of public library users seems to be much closer than previously. Some observers believe that this 'tipping point' for the e-book clearly offers the public library a major opportunity to reassert its position as an organization fit for the 21st century:

> 'What better institutions to evangelize new reading than libraries . . . Libraries have a proud history of education . . . they're not afraid to test new technologies because they're not concerned with profits.'
>
> (Steve Potash, quoted in Rogers, 2004, 23)

As the Chief Executive Officer of OverDrive, it might be expected that Steve Potash would support the role of libraries in the development of e-book take-up, but he is not alone in believing this. Indeed, some publishers such as Macmillan in the USA are only too aware of its implications: 'You get the book, read it, return it and get another, all without paying a thing. It's like Netflix, but you don't pay for it. How is that a good model for us?' (Sargent, 2010).

Either way, if the take-up of e-books by the general public is now finally reaching a tipping point, it provides public libraries with both an excellent opportunity and a challenge. The full benefits of e-books have only just begun to be fully exploited by public library practitioners, but they do seem to offer much more potential to engage with readers.

The challenge is to ensure that this actually happens. At the time of writing, it could be argued that although the signs are promising quantitatively (in terms of increasing levels of loans for e-books), there is still much more to do qualitatively. In fact, some may feel that there has been little improvement in the use of e-materials to engage readers in the time that has elapsed since the following statement appeared in one of the earliest titles on reader development, when the potential of technology appeared to be much stronger than its actual take-up:

> There are evident tensions between the new technologies and reader
> development, particularly in the field of children's reading. However, it is
> clear that there are many innovative technologies which make use of the
> opportunities provided by the new technologies to engage with readers.
>
> (Denham, 2003, 193)

Useful links

DNL www.DNLebooks.com
Electronic Literature Organization www.eliterature.org
Free e-books www.e-book.com.au/freebooks.htm
Penguin Readers' Group http://readers.penguin.co.uk
Public Library Online www.exacteditions.com

References

Berube, L. and Palmer, M. (2004) E-books: some stock management questions, *Taking Stock*, **12** (1), (Summer), 9–11.

Cavanaugh, T. and Weber, C. (2006) Promoting Reading: using e-books with gifted and advanced readers, *Gifted Child Today*, **29** (4), 56–63.

Collinge, M. (2002) quoted in 'Discussion following the paper by Penny Garrod'. In Brewer, S. (ed.) *E-books and Public Libraries: proceedings of a seminar held at Stamford, Lincolnshire on 29 November 2001*, Capital Planning Information.

Dearnley, J. et al. (2004) Electronic Books in Public Libraries: a feasibility study for developing usage models for web-based and hardware-based electronic books, *New Review of Information Networking*, **10** (2), (November), 209–46.

Denham, D. (2003) ICT and Reader Development. In Elkin, J., Train, B. and Denham, D. (eds), *Reading and Reader Development: the pleasure of reading*,

Facet Publishing, 171–93.

Ebooks About (2008) *Enhanced E-books – Penguin style*, http://ebooksabout.blogspot.com.

Electronic Literature Organization (n.d.) *About the ELO*, www.eliterature.org/about.

Genco, B. (2009) Summit Paints Picture of Ebook Future, *Library Journal*, 21 December, www.libraryjournal.com/article/CA6712593.html.

Hill, H. (2010) My iPhone has Revolutionised my Reading, *The Guardian*, 6 April, www.guardian.co.uk/education/2010/apr/06/iphone-makes-reading-books-easier.

Jones, P. (2010) E-book Sales in US Overtake Sales of Audio Books, *The Bookseller*, 8 April, www.thebookseller.com/news/115933-e-book-sales-in-us-overtake-sales-of-audio-books.html.

Landoni, M. and Hanlon, G. (2007) E-book Reading Groups: interacting with e-books in public libraries, *The Electronic Library*, **25** (5), 599–612.

London Borough of Richmond upon Thames (2003*) E-book and E-audio Services Review, March–June 2003.*

McHugh, J. D. (2005) J K Rowling Refuses E-books for Potter, *USA Today*, 14 June, www.usatoday.com/life/books/news/2005-06-14-rowling-refuses-ebooks_x.htm.

Neilan, C. (2009) E-book Users want Better Content and New Devices, *The Bookseller*, 8 September, www.thebookseller.com/news/96325-e-book-users-want-better-content-and-new-devices.html.

Neilan, C. (2010a) PA: digital book industry now 5% of total sales, *The Bookseller*, 16 April, www.thebookseller.com/news/116506-pa-digital-book-industry-now-5-of-total-sales.html.

Neilan, C. (2010b) Walker Launches Enhanced E-book Apps, *The Bookseller*, 24 March, www.thebookseller.com/news/114941-walker-launches-enhanced-e-book-apps.html.

Opening the Book (n.d.) Definition of Reader Development, www.openingthebook.com/about/reader-centred-approach/definition/default.aspx.

Page, B. (2008) Penguin Launches Enhanced E-book Classics, *The Bookseller*,

13 March,
www.thebookseller.com/news/54909-penguin-launches-enhanced-e-book-classics.html.

Page, B. (2010) Rowling Opens Door to Digital Harry Potter Books, *The Bookseller*, 31 May,
www.thebookseller.com/news/119581-rowling-opens-door-to-digital-harry-potter-books.html.

Peters, T. (2009) The Future of Reading, *Library Journal*, 1 November,
www.libraryjournal.com/article/CA6703852.html.

Relaxnews (2010) Enhanced E-book Apps Anticipate a New Generation of E-readers, *The Independent*, 28 March,
www.independent.co.uk/arts-entertainment/books/enhanced-ebook-apps-anticipate-a-new-generation-of-ereaders-1929810.html.

Rogers, M. (2004) Librarians, Publishers, Vendors Revisit E-books, *Library Journal*, **129** (7), 15 April, 23–4,
www.libraryjournal.com/lj/ljinprintcurrentissue/871862-403/librarians_publishers_and_vendors_revisit.html.csp.

Rowling, J. K. (2005) Harry Potter E-book Scam,
www.jkrowling.com/textonly/en/news_view.cfm?id=84.

Sargent, J. (2010) E-books in Libraries a Thorny Problem, says Macmillan CEO,
http://go-to-hellman.blogspot.com/2010/03/ebooks-in-libraries-thorny-problem-says.html.

Smashwords (2009) J K Rowling Publishes Harry Potter Ebooks on Smashwords,
www.smashwords.com/press/release/8.

12

Engaging students with e-books in further education

Sue Caporn, Lee Bryant, Karen Foster and Emma Ransley

Intoduction

This chapter examines the experiences of two FE colleges, City of Bristol College and Yeovil College, both situated in the west of England.

City of Bristol College has nearly 30,000 students based at six main centres across the city. As well as providing a full range of academic and vocational FE courses, the College works with five universities, including the University of Plymouth, to provide HE courses to 1200 students. Yeovil College has over 7000 students and has two main campuses situated in Yeovil, one of which is focused on the provision of HE courses, as well as two sites outside the town.

A range of strategies are used to engage students with e-books, including holding workshops and training sessions, embedding the use of e-formats into the curriculum, linking titles from the VLE, and verbal and visual promotion.

Engaging foundation degree students with e-books: the experience at City of Bristol College

This section draws on both the results produced and the experience gained during a research project which ran from February 2009 to February 2010. The aim of the project was to explore how e-books can effectively support HE students on foundation degree courses delivered in FE colleges. The project was funded by the Higher Education Learning Partnerships Centre for Excellence in Teaching and Learning's Award

Holder scheme, which is based at the University of Plymouth.

There is a relatively small but increasing body of research on the impact of e-books on students, and on the LRCs and libraries supporting them. This is generally focused on students in HE, the two most comprehensive UK studies being the CIBER SuperBook project, a survey of students and staff with 1818 respondents carried out at University College London (Rowlands et al., 2007), and the JISC-funded UK National e-Books Observatory Project (JISC, 2009). Another recent research project was carried out by librarians at the University of the West of England, employing an online survey of students (Briddon et al., 2009).

Project methodology

The project investigated the perceptions and use of e-books among students on three University of Plymouth foundation degrees taught at the College: Business, Administration and Business Technology (collectively designated Business and Administration in the following study), and Early Childhood Studies (ECS). The study aimed to engage students, both first and second years, with e-books, ascertaining the ways in which e-books could support their learning, and investigating their perceptions of the advantages and disadvantages of e-books and any barriers to their use. LRC staff also hoped to gain an insight into any training and support needs that the students had relating to e-books.

LRC staff worked with the programme co-ordinators of these three courses, planning and delivering an introductory one-hour workshop on e-books in early October 2009. The hands-on workshop covered the two e-book services available via Blackboard, the College's VLE. These included books purchased by the College from MyiLibrary as well as the 3000 e-books available on the ebrary platform, provided by the JISC-funded FE e-book project. After the workshop, the students were asked to complete an online questionnaire, to find out whether they had any previous experience of e-books, their perceptions of how they might use the new format, and opinions on the advantages and disadvantages that books in e-format might have. The students were then expected to use e-books alongside other resources in their first assignment of the term. Six weeks later, they were asked to complete a second questionnaire to follow up on the issues raised in the first, and ask them about their experience of using (or not using) e-books. The survey data was supplemented by interviews with the programme co-ordinators, who gave their perspective on the students' experience as well as their own views on the benefits or otherwise of e-books.

The project started with nearly 50 students, with 24 completing both questionnaires. The data was analysed to explore whether students' perceptions changed as they made use of e-books during the course of the project. Comparisons were made between the responses from first and second year students, and across age groups and courses.

The first questionnaire

The first questionnaire established that all of the students were experienced IT users – all used the internet and Microsoft Office, and 92% of the youngest age group (18–21) used social networking tools, such as Facebook. Second year students were more likely to have used e-books previously (50%) than first year students (33%).

Despite the novelty of e-books, confidence levels in their use were high after the workshop (see Figure 12.1).

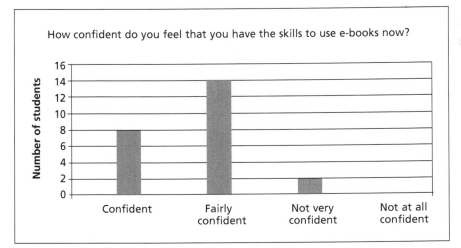

Figure 12.1 *Confidence of students after the e-books session*

After the session, 22 of the students expected to change the approach that they took to searching for information; indeed when asked which format would be their first choice, 13 out of 24 said that they would begin with e-books, compared with 11 who would prefer print books. This preference was particularly strong for the youngest age group and also for the first year students. All of the first years said that they would change the way in which they carried out research, compared with 75% of the second year students. Taken together, these findings demonstrated the value of the workshop in promoting e-books and training students how to use them, particularly at the beginning of the HE course.

Other findings of the first survey included a belief by some of the 18–21 age group (17%) that they would read whole books online. None of the students in the over 22 age group were of this opinion.

The second questionnaire

Six weeks later, in mid-November, the students were asked to complete the second online questionnaire, which asked them whether they had used e-books for their first assignment of the term; if so, how many; where they had accessed them; and how they had accessed them. Again they were questioned about their views on the advantages and disadvantages of the e-format. In addition the questionnaire explored their satisfaction with e-books and how likely they were to use them again. If they had not used e-books, they were asked to state the reasons why.

Results

Of the group of 24 students, 14 had used e-books for their assignment and 10 had not. These two groups were analysed separately, and then responses were further analysed by age, year of study and course. A relationship was identified between age and use of e-books, as demonstrated by Figure 12.2.

Greater use was made of e-books by the 18–21 age group (67%), than by the others, with 57% of 22–30s and 50% of 31–40s having used them. A similar relationship was recorded with the year of study, with more first year students having used e-books than second year students. This might indicate that first year and younger students were more open to

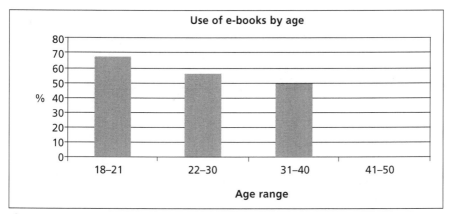

Figure 12.2 *Use of e-books by age*

new ways of studying and trying out new technologies. The Early Childhood Studies students had used e-books more than the Business and Administration students (75% versus 42%).

The role of the LRC in promoting the accessibility of e-books to students is shown to be crucial, as all but one of the e-book users said that they had accessed them via the college's VLE, Blackboard. Of these, nine students had gained access via the LRC catalogue embedded within the VLE and six students via the e-books link on the eResources tab in the VLE, which is managed by the LRC. Most students had one preferred way of accessing e-books, although two students used both.

Regarding methods of reading e-books, none of the students had read a whole e-book online, despite the opinions expressed in the first questionnaire. Figure 12.3 overleaf summarizes the preferences of students.

The data indicates the willingness of students to read from the screen, with most expressing a preference for a combination of reading online and printing out sections. Some (29%) preferred to read online and only 14% always preferred to print out and read from paper. It seems students are happy to read at least some content online and that this is not an impediment for most. This reflects, albeit to a lesser extent, the willingness to read from the screen found by the CIBER SuperBook Project (48% read from the screen only and 39% from both screen and printouts). Analysing the results of the City of Bristol College study further, both year groups and all ages displayed similar preferences in

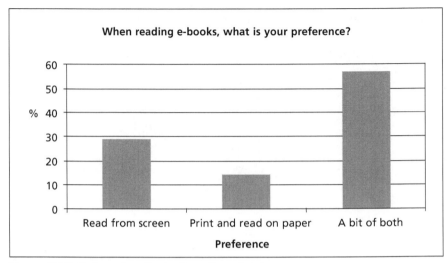

Figure 12.3 *Preferred methods of reading e-books*

relation to reading e-books. However, there was a marked difference between the Business and Administration students, 80% of whom preferred to read from the screen, and the ECS students, none of whom preferred to read from the screen. Does this reflect the nature of the information needs of the two courses – factual versus descriptive – or the nature of the students themselves? This is an interesting subject for further research, and a future project will extend the scope of the study to include a greater range of disciplines.

The importance of remote access to e-books was clear from survey responses: 36% of students had used e-books mostly at home and 50% had accessed them both at home and at the college, making a total of 86% of students using remote access. Only 14% of students had accessed them mostly at the college. This finding indicates the importance of clear links to e-books within the College VLE, supported by helpsheets and tutorials online, so that students can use them independently, outside of the opening times of the LRC.

The Business and Administration students had accessed e-books more at home, whereas most of the ECS students had used them both at the college and at home. This could be explained by the fact that some of the Business and Administration students are part-time, and therefore have little free time for research whilst at college.

Those who used e-books expressed high levels of satisfaction with them (92%), with no difference between the courses or the year groups. However, it is worth noting that all of the 18–21 age group were very or quite satisfied with e-books. Even among those who had not used them during the project itself, 60% were quite satisfied with their subsequent use of e-books. A very high number of people said they were quite likely or very likely to use e-books again; see Table 12.1.

Table 12.1 *Likelihood of future use of e-books*

Likelihood of use	Number of students: users	Number of students: non-users
Very likely	9	3
Quite likely	4	3
Possibly	0	2
Unlikely	0	1
Non-respondents	1	1

What do students like about e-books?

It is clear from both surveys that students like both the idea of e-books and the reality of using them. In fact, a higher proportion of students mentioned advantages in the second survey, particularly the real benefits (no fines, no heavy books to carry, no special trips to the library), which they had enjoyed whilst using them. Their comments are summarized in Table 12.2.

Table 12.2 *Advantages of e-books mentioned by students completing Questionnaire 2*

Advantage	Number of students
Convenience (no need to visit library; no fines; no carrying)	10
Accessibility (accessible 24/7 anywhere)	9
Ease of searching (including within books)	5
Widening the range of resources	3
Ease of referencing	1

Convenience and portability was seen as the most significant advantage over printed books. In the students' own words:

If they are not available in the library and you do not wish to buy them then this is a good way to access them. Also, if you are at home and cannot go to a library they are easy to access.

You can save relevant pieces to your computer and they are available when the printed books might not be.

Accessibility was seen as a big advantage. One student commented:

I can search it at any time of day unlike the library which has opening times and is harder to get to.

Ease of searching was mentioned by five students; one made the following comment:

You can easily search a term, rather than using the index in books.

Increased range of resources through the provision of e-books was mentioned; comments included:

You can only take five books out from City of Bristol College, so they allow you to use more sources for your research.

Ease of referencing was also mentioned.

What do students dislike about e-books?

As for the disadvantages of e-books, it was clear from the second questionnaire that technical issues were the main problem, with six students mentioning this, a much higher proportion than in the first questionnaire (see Table 12.3 overleaf).

Technical issues were mentioned by six of the students, some really struggling to access e-books from outside the College, owing to a series of technical problems resulting from the implementation of federated access. It is possible that if access to e-books had been more reliable throughout the project, students would have used them more and would have had more positive experiences. Comments included:

Table 12.3 *Disadvantages of e-books*
(NB: number of students only recorded for those who mentioned a disadvantage in Questionnaire 2)

Disadvantage	Number of students
Technical issues, including unreliability/problems with remote access	6
Not enough relevant e-books available	3
Prefer reading from print	3
Can't print enough pages	2

> Not being able to access it most of the time is very frustrating. I have reported the problem several times but I am still having problems.

Lack of relevant e-books available was mentioned by three students, one of whom commented:

> It would be useful to have more books from my course recommended reading lists.

The LRC does have a policy of buying electronic copies of all books requested if available. However, currently not all titles are available electronically and student expectation therefore has to be managed.

Preference for reading from print was mentioned by three students, commenting on the fact that they were used to reading print and liked printing out pages, even if they knew that this was wasting paper. One wrote:

> I see e-books as saving paper. However, I personally find it more useful getting research by printing off what I have found or photocopying pages and then highlighting the important points by hand and then continuing with my work. So in one sense the use of e-books is defeated because of printing pages off.

However, only three students mentioned that they preferred reading from print, compared with seven students in Questionnaire 1. It seems that the students soon adapted to reading from the screen in practice.

Inability to print many pages because of restrictions in place was also mentioned as a source of frustration:

I can't print out enough pages, or save them.

These likes and dislikes are comparable to those found by the larger-scale research projects cited above, which found that students like the convenience, searchability and 24/7 online access offered by e-books, but identified disadvantages of a technical nature, such as limits to downloading and printing. Some students in all three studies preferred the physicality of printed books, finding them easier to read, particularly when reading a whole book.

Views of teaching staff

The programme co-ordinators of the three courses were also interviewed about their views on the use of e-books by their students. They felt that the students had a positive approach to e-books, had enjoyed the e-books workshop, had felt 'supported and valued' and had 'bought in' to e-books as a result. They did say that the students had encountered problems using the e-books, particularly accessing them remotely, because of technical difficulties. One co-ordinator commented that some students had reported back that it was difficult to read online, although the survey showed this to be a minority view.

After marking the students' assignments, the programme co-ordinators were positive about the value of e-books. One commented: 'It did improve the quality of their work, particularly in their use of a wider range of resources.' This programme co-ordinator did feel that students were affected by the fact that some textbooks were not available electronically. Another co-ordinator felt that students' referencing had improved but could not say with any certainty whether this was as a result of the project.

All of the interviewees felt that they would make further use of e-books. One programme co-ordinator gave an example of how an e-book had been used as part of a study skills session, indicating that e-texts are now seen as a key resource. She also mentioned that she, like the students, valued the ability to search through books by keyword. Another was keen to introduce e-books to all of her students and make use of them herself. Interestingly, one programme co-ordinator felt that he would encourage the use of e-books with the younger students but that mature students preferred to use traditional resources such as handouts and printed books. Although there is a link between the age of students and their overall use of e-books, the high satisfaction ratings do suggest that mature students are happy to use e-books in certain circumstances, so it may be that this co-ordinator had transferred his own view of e-books onto his mature students.

Overall, the positive views and concerns of the programme co-ordinators matched those of the students. All of the interviewees were pleased to have been involved in the project and felt that there was kudos attached to a project using new technology, a fact that could be used in the promotion of e-books. Another significant finding was the positive impact of having a workshop delivered to the students in the classroom. Finally, it is clear that in some cases the views of teaching staff can impact on how new resources such as e-books are promoted to students, and therefore teaching staff need to be convinced of their value.

Summary

Several key points have been highlighted by this research project. The first is that the e-books workshop session made a real difference in raising students' awareness of e-books and giving them the confidence to use the e-format. In the words of one student: 'The introduction was very useful, as I doubt I would have thought of using e-books if we had not had this session.'

The project found differences between students according to age, year of study and course. Interestingly, although the younger students did use e-books more during the course of the project, age was not the major differentiating factor in e-book use. However, there was a difference between the two year groups in their willingness to change the way they studied after the e-books workshop, with first year students being more open to change. This finding indicates a need for early, effective information literacy sessions, which is also mentioned by Karen Gravett in Chapter 9 and Anne Worden and Timothy Collinson in Chapter 13.

The main differentiating factor in use and perceptions of e-books was the subject of study. Compared with the Business and Administration students, the Early Childhood Studies students were more likely to make use of social networking sites, had made more use of e-books previously and during the project they used more books, both electronic and print. However, the Business and Administration students thought they were more likely to use e-books remotely and actually did so, used more e-books than print books, preferred to read from the screen and were more likely to use them again. This would appear to reflect the findings of the JISC National e-Books Observatory Project (2009), which identified Business students as 'super-users' of e-books.

The importance of remote access is also reflected in the students' use of e-books. A minority of students accessed e-books mainly at college, while most accessed them both at college and at home. With the likelihood of more flexible modes of delivery in the future, and of students having greater commitments outside their studies, remote access to resources will continue to be a key consideration for students.

One of the main perceived disadvantages of e-books at the start of the project, by both students and staff, was reading from the screen. However, in reality only a minority of students preferred to print out sections to read. The majority read directly from the screen, at least some of the time, with the Business and Administration students stating a preference for reading from the screen.

The likes and dislikes of students relating to e-books correspond with those found by the other studies cited. The main advantages recognized by students in both questionnaires were remote access at any time, ease of searching, no library fines and the physical advantages of e-books over printed books, for example that there was no need to borrow or carry heavy books The fact that students encountered access problems during the course of the project did not appear to impact on these particular perceptions. However, in terms of disadvantages, students stated above all the technical difficulties in accessing e-books remotely, a lack of relevant titles and limitations on downloading and printing.

The interviews with the programme co-ordinators reflected the concerns of the students, with the same advantages and disadvantages being cited. It emerged that the attitude of teaching staff towards e-books shapes the student experience. It is therefore important that LRC staff work closely with teaching staff to convince them of their value to students.

So how will this research project change the way that HE students are supported at City of Bristol College? Building on this research, the LRC will continue to work closely with teaching staff to ensure that e-book workshops are delivered to first year students. Good links, particularly from course pages on Blackboard, will be crucial, as will promotion by LRC staff. The LRC will endeavour to obtain more relevant e-book titles, to address the concerns raised about the lack of appropriate texts available. A further research project is also planned, following the Early Childhood Studies, Business and Administration students into their second year, and extending the original research to include two technical programmes taught at the college.

It is hoped that these research projects, as well as changes to the information literacy programme, will help HE in FE students at the City of Bristol to fully utilize all of the advantages of e-books in the very near future.

Using the virtual learning environment to encourage e-book use: the experience at Yeovil College

Introduction

Despite the many advantages of e-books, such as those identified by students and staff at City of Bristol College, there can be some difficulties in encouraging learners to engage with them initially. For example, at a recent focus group at Yeovil College, a learner made the comment, 'I don't really get on with e-books', even in a situation where there was little choice but to use the e-format because there were insufficient printed copies of their desired texts in the Library.

LRC staff need to explore this attitude further to establish why some learners just 'do not get on with e-books'. Is it that they cannot log in to them, find it difficult to search for the right book, do not like reading from the screen, or are restricted to printing too little? Is the requirement to have either a computer or an e-reader available to access them the real issue? Or is it ultimately the need to get used to something new and different, rather than continuing to use a resource that has been comfortable to access for most learners from childhood – the printed book?

In fact, it is likely to be a combination of factors – but LRC staff can strongly influence attitudes and approaches to e-books in order to give a more positive impression. At Yeovil College, a range of initiatives have been put in place to promote engagement by both learners and teaching staff. For example, as City of Bristol College have found, information skills sessions are the ideal way to provide information on how to access and navigate e-book platforms, and a range of sessions have been offered at Yeovil College, which include drop-in sessions and sessions delivered to groups to support specific assignments.

The LRC also carries out awareness-raising activities, for example regularly producing posters, instructional guidelines and newsletters to inform the wider community of the growth of the e-book collection – including an 'E-book of the week'. In addition, pictures of book covers have been embedded in the relevant sections of the college VLE. Learners can click on the image of the cover and are directed straight to that particular e-book. Feedback from learners shows that this is an appealing way of accessing e-books, and is also an easier option for those with poor information literacy skills.

Support from teaching staff is also essential to make e-books a success. Students are encouraged to engage with e-books when they form part of the recommended reading provided by their tutor, and co-operation is required to ensure that titles are embedded in the relevant space on the VLE. At Yeovil College tutors have been sent lists of the specific e-book titles that are available in their subject areas, so that these can then be brought to the attention of students.

However, one of the most effective ways to persuade students that e-books are useful for their study is to ensure that there are relevant, easy-to-access links embedded in the space where they carry out a large proportion of their independent learning, the course-specific areas of the virtual learning environment.

Virtual learning at Yeovil College

It is now commonplace in FE to use a VLE as a focus for curriculum-based information, which learners can access at times that suit their learning style. The take-up of VLEs was fuelled by allocations of funds to FE specifically for this purpose in 2001 (JISC, 2003). The past decade has seen teacher engagement within technology and the increasing sophistication of VLEs, adding more value to the educational process.

At the same time, there has been a shift in emphasis towards learners being more self-directed in their study. An increased use of personal learning plans and blended learning techniques, and an emphasis on informal learning mechanisms, all support this goal. Yeovil College, in common with many other further education colleges, uses the VLE platform Moodle to support all aspects of curriculum activity. This includes provision of course pages, homework, assessment activities, reports, initial assessments, personal learning plans and work portfolios.

Strategically it is important that LRCs are at the heart of teaching and learning within the further education college and that they have a key role in organizing the development of the college VLE as an educational tool. The learning resources manager should be able to influence the way in which all learning resources, not just e-books, are embedded, organized, developed and promoted within the VLE for all courses, at all levels and for all learners.

The very nature of VLEs lends them to easy accessibility by learners on-campus, at off-site locations and, critically to learners, at home or in the workplace. There is an opportunity for LRCs to capitalize on this accessibility and enhance the overall learning experience by integrating key curriculum texts into spaces within the VLE.

This could be achieved by simply adding reading lists to VLE pages and linking them back to the library catalogue. The National e-Book Observatory study (JISC, 2009) shows that e-books are most likely to be used by those who actively seek them through a library catalogue. However, it is important to recognize that this study was conducted within the HE community. Learners in the FE environment are studying at a lower academic level; often their course of study does not require independent research beyond the recommended texts, and any such research is often carried out in the simplest way available, through using a search engine such as Google. Therefore LRC staff may find that simply making the catalogue available through the VLE will not be enough to engage learners with e-book content.

An alternative is to embed links to specific e-book titles at key points of learning contact within the VLE, actively promoting these titles to learners. This could be through links added to a page dedicated specifically to learning resources, or the titles could be linked to a page embedded within a teaching course for a specific subject.

Embedding e-books in a generic learning resource centre course

LRC staff may prefer to create a course dedicated to LRC services, and then embed links to e-books within it. There are benefits to this approach; for example it means that there is a single place to which learners can be referred, making it easier for LRC staff to carry out training and answer enquiries. A single generic course allows for easy upkeep and development, as it means that housekeeping and checking the accessibility of resources can be done without keeping a record of where each has been linked in multiple subject-based courses. It also means that housekeeping can be carried out without having to access teachers' pages (which can be difficult to achieve) and the resources or layout can be changed without the explicit permission of teachers.

The main disadvantage of this approach is likely to be lack of use. In the FE sector the amount of information that learners have to find and use independently is currently limited, and if they are allowed to cite information found through 'quick and dirty' searches on Google (Brophy, 2004; Rowlands and Nicholas, 2008), then it is unlikely that they will exert energy on accessing a generic course on the VLE and trawling through several pages of resources that may be irrelevant to them.

A less obvious disadvantage of having a single generic learning resource page is the over-enthusiastic librarian who will continue to add resource after resource without considering how the learner is going to find what is actually relevant to them. It may be necessary to set appropriate boundaries and policies on how much material may be listed to avoid creating an unusable resource. As Emma Ransley, Deputy Learning Resources Manager, says:

> When I arrived at Yeovil College there was a huge web-based resource site, which at first glance looked fantastic. But greater investigation found that learners just did not use it and the 'hit' counts per page were low. The reason was investigated and it seemed that too much information was confusing learners, who did not want to look through lots of irrelevant links before finding the one that suits. Ironically this is exactly what they would go ahead and do with the results of a Google search anyway.

Embedding e-books in a subject-specific teaching course

The approach of embedding e-books into the main course page for a subject again has advantages and disadvantages. The key positive aspect of doing this is the ease of access to relevant e-books for all learners studying that particular subject. Learners often find it hard to carry out independent research effectively, and embedding pre-selected links overcomes this problem. However, this approach may not be appropriate for all courses, especially as in some cases it may be integral to the course to aim for developing independent research skills.

It follows that this approach could be implemented in different ways depending on the long-term outcome required:

1 Relevant e-books could be embedded into the course page throughout the course of study, for fully supported learning.
2 Specific e-books could be embedded in year one and then links to a relevant e-book collection or database provided in year two, promoting greater independence in a staged approach.
3 A link to a relevant e-book collection or database could be added from the beginning of the course and additional independent research encouraged from this point.

The primary disadvantage of embedding resources within subject-specific course pages is the time that learning resource staff will need to spend on tracking the links to ensure that they are all kept up to date. A college may host in excess of a thousand VLE courses and it would be hugely challenging to keep track of all of them with limited staffing.

A compromise solution

Yeovil College has attempted to find a compromise by implementing elements of the two principal approaches described above. Teaching staff retain control over their course pages, but LRC staff have set up their own subject-specific resource pages under broad themes within Moodle. These pages are then meta-linked to the relevant course-specific pages. For example, there might be ten separate courses for Biology within Moodle: an AS level course, an A level course, courses for different sets, courses for evening classes and so on. However, there will be just a single learning resource page for Biology, meta-linked to all ten individual course pages, significantly reducing the need for housekeeping.

In the future, changing business models for e-books may mean that there is less need for LRC staff to decide where best to place links. Increasingly it is possible to review and purchase just one chapter of an e-book, making it economically viable for learners to download and save their own material. The next step on from this will be the ability to create customized resources from a series of chapters from various e-books, producing a tailored solution for specific courses, which is likely to be of interest only to the learners studying that programme, and will reduce the need for them to spend time hunting for relevant material.

Conclusion

In both City of Bristol and Yeovil Colleges, the crucial role of LRC staff in engaging both teachers and students with e-books is made clear. The relative invisibility of the e-format means that it is necessary to raise awareness of their very existence through a range of promotional activities aimed at all parts of the college community, as well as by pointing out to teachers that e-books can provide answers to some of the problems of access to learning resources that are common in the FE sector.

The next stage of the process is to ensure that learners have the skills to find and use e-books, through information skills training at various levels. Finally, the right e-books need to be made available in the college's VLE, which the majority of students now use to access curriculum resources at a time and location to suit their learning style and individual circumstances.

Bibliography

Bristol:

Briddon, J. et al. (2009) 'E-books are Good if There are No Copies Left': a survey of e-book usage at UWE Library Services, *Library and Information Research*, **33** (104), 45–65.

Jamali, H. R., Nicholas, D. and Rowlands, I. (2009) Scholarly E-books: the views of 16,000 academics: results from the JISC National e-Book Observatory,

Aslib Proceedings, **61** (1), 33–47.

JISC (2009) *JISC National E-books Observatory Project: key findings and recommendations, final report.*

Nicholas, D. et al. (2008) UK Scholarly E-book Usage: a landmark survey, *Aslib Proceedings*, **60** (4), 311-34.

Rowlands, I., Nicholas, D., Jamali, H. and Huntington, P. (2007) What do Faculty and Students Really Think about E-books?, *Aslib Proceedings*, **59** (6), 489-511.

Yeovil:

Abdullah, N. and Gibbs, F. (2006) A Survey of E-book Awareness and Usage amongst Students in an Academic Library. In *Proceedings of International Conference of Multidisciplinary Information Sciences and Technologies*, 25–8 October, Merida, Spain, http://strathprints.strath.ac.uk/2280/1/strathprints002280.pdf.

Brophy, P. (2004) Evaluating the Joint Information Systems Committee's Information Environment: the EDNER and EDNER+ projects, *Vine*, **34** (4), 143-7.

JISC (2003) Virtual Learning Environment Activity in Further Education in the UK, www.jisc.ac.uk/media/documents/programmes/buildmlehefe/vleinfe.pdf.

JISC (2009) *Libraries of the Future: a vision for the academic library and information services of the future*, www.jisc.ac.uk/news/stories/2010/01/lotf.aspx.

Rowlands, I. and Nicholas, D. (2008) *Information Behaviour of the Researcher of the Future - executive summary*, CIBER briefing paper, UCL, www.jisc.ac.uk/media/documents/programmes/reppres/gg_final_keynote_11012008.pdf.

13
Engaging staff and students with e-books in a university setting

Anne Worden and Timothy Collinson

Introduction

This chapter outlines the strategies in place at the University of Portsmouth that have led to a 1700% increase in e-book use between 2004–5 and 2009–10, with just under 2 million pages viewed in the 2009–10 academic year. Results from a 2009 survey of 1111 students are presented, together with a brief snapshot of feedback from academic staff as well as ebrary usage statistics, all of which help to provide a summary of the state of engagement with e-books at Portsmouth.

An online survey about e-book use carried out at the University in 2005 elicited 110 responses from students. In contrast to results obtained in several other surveys of e-book use in universities (e.g. Abdullah and Gibb, 2006; Briddon et al., 2009), the largest percentage of replies (40%) was from the Faculty of Humanities and Social Sciences, and the next largest from the Faculty of Technology (at 24%). The response rate suggested that Humanities and Social Sciences students were heavy users of e-books, and this was confirmed by tracking Athens account prefixes and ebrary log-ins by department. This is a departmental usage pattern that has been prevalent at Portsmouth ever since.

Meanwhile, Portsmouth has had the second highest ebrary use of all UK universities for three consecutive years. It was decided to investigate the reasons behind this clear indication of the enthusiasm for e-books at Portsmouth, so the faculties with the highest usage rates were selected for a survey in spring 2009.

Background context

The University of Portsmouth is a post-1992 university with 21,000 students, including distance learners located both in the UK and around the world. There are five faculties which are, in order of size: Humanities and Social Sciences (HSS); Science; Business; Technology; and Creative and Cultural Industries. There are five faculty librarians, plus a law librarian, who are responsible for stock selection, academic liaison and information literacy training for their particular faculty or department.

In 2004 the Library began a trial of e-books, and by spring 2009 there were around 40,000 titles available, the bulk of which were from ebrary's Academic Complete collection, but also included 2000 titles purchased from MyiLibrary and around 100 books from NetLibrary. The University Library has purchased no e-books for handheld reader devices as yet.

The survey

To encourage completion, the survey took up just one side of A4 paper, and, for comparative purposes, repeated a number of questions from the 2005 survey. Distribution on paper was chosen rather than asking participants to fill in an online survey as this approach had resulted in higher response rates in previous research. Because the Library wanted to capture views from whole cohorts, regardless of whether they were e-book users or not, co-operation was sought from academics to allow faculty librarians to drop in at the beginning or end of lectures to give the survey to students – a methodology that also favoured the distribution of the survey on paper.

Students responded anonymously but were asked to state their course, level of study and gender so that the possibility of these as variables could be analysed. A total of 1111 responses were received, 835 from HSS and 208 from Technology. The subject breakdown is given in Table 13.1.

A further 68 responses were obtained from international students, mainly from China, studying English Language plus International Trade. These responses were tracked separately to see whether there was any difference between responses from international students and those of students from the UK.

The survey found that 90% of student respondents across the two faculties were using e-books to a greater or lesser extent in their academic

Table 13.1 *Subject area studied and gender of students submitting responses to survey*

Subject area	Male students	Female students	Total for subject
Childhood and Youth Studies	2	22	24
Criminology	22	48	70
English Literature	52	187	239
History	30	31	61
Languages and Area Studies	71	136	207
Politics/International Relations	77	40	117
Sociology	26	60	86
HSS MA	9	22	31
Humanities and Social Sciences Total	*289*	*546*	*835*
Technology	166	28	194
Technology MSc	14	0	14
Technology Total	*180*	*28*	*208*

work (compared with 78.5% in 2005), with 42% of female HSS students, 40% of male HSS students, 25% of international students and 20% of Technology students claiming to use them for every assignment. This figure rose to 51% for first year HSS students, supporting the finding reported by Bryant and Caporn in Chapter 12 that first year students were more engaged with e-books than second years (see Figure 13.1 overleaf).

Ebrary usage statistics show that use varies significantly throughout the year with certain months, such as January and May, and certain days, for example the Monday before the Christmas vacation, experiencing the highest use. The academic year is divided into two semesters at Portsmouth, so January and May are the times when most students are submitting work for end of semester deadlines (see Figure 13.2). This highly seasonal pattern of e-book use in universities is highlighted in the executive summary of the JISC National e-Book Observatory Project report (JISC, 2009), which notes that variation from month to month can exceed 50%.

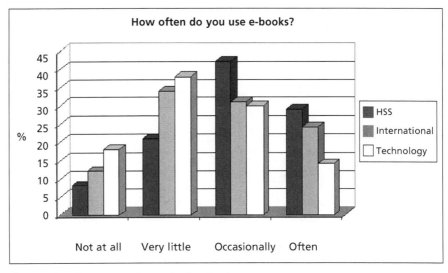

Figure 13.1 *Frequency of use of e-books*

When asked how useful they found e-books in relation to their academic course, 71% of female HSS students, 65% of male HSS students, 62% of international students, 60% of HSS postgraduate students and 50% of

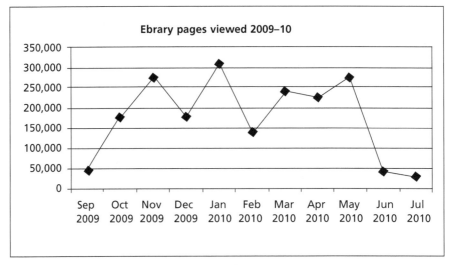

Figure 13.2 *Ebrary usage by month for academic year 2009–10*

Technology students chose either 'very useful' or 'quite useful'. (Again, it should be noted that first year HSS students were the course level that indicated most enthusiasm for e-books, with 76% choosing 'very useful' or 'quite useful'.)

The subject groups which found e-books most useful were Politics/International Relations and English Literature. These two groups also tended to use e-books most often and therefore the Portsmouth 'super-users' of e-books could be deemed to be female and studying either Politics or Literature, in contrast with the findings of the JISC Observatory (JISC, 2009), which found male students, and those in the subject areas of Business and Engineering, more likely to be the super-users. It is noteworthy that Rowlands et al. (2007, 490) in their literature review covering other e-book surveys report only Gibbs' (2001–2) finding that Literature was 'among the most popular subject areas'. Indeed, Nicholas et al. (2008, 314) report Levine-Clark's (2006) finding of greater awareness of e-books among humanities users but note that this 'did not translate to greater use'. In their 2006 online survey of 1372 students at the University of Strathclyde, Abdullah and Gibb (2006) report only 2% of responses coming from students studying humanities subjects and imply that these students are less interested because they are less comfortable with online resources. The next section proposes some possible reasons for the difference observed at Portsmouth.

Why are students, particularly in Humanities and Social Sciences, so engaged with e-books at Portsmouth?

In Chapter 12 Caporn and Bryant list factors that make e-books popular with foundation degree students in an FE college, and some of the same factors are cited by undergraduate and postgraduate students at Portsmouth. Convenience, accessibility and ease of searching all feature prominently in responses from users at Portsmouth.

Although convenience is the number one reason for both HSS and Technology students, two other reasons stand out that are more pertinent to the subject studied. For HSS students, the fact that relevant printed books have already been taken out by others is the second most common reason; one Languages final year student commented: 'So useful, especially if it's a book everyone on the course needs and there are not enough hard copies.' For Technology students on the other hand, the fact that they simply prefer to access information online is a significant reason. Meanwhile, for international students, ease of searching is the number one reason for using e-books. Figure 13.3 shows the relative distribution of responses.

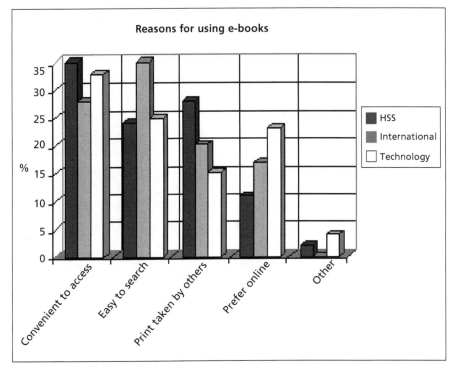

Figure 13.3 *Reasons for using e-books*

There are also some categories of user who particularly benefit from the availability of e-books, for example distance learners. When ebrary usage statistics for Portsmouth are examined to identify the most popular books accessed, those required for distance learning courses dominate the top ten every year. It has also been noticeable that when new distance learning courses have been set up over the past five years, lecturers have deliberately populated reading lists with items that are available in our e-book collections. Naturally, the convenience factor that makes e-books ideal for distance learners is also appreciated by non-distance learners who sometimes find it difficult to get to the university library as often as they might wish. One student, for example, commented:

> As a mature student living outside the city and with domestic commitments it is not always convenient to travel to the library so e-books are a very useful asset. (MSc Computing student)

We will now look at four key factors which we believe have been highly significant in creating the high usage of e-books at Portsmouth.

Influence of lecturers

Within a year of e-books becoming available in Portsmouth the Faculty Librarian for HSS subjects began running hands-on sessions for subject groupings of lecturers in order to convince them of the benefits of e-books. Lecturers at these sessions quickly discovered how the collection available on ebrary could go some way towards meeting their reading list needs. Some older staff, who might previously have been regarded as late adopters of new technology, surprised their colleagues by their enthusiastic adoption of e-books that they had discovered as key weekly reading for their units. When asked why e-books were so popular with their students, one of the Politics lecturers commented:

> X introduces them to e-books in Level 1 Semester 1 and his reading lists reflect this . . . . The fact that his units come at the start ensures that students are very exposed to e-books. And as they like them they then take that knowledge into the rest of their units.

It should be noted that Dr X is one of the older, enthusiastic adopters and one of the books on his reading list, Modern Political Thought: a reader, has consistently been in the top ten ebrary books accessed at Portsmouth for the past four years.

The Portsmouth survey findings showed that 18% of female HSS students, 25% of male HSS students, 20% of international students and 31% of Technology students first found out about e-books through their lecturers, whose influence cannot be underestimated. Briddon et al. (2009, 63) state: 'As academic staff are likely to be instrumental in drawing students' attention to e-books, promoting e-books firstly to academics is likely to reap the highest rewards.' The evidence from usage patterns at Portsmouth supports this case, as do the experiences at the University of Surrey mentioned in Chapter 9 and at City of Bristol College mentioned in Chapter 12 in this book.

It is evident that HSS lecturers now regard e-books as an essential element of course provision. For example, lecturers now typically respond to student complaints about not having enough print copies of course texts by stating that the Library invests in e-books in order to give all students the chance of accessing relevant information. Also, when the results of this survey were presented at the 2009 HSS Faculty Learning and Teaching conference, lecturers were asked to use an interactive voting system to give feedback. In answer to the question, 'Can you see the benefits of e-books in your students' work?', 84% of those present replied 'Yes'.

The library factor

Alongside convincing academics of the benefits of e-books, the 2009 survey results indicate another probable reason behind the high usage – hands-on training sessions given by librarians. A total of 47% of male HSS students and 46% of female HSS students responded that they first found out about e-books in a library lecture or workshop. For Year 1 HSS students this rose to 53% and for HSS postgraduates it rose to 58%. In contrast, only 13% of Technology students and 32% of international students chose this option and both these groups had lower usage overall.

Whilst Technology and international students are introduced to e-books during a lecture that also includes many other library topics, both undergraduate and postgraduate students in HSS are timetabled to attend hands-on workshops run by their librarian, which cover e-books and e-journals, during the early stages of their courses. The survey findings appear to suggest that information literacy training that includes hands-on practice is giving HSS students encouragement to use e-books for their academic work (see Table 13.2).

Table 13.2 *Source of initial discovery of e-books*

Discovery method	HSS female, %	HSS male, %	HSS international, %	Technology, %
Library sources	61.5	59	56	24
Faculty sources	27	32	3	36
Other students	10	7	13	18
Other	1.5	2	0	22

Both the UCL SuperBook study (Rowlands et al., 2007) and the JISC National e-Books Observatory (Nicholas et al., 2008) found library sources, then lecturers, to be the main methods of initial discovery. So, whilst lecturer influence is important, the contrasting findings between the HSS and Technology departments in the Portsmouth survey seem to indicate that a hands-on introduction as part of a library workshop can lead to even greater use.

Volume of e-books

The third key factor that has encouraged student engagement with e-books at Portsmouth is the sheer number of books available (40,000 at the time of the survey but at least 15,000 from the outset). This means that many students are able to find something to help them whenever they search the online collections. Visibility is high because all of Portsmouth's e-books are available on the library catalogue and there are prominent links to e-books on the front page of the library website. The importance of this factor is highlighted by Nicholas et al. (2008) when reporting the finding of the JISC National e-Books Observatory that the use of catalogued e-books is double that of books not on the catalogue.

Facilities within e-books

The final reason for the popularity of e-books at Portsmouth may be the availability of additional features. Ebrary includes tools that allow students to make notes, use virtual highlighter pens, apply sticky notes to pages and add useful items to a personal bookshelf accessible wherever they are working. These facilities are popular with students, particularly once pointed out to them in training sessions. Of the Portsmouth students who responded to a survey question about ebrary tools, one-third of HSS students selected the highlighter pen as their favourite, with copy-and-paste being the second most popular tool. In contrast, one-third of Technology students chose copy-and-paste as their favourite tool, with highlighter pens coming second, closely followed by dictionary definitions. A Computing MSc student commented that 'being able to cut-and-paste both the quote and the details for the reference cuts down on errors and typos', whilst a final year Literature student wrote that 'it is easy to bookmark pages and highlight [them] so that you can go back to research [quickly]'.

Keyword searching is another feature of e-books that students value highly. A final year Sociology student commented: 'The word search is very useful and often saves time reading irrelevant pages.' However, the second part of this quote illustrates one of the pedagogic concerns about e-books that have been raised in various articles; although students perceive keyword searching to be a time-saving feature, lecturers worry about the consequences of the resulting highly targeted quotation grabbing. Briddon et al. (2009) note lecturers' concerns that keyword searching results in students taking information out of context and possibly drawing incorrect conclusions, while Walton (2008, 27) comments that 'in a cut-and-paste world, critical thinking is lacking'.

A time for 'e' and a time for print

Despite the popularity of and support for e-books at Portsmouth, neither staff nor students are ready to go down the e-only route just yet. When replying to the question, 'Given a choice, which would you prefer to use?', with the options 'e-book', 'printed book', 'no preference' and 'it depends', 56% of student respondents said that they would prefer a printed book (rising to 63% for HSS), whilst 16% chose the e-book option. A comment from a final year Literature student appears to sum up the feelings of many students across HSS: 'I think they're useful and easy to access, however I personally prefer printed books.' When polled with the same question during the 2009 HSS Learning and Teaching Conference, 48% of lecturers chose printed books, with only 5% choosing e-books.

However, the survey also recorded a preference for reading e-books on-screen from 65% of HSS female respondents, 72% of both HSS male respondents and Technology respondents and 78% of international respondents, which reflect the JISC Observatory findings that e-books are read mainly on-screen (Nicholas et al., 2008). It could be, therefore, that users in an academic context are becoming more comfortable with on-screen reading or it could be that the preferences of the 'millennial' generation for reading on-screen are starting to emerge, as reported by Buzzetto-More, Sweat-Guy and Elobaid (2007, 244): 'Ninety-eight percent of the respondents reported that they feel comfortable reading off a computer screen.'

Overall, 9% of student respondents and 47% of lecturers surveyed indicated that their use of e-books would depend on circumstances. Typical comments included:

> For reading I prefer printed copies. For extracting quotes, e-books are better.
> (Politics year 1)

> When revising I prefer to have a hard copy. (Computing final year)

> Large books are better to read from paper copy – foreign language sources are easier to read from paper copy. (Languages year 2)

This final quote about foreign language texts being easier to read in printed form may indicate why the international students' selection of the option 'Depends on circumstances' was double that of other students, at 19%.

Literature students' comments also reveal that they clearly differentiate between primary and secondary sources when choosing between print books and e-books:

> For reading a novel, I would have a printed version, but for research I would use an e-book. (Literature year 1)

> For critical works yes, but literary texts no. (Literature year 2)

Student use of e-books for extracting quick facts rather than extended reading, which comes through in a number of comments in the

Portsmouth survey in addition to the example shown above, is also one of the findings highlighted in the JISC Observatory (JISC, 2009, 6). The executive summary of the report comments: 'They are being used as though they are encyclopedias or dictionaries rather than extended continuous text.'

What is stopping students using e-books?

One part of the survey asked about reasons for not using e-books. Surprisingly, the most common reason chosen by Technology students was that they were not aware of e-books: 24% chose that option. In contrast, only 8% of male HSS students chose that option, although it was still their most common reason for not using e-books. For female HSS students the most common reason for not using e-books was that they were put off by technology; 10% chose this option.

Free-text comments provide other clues about what students do not like about e-books. The most common negative points raised were:

- *Computer access problems*: 37 comments received, typical examples being: 'Takes too long to load – then crashes' (Politics year 2) and 'Complicated login method' (Languages and Area Studies final year).
- *Not enough e-books*: 37 comments received, a typical example being: 'Not always the books I need' (English Literature year 1).
- *Preference for print books*: 21 comments received, a typical example being: 'Don't like reading off computer, prefer holding book – paper. I find it easier to make notes' (Languages year 2).
- *Discomfort with reading on a computer screen*: 17 comments received, typical examples being: 'Reading computer screens hurts my eyes after a short time' (Technology final year) and 'Sitting at the PC for hours really hurts your back' (Languages and Area Studies final year).

Since the survey took place, Shibboleth authentication has been fully implemented for ebrary, which means that users no longer need to log in as an extra step on-campus at the point when they choose to connect to e-books. In addition, ebrary introduced their Quick View facility, which means that users no longer need to download a separate e-book reader onto their home computer if they wish to read e-books. These two measures should mean that many of the computer access problems are no longer experienced. Easier access should, in turn, lead to even greater use of e-books.

Perhaps surprisingly, none of the respondents explicitly mentioned being unable to download e-books for reading offline or in transit, although many studies have mentioned the need to be online in order to access e-books as a disadvantage (Tedd, 2005; Ball, 2009; JISC, 2009; Soules, 2009). Possibly other technical difficulties have eclipsed this as an issue of primary concern.

Conclusion

Overall, evidence from both the survey and usage statistics indicates that e-books have become a very useful academic tool at Portsmouth. In the words of Nicholas et al. (2008, 333): 'The e-book revolution has already happened . . . the touch-paper has been lit.' Owing to a combination of both lecturer and library input, students in Humanities and Social Sciences – the subject areas that traditionally account for the highest print book use in libraries – have become highly engaged with e-books and are the reason why Portsmouth has a leading place in the UK table of use for ebrary e-books.

E-books are firmly embedded in the information landscape of both students and staff because of the convenience of being able to access them whenever and wherever they want; this is particularly valued by groups such as part-time students, mature students, distance learners and disabled students, who can find accessing the physical library problematic. Specific features of e-books such as virtual highlighter pens, bookmarks and bookshelves enhance the user experience, by allowing them to replicate their behaviour with printed books. Meanwhile, the ability to search for individual words and phrases and to use copy and paste greatly assists those students who may be completing assignments just before the submission deadline.

As student numbers have grown, e-books have become the only practical way to meet demand, reducing complaints and increasing student satisfaction. They have become a crucial way of ensuring that students are able to complete their assignments using academic sources, so much so that they would like even more books on their reading lists to be made available online, ensuring fair access for all. The words of an MSc Computing student underline two key benefits for students: 'There is no waiting time and the stress of having a printed copy recalled is eliminated', while a first year Literature student neatly encapsulates the principal reasons why students love e-books: 'Easier to find relevant information for my essays and never out on loan when really needed.'

Acknowledgements

We wish to thank Sarah Weston, the Data Management Assistant at the University of Portsmouth Library, and Chris Jones and Sara Bowler of 2info, ebrary's UK re-seller, for their help in gaining access to usage data.

Bibliography

Abdullah, N. and Gibb, F. (2006) A Survey of E-book Awareness and Usage amongst Students in an Academic Library. In *Proceedings of International Conference of Multidisciplinary Information Sciences and Technologies*, 25–8 October, Merida, Spain, http://strathprints.strath.ac.uk/2280/1/strathprints002280.pdf.

Abdullah, N. and Gibb, F. (2008) Students' Attitudes Towards E-books in a Scottish Higher Education Institute: part 2, *Library Review*, **57** (9), 676–89.

Armstrong, C. and Lonsdale, R. (2010) E-books – a way to go, *Library & Information Update*, July, 30–2.

Ball, R. (2009) E-books in Practice: the librarian's perspective, *Learned Publishing*, **22** (1), 18–22.

Briddon, J. et al. (2009) 'E-books are Good if There are No Copies Left': a survey of e-book usage at UWE Library Services, *Library and Information Research*, **33** (104), 45–65.

Buzzetto-More, N., Sweat-Guy, R. and Elobaid, M. (2007) Reading in a Digital Age: e-books are students ready for this learning object?, *Interdisciplinary Journal of Knowledge and Learning Objects*, **3**, 239–50.

Carlock, D. M. and Perry, A. M. (2008) Exploring Faculty Experiences with E-books: a focus group, *Library Hi Tech*, **26** (2), 244–54.

Dillon, D. (2001) E-books: the University of Texas experience, part 1, *Library Hi Tech*, **19** (2), 113-24.

Gibbs, N. J. (2001-2) Ebooks Two Years Later: the North Carolina State University perspective, *Against the Grain*, **13** (6), 22-6.

JISC (2009) *JISC National E-books Observatory Project: key findings and recommendations, final report.*

Levine-Clark, M. (2006) Electronic Book Usage: a survey at the University of Denver, *Libraries and the Academy*, **6** (3), 285-99.

Mayfield, I. (2006) *Opening the E-library: a pilot on the impact of electronic books on learning and teaching*, unpublished internal document, University of Portsmouth.

Nicholas, D. et al. (2008) UK Scholarly E-book Usage: a landmark survey, *Aslib Proceedings*, **60** (4), 311-34.

Rowlands, I. et al. (2007) What do Faculty and Students Really Think about E-books?, *Aslib Proceedings*, **59** (6), 489-511.

Safley, E. (2006) Demand for E-books in an Academic Library, *Journal of Library Administration*, **45** (3), 445-57.

Soules, A. (2009) The Shifting Landscape of E-books, *New Library World*, **110** (1/2), 7-21.

Tedd, L. A. (2005) E-books in Academic Libraries: an international overview, *New Review of Academic Librarianship*, **11** (1), 57-79.

Walton, E. W. (2008) From the ACRL 13th National Conference: e-book use versus users' perspective, *College & Undergraduate Libraries*, **14** (4), 19-35.

Part 5
The future of e-books

Contributors' views

To elicit a range of views on the future of e-books, two questions were asked of contributors:

- What needs to change before e-books become universally and easily read?
- What will the e-book landscape look like in ten years' time?

Without exception, the contributors to this book predict a rapidly increasing uptake of e-books, facilitated by the spread of internet-enabled mobile devices. However, most contributors feel that in order to make e-books a truly universal feature of leisure, study and work, improvements in standardization and usability, combined with an easing of DRM restrictions, are essential.

Chris Armstrong and Ray Lonsdale

To help achieve greater universal use, the range of e-book publishing needs to extend more broadly across the disciplines to ensure an adequate critical mass for academic non-fiction (in particular in the arts and the humanities), general non-fiction and both general and genre fiction. Another area for growth would be in the primary and secondary school sectors, especially for the lower key stages and less academic children. To encourage greater use, there need to be significant improvements in the screen and navigation interface, principally to allow more content to be visible on the screen as well as in catering for users with special needs, such as those with visual impairments or specific learning difficulties. Greater, and perhaps more imaginative, interactive content is required, not only for fiction but for non-fiction, and this will necessitate the development of new authoring skills and possibly a shift in the traditional publisher–author relationship. The development of systematic bibliographic listings for commercial and free e-books will facilitate easier selection and thus easier use. So far as libraries are concerned, one of the major hurdles has been adding e-book MARC records to their catalogues, and publishers must continue to address this.

In ten years' time, e-books will no longer be the occasionally used exception, but an expected part of book collections in all kinds of libraries, although print will probably still dominate. In this period, too, we can expect to see a greater emphasis on the born digital e-book, offering enhanced interactivity. Users will be considerably more *au fait* with the format, having acquired familiarity and the fundamental skills to successfully exploit e-book collections. We would expect to see much greater use of handheld e-book readers, probably converging to a new model with aspects of both iPad and e-book reader and probably owned by users as a consequence of reduced pricing. Libraries will provide loans through download access to their e-book collections. The lending of pre-loaded readers will diminish. Whilst not necessarily condoning the idea, it seems likely that there will be a convergence of e-formats (e.g. e-books, e-journals, e-audio books) into e-content, or at the very least aggregators will be making many formats available together on one platform.

Lee Bryant and Sue Caporn

As our research at the City of Bristol College shows, students are now prepared to read from the screen. Although this was not their perception prior to use, their responses after using e-books for their assignments clearly demonstrated that they were comfortable in doing so. As the age of first contact with technology continues to decrease, it is likely that the ease with which people read from the screen will only continue to increase. In addition, technology is becoming more mobile with smartphones becoming the norm and with the iPad on the market. Access to laptops is now commonplace and arguably replacing the desktop as the standard access to technology. These factors suggest a bright future for e-books and it is not difficult to imagine a similar move from print to e-books as has already happened in music with the move from CDs to MP3 files.

This raises a number of issues not dissimilar from those faced by the moving images and music industries. These issues include copyright, cost and ease of download. These have not yet been fully resolved by these industries and which are unlikely to be resolved by publishers in the near future. However, just as in other industries, publishers will have to embrace the technology in order to survive. Pricing models need to be established that are viable for publishers, but also affordable for academic institutions and individual customers. To meet the mobile, connected needs of the students and consumers of the future, a shift from paper to electronic format will be essential.

James Clay

Predicting the future is always difficult. However, if we look at other sectors we can see that digital versions of traditional media often result in new and exciting ways of consuming those products. YouTube, iTunes, Freeview and BBC iPlayer show how the format and delivery of audiovisual media has fundamentally changed the film and television viewing experience. We can now access video at a time and place to suit us, download it, and play it back on a range of devices. There are also trends for music lovers to download individual tracks rather than buying complete albums, and for television viewers to buy boxed sets of television series on DVD rather than watching the series as it is broadcast. Importantly, despite this ease of access to digital and time-shifted versions, a great many people still enjoy a trip to the cinema, still want to sit down on the sofa and watch television programmes as they are broadcast, and still like to listen to music on the radio.

We can expect that the same will happen with books and e-books: the format, delivery and consumption of books will change in the future. The exact details of this can be intelligently guessed at, but nobody knows for sure. We just need to be ready to embrace that future.

Jim Dooley

Although forecasting the future is not without risk, it does appear possible to make certain predictions about e-book development with some confidence. Some of these predictions come from the general development of e-books during the past ten years. Others come from changes in technology and modes of scholarly communication. The main prediction is that the e-book marketplace will continue to mature in the following ways:

- Publishers will increasingly see e-books as an important contributor and not as a threat to their income.
- E-books and print books will increasingly be published simultaneously.
- E-books will increasingly be published DRM-free so the user experience will be similar for all vendors.
- Born digital e-books with active linking to source documents, audio, video and so on will become much more common.
- Open standards such as XML will increasingly replace proprietary systems.
- Electronic content will be increasingly disaggregated.
- E-books and e-journals will look increasingly similar and be available on the same interfaces.
- E-book packages will act more like databases and less like collections of discrete objects.
- New business and pricing models will be developed in response to these factors.
- Increasing amounts of digital content will be optimized for use on mobile devices.
- There will be buy-outs, mergers and sales among e-book providers.

Several other predictions can also be made with reasonable certainty. One is that mass digitization will have an increasingly significant impact on libraries and readers regardless of the outcome of the litigation in the USA involving Google. The impact will be felt differently in different countries because of variations in copyright laws, but ultimately large numbers of digitized works will become available. This will greatly increase access to texts that are not widely held and significantly affect the way in which scholarship is conducted. For example, it will be possible to use data-mining techniques to search massive numbers of titles at the same time. Mass digitization will also require libraries to address how they manage extensive duplicate collections of print monographs.

The development of a new generation of portable e-book readers promises to increase interest in and use of e-books. Many of these devices have page-turning mechanisms that mimic the way a person reads a printed book. Over time, this is likely to challenge the conventional wisdom that people will not read entire books on a screen. Current practices of selling e-books in the retail sector for less than the cost of a print book will also attract customers.

Another reasonably certain prediction is that interest in e-textbooks will increase significantly. Responding to user complaints about printed textbooks, most publishers now offer some e-textbooks. Consensus regarding pricing and access models has yet to develop, but this will emerge in response to market forces in a relatively short time.

The final prediction is that, based on the above, acceptance of e-books by users and libraries will increase at a rapid pace. E-books will not replace print books, but they will become an increasingly important format for the dissemination of information.

Karen Foster and Emma Ransley

In FE the question of what needs to change in order for e-books to become more universally used is simply answered; core textbooks need to be made available in e-formats, as there is a significant lack of suitable material for learners studying English qualifications (for example, National Vocational Qualification Levels 1 to 3). In addition it would be helpful to have a more seamless experience of authentication to the e-book resources. Although Shibboleth has eradicated the need for yet another username and password, it is still not fully intuitive.

It is likely that the e-book as a static, isolated resource will no longer exist in ten years' time. Users will have the ability to create their own 'live' book or journal by accessing a selection of snippets from a variety of materials online including e-books, journals, videos and websites. The 'journal' of resources that they create will have seamless authentication and allow the user to manipulate text in ways that they can use for study or recreation. There will be no need for dedicated e-book readers or similar devices as clarity of screen resolution will be available on all mobile devices, as will the ability to project from these to tables and work surfaces for a complete mobile study experience that can be shared with others.

Karen Gravett

In the future e-books will be used more easily and more flexibly, owing to their availability through standardized platforms and discovery services. It will also be because of the relaxation of DRM restrictions meaning that e-books can be printed, e-mailed and downloaded with ease, and that they can be read on a range of different portable devices. Hardware improvements and developments in e-ink technologies will mean that on-screen readability is also improved. Publishers will also become more confident about the e-format and more e-texts will be available for purchase. Ultimately all of these positive developments will see a surge in the popularity of e-books and they will be viewed as a core resource on an equal footing to printed library collections. Information professionals will still be needed to train and support users, but this will be less focused on overcoming barriers and more time will be freed up for extended information literacy work and support.

Anna Grigson

In 1995 I wrote a dissertation looking at the future of e-books. Fifteen years later it is interesting to see what has changed, and consider what the next ten to fifteen years will bring. In the early days e-book hardware was a major limiting factor – no one wanted to read from a poor quality screen, sitting at a desktop computer. Nowadays high-quality mobile devices make it possible to carry an e-book library in your pocket. This convenience is perhaps the key driver for increased acceptance of e-books, and for many readers it is likely to outweigh any preference for reading from the printed page.

But current proprietary devices and standards are still a barrier, and in the next few years I would hope to see a move towards open standards that enable e-books to be read on a range of generic devices including phones and tablets – although some content may still be exclusive to a limited number of suppliers.

In 1995, very few texts were available as e-books. In some areas availability is still limited, but mass digitization is rapidly changing both availability and user expectations, and in the next few years it is likely to be the norm to expect all new books (and many library collections) to be online in some form.

Change will not necessarily happen at the same pace in all sectors of the market. E-books are likely to replace print for reference works, whilst fiction may continue to be published in both print and e-book form for some years. Specialist academic texts may move towards more print on demand, with textbooks disappearing to be replaced by multimedia online learning objects.

A diversity of formats will result in new business models too. No longer tied to the 'book' as the unit of sale, there will be increasingly flexible options to buy selected parts of books or to rent them on a temporary basis. In ten years' time, the book as we now know it may well have ceased to exist.

Virginia Havergal

I recently visited one of a well known chain of bookstores and was fascinated by a conversation between an 80-year-old woman and her son regarding the merits of her Sony Reader and the books she planned to download. There is no doubt that e-books and e-book readers are starting to make their mark – for me personally the advent of e-books has been an exciting development, at the very least the availability of PDF documents that I can bring together on one portable e-book reader has considerably lightened the load while traveling by train! In the future, as a personal consumer of e-resources I will be downloading from Google Books, accessing interactive versions of print-based resources according to my own needs and the nature of the situation. This is the crux of the matter for me – there will be times when I will still want a novel in print form but I want to be able to have the *choice*.

This concept of choice has significantly altered my workload as an information specialist as I seek to manage a continually evolving collection involving alternative formats, both print-based and electronic. At present, we are fortunate in the FE world to have access to a large collection of e-books made available through JISC, which has been made possible through a consortium approach. I believe that such consortium arrangements will continue to grow and will be a necessary feature of the e-book landscape, in order to address the practical implications of e-book provision as discussed in this book. For example, North Carolina libraries provide online texts (and other resources) via the NCLive portal (www.nclive.org) and this is the direction that libraries could take in the future, particularly as public libraries seek to adjust to a world of tighter budgets and limited staffing.

Whilst it is always difficult to predict the future, if libraries are to survive in the digital world it is imperative that we continue to embrace new methods of accessing and providing information to our users in an appropriate range of formats to suit their needs and the choices that they seek to make.

Günter Mühlberger

Just a year ago, after having bought a Sony Reader and read some thousands of pages on it, I had the following wish list: e-book devices should come with a much larger, coloured display so that PDF files and websites could be read easily; they should be navigated using an intuitive touch screen rather than buttons; and they should always be connected to the internet. Today, with the introduction of iPad, those wishes are fulfilled.

In ten years e-book readers or tablet PCs or whatever one may call these advanced reading devices will be as popular as TV sets. One or more will reside in every living room, offering the opportunity to comfortably read any kind of electronic text. The books themselves will offer additional features, such as links, pictures, videos and background information, and this will significantly increase the attraction of reading them electronically. Nevertheless, the e-book will not replace the printed book, but will become its alter ego. In ten years books will always come in an electronic *and* a printed version and the user will be able to decide exactly when, where and how much of either version they choose to read.

Martin Palmer

For e-books to become universally accepted, the technology needs to become simpler and more intuitive, with a single file format for downloads. Although the music and film industries almost imploded in getting to that point for their products, providers of both e-book content and hardware should use the lessons learned from digital developments in other media to provide a universal solution that will benefit consumers and publishers alike.

In ten years' time the further development of e-ink will have made the difference between print and e-books almost undetectable. As a result, a new product will have evolved offering all the benefits of digital content while still retaining everything that makes printed books so attractive, and requiring no expertise on the part of the user. There will, therefore, be no need to talk about separate e-book and print book landscapes, because they will be one and the same.

Kate Price

In order for e-books to be fully accepted in the academic environment, students and researchers must be allowed to use the contents in a way that furthers their learning and helps them in the process of synthesizing existing information to create new knowledge, recognizing that e-books may be used differently from the printed equivalent. Students and researchers must be allowed to copy parts of the text and paste this into new documents for a range of uses from writing assignments to keeping personal notes; to print out parts of the text to share, annotate, discuss and revise from; to jump quickly from page to page before identifying a part of the text to concentrate on rather than reading each page in a linear fashion; and to harvest and manipulate information in new ways to investigate trends and extrapolate data from the text itself. The current inflexible application of DRM software to many e-books often restricts these activities up front without any indication that there is any malicious or illegitimate intent, and this is causing frustration with a resource that has huge potential.

In the future, e-books will be used on multiple platforms, according to the preference of the reader and the purpose of the book. As well as accessing text in a customizable format, readers of fiction will make real time comments to the other members of virtual book clubs, read reviews and participate in online communities built around fictional worlds. Textbooks and academic works will be made available simultaneously in different formats – print-on-demand, online as simple text, and online as a file that can be discussed, manipulated, shared and built on as study and research takes place in a collaborative way. Reference works with individually tailored visual interfaces will be available as constantly updated applications (apps) for many practical professions from astronomy to zoology, allowing users to upload information in text, audio and visual formats; carry out searches and calculations; consult colleagues; and gain instant access to the facts required to solve a problem in real time. As the same person could be a reader of fiction for leisure, a lifelong learner studying in their spare time, and a professional, they will be able to carry out all of these activities using a single, portable, web-enabled device, which can also be connected to a desktop machine should additional software or computing power be required.

Anne Worden and Timothy Collinson

There is often confusion between e-book devices and e-books themselves but it is as both develop rapidly in parallel that we are finally beginning to see e-books taking off. Sony's Reader and the Amazon Kindle show a possible way forward for screen readability and battery life; the iPad demonstrates great purchase models and usability (in a more generally useful multi-purpose device). But the cost of both devices and e-book texts must come down, there must be greater availability of titles, and DRM issues must be resolved so that books are easy to access, annotate and can be legitimately shared with friends, before there is universal take up.

In ten years' time e-books will make much more of their electronic nature rather than 'merely' being print books in an online format – which is particularly the case with many academic e-books at present. Multimedia, hyperlinks and social network connections allowing comments, tagging and sharing will become much more prevalent, with authors and publishers creating e-books from scratch rather than simply converting a print original, but this will also mean that text may become much more fragmented. E-books will have become much more straightforward to use – from access (Apple's iBooks model is one to watch here) to the practical side of note-taking and extracting quotations. In academia, findability and cross-searching with other e-resources will be crucial to ensure that e-books become an effective tool for teaching, learning and research.

Part 6

Useful information

Glossary

3G

3G or 3rd Generation is a collection of standards for mobile phones and other mobile telecommunications services, developed to specifications determined by the International Telecommunication Union (ITU).

Access management

A system or process for ensuring that only authorized users can access online resources.

Adobe Acrobat and Acrobat Reader

Software for creating and viewing Portable Document Format (PDF) files. Acrobat Reader is freely available online, and versions are available for most computer operating systems. See also **PDF**.

Aggregated search

A means of searching a variety of sources for information and placing the results of that search into a single interface.

Aggregator

A business supplying electronic content from a range of publishers, specifically for the library market. E-book aggregators offer a range of access and licensing models. Content can usually be purchased as a collection or on a title-by-title basis. Subject coverage ranges from specialist content to popular fiction and non-fiction titles.

Athens

An access and identity management service provided by the

Eduserv organization in the UK, primarily used by educational institutions and the National Health Service (NHS). Athens can be nominated as an outsourced service provider for access to Shibboleth/federated access management protected resources. The framework of access and identity management products available from Eduserv is now known as OpenAthens. See also **Shibboleth** and **Federated access management**.

Authentication

A process for verifying the identity of a user, often as a prerequisite to allowing access to resources on a computer network.

Backwards and forwards compatibility

Backwards compatibility is the ability for a new device or technology to work with data generated using an older device or software release. The reverse of this is forwards compatibility: the ability of older devices to access data generated by using a newer device or software release, whilst not necessarily supporting all of the features.

Becta

Formerly known as the British Educational Communications and Technology Agency, Becta was the UK Government's lead agency for information and communication technologies (ICTs) in education from 1998 to 2010. The aim of the organization was to develop a national infrastructure and supply framework that would allow schools and colleges to make the most of technology.

Born digital

Materials that originate in digital form, rather than being produced in print and then digitized through scanning.

CLOCKSS (Controlled LOCKSS)

A not-for-profit partnership between publishers and research libraries, which aims to build a dark archive for the preservation of web-based scholarly publications such as e-journals and e-books. See also **Dark archive** and **LOCKSS**.

Copyright Licensing Agency (CLA)

An independent organization, which represents a large number of UK and overseas publishers. The CLA provides licences to educational and commercial organizations in the UK, which enable them to photocopy or scan and then distribute copyrighted material to their members within strict guidelines. The revenue gained from the licences is redistributed back to the publishers.

COUNTER (Counting Online Usage of NeTworked Electronic Resources)

An independent organization that oversees an agreed international set of standards and protocols governing the recording and exchange of online usage statistics, collectively known as the COUNTER Codes of Practice.

Dark archive

An online archive that is hidden from public access and suppressed from search engines as it is used to store commercial or private data. See also **CLOCKSS**.

Digitization

A technical process for creating a digital representation of a picture, drawing, film, audio recording, text or three-dimensional object.

DOI (digital object identifier)

An alphanumeric identifier for digital content, such as e-book chapters and e-journal articles. The DOI is paired with the content's URL in a central directory, and is published in place of the URL in order to avoid broken links while allowing the content to move as needed.

DRM (digital rights management)

This term covers the description, identification, trading, protection, monitoring and tracking of all forms of rights usages relating to digital materials (including intellectual property rights). DRM software is often used to 'wrap' e-book content in such a way that actions such as printing, downloading and re-using the content on different devices are restricted.

E-book (e-Book; eBook; electronic book)

This term can be used to describe a range of digital objects, from a digital version of a printed book to a program that includes interactive content and multimedia. E-books are available in a wide variety of formats. Some may be downloaded in full to be read offline, while some may only be read online whilst connected to the internet. The term may also be used to refer to an electronic reading device such as a Kindle or Sony Reader.

See also Chris Armstrong (2008) Books in a Virtual World: the evolution of the e-book and its lexicon, *Journal of Library and Information Science*, **40** (3), 193–206, http://hdl.handle.net/2160/647.

E-book reader (e-reader)

An electronic device designed primarily for the purpose of reading digital books and periodicals. The most recent devices use e-ink technology to display content. The main advantages of these devices are portability, screen readability in bright sunlight and long battery life. See also **e-ink**.

EDI (electronic data interchange)

The structured transmission of data between organizations by electronic means. EDI is often used in the library environment to facilitate ordering and invoicing using the library management system (LMS).

Eduserv

A not-for-profit organization based in the UK, which develops and delivers technology services for education, health, local authority and commercial organizations. Eduserv supplies the access and identity management service OpenAthens, and also license negotiation services for both software and electronic content, through a range of agreements with suppliers and service providers.

E-ink (electronic ink; electronic paper)

A display technology designed to mimic the appearance of ordinary ink on paper. Unlike a conventional flat panel display, which uses a backlight to illuminate the pixels, e-ink reflects light in the same way as ordinary paper. It is capable of holding text and images indefinitely without drawing electricity, while allowing the image to be changed later.

EPUB (e-Pub; e-pub; EPub; epub; ePUB)

An open e-book standard from the International Digital Publishing Forum (IDPF). EPUB is designed to produce reflowable content, meaning that the text display can be optimized for different devices. Files have the extension .epub.

Federated access management

A method of authentication and authorization for access to online resources. Federated access management builds a trust relationship between identity providers such as universities and colleges, and

service providers such as e-book vendors. It devolves the
responsibility for authentication to a user's home institution, and
establishes authorization through the secure exchange of
information (known as attributes) between the two parties. See also
Shibboleth.

Federated search

A method of searching across multiple online databases or web
resources simultaneously, receiving a single set of results.

Information and learning technology (ILT)

A collective term used to describe a variety of different ways of
using technology to enhance the learning experience for students
at different levels of education.

Intellectual property rights (IPR)

The legal framework for protecting the results of creative processes,
such as inventions, literary and musical works and the images and
icons used in commercial activities. Includes laws on copyright,
patents and trademarks, and is intended to prevent unauthorized
use and plagiarism that may violate the moral and/or commercial
rights of the originator.

International Digital Publishing Forum (IDPF)

A trade and standards organization focused on the development
and promotion of electronic publishing and access to content. The
IDPF develops and maintains the EPUB standard for e-books.

Internet Protocol (IP) authentication

An IP address is assigned to any device connected to the internet,
and takes the form of a series of numbers. Users can be allowed
access to online information resources on the basis of the IP
address from which the authentication request comes – for
example a computer connected to the network of a university,
college or business that has the right to access the content.

ISBN (international standard book number)

A 13 (formerly 10) digit number that uniquely identifies books
that have been published internationally.

JISC (Joint Information Systems Committee)

A body funded by the post-16 education funding councils in the
UK, which provides infrastructure, advice, consultancy and
support for learning and research focusing on the innovative use

of digital technologies in education. JISC Collections is a consortium that negotiates with publishers and service providers to provide electronic content at no or reduced cost for the education community.

LibX

An open-source extension for the Firefox and Internet Explorer browsers, which enables users to add a toolbar that can be used to search library catalogues and databases directly.

Link resolver

An online utility that uses the OpenURL standard to link between a citation and the electronic full text of the resource cited (such as a journal article or book chapter). A link resolver is typically set up by a library in such a way that only the text to which its users are entitled is linked to, thus avoiding dead ends.

LOCKSS (Lots of Copies Keep Stuff Safe)

An international community initiative that provides libraries with digital preservation tools and support so that they can easily and inexpensively collect and preserve their own copies of authorized e-content. See also **CLOCKSS**.

MARC record (MAchine Readable Cataloguing record)

A bibliographic record created using an international standard digital format.

Metadata

Structured information that describes an individual data item or a collection of data items.

Mobile device

A pocket-sized computing device, typically having a display screen with touch input and/or a miniature keyboard. The term can refer to smartphones, personal digital assistants (PDAs) and tablet computers.

Mobile learning

Any sort of learning that happens when the learner is not at a fixed, predetermined location, or that happens when the learner takes advantage of the opportunities offered by mobile technologies.

National Vocational Qualification (NVQ)

Work-based qualification awarded in England, Wales and Northern Ireland, with levels from 1 to 5.

OCLC WorldCat
A union catalogue that itemizes the collections of over 70,000 libraries in over 100 countries that participate in the Online Computer Library Center (OCLC) global co-operative. It is built and maintained collectively by the participating libraries.

OCR (optical character recognition)
The process of scanning printed or handwritten text and submitting it to a mechanized process to produce machine-readable text, which can then be further manipulated, for example to provide keyword searching.

ONIX (ONline Information eXchange)
A family of standards that supports computer-to-computer communication between the parties involved in creating and distributing books and serials.

Open access
Online resources made openly available to users with no requirements for authentication or payment. Examples of open access resources include those provided by OAPEN, a project for the development of a sustainable open access publication model for academic books in the humanities and social sciences (see Chapter 4).

PDA (personal digital assistant)
A mobile device that functions as a personal information manager. PDAs often have the ability to connect to the internet and provide access to a wide range of information including e-books.

PDF (Portable Document Format)
A file format created by Adobe Systems in 1993 to be independent of specific hardware and operating systems. PDF has become one of the most commonly used e-book formats.

Pre-harvested system
A method of searching a centralized database of metadata taken directly from vendors and publishers, which can also be integrated with search results from a local library catalogue.

Proxy
A firewall mechanism that replaces the Internet Protocol (IP) address of a host on the internal (protected) network with its own IP address for all traffic passing through it. A proxy server can

therefore facilitate IP authentication from remote locations. See also **IP authentication**.

RDA (Resource Description and Access)

A set of instructions for cataloguing both physical and virtual items, intended to replace AACR2 (Anglo-American Cataloguing Rules, 2nd edn).

Reflow

Used to describe the way that the content of a page can resize (or reflow) to fit the screen on which it is displayed, depending on the device itself, or user preferences.

RSS (really simple syndication)

A collection of web feed formats used to publish frequently updated works such as blog entries, news headlines, audio and video in a standardized format.

Screen reader

A software program that allows users to access the contents of a computer screen and navigate around its structure using synthetic speech, most often used by people with visual impairments.

Search engine

An information retrieval system for finding information stored on a computer or network.

Service provider

A business that provides subscription or web services to other organizations or individuals.

Shibboleth

An open-source software program, which uses the SAML (Secure Assertion Markup Language) protocol to enable federated access management. It both triggers the authentication process within an institution, and supports the secure exchange of information to establish authorization. See also **Federated access management**.

Smartphone

A mobile phone with advanced software, usually providing facilities for connecting to the internet and browsing websites.

URL (Universal Resource Locator)

A string of characters that represents the location of a resource on the internet and indicates which program should be invoked to access the resource.

VLE (virtual learning environment)

A software system designed to support teaching and learning through the provision of tools to help develop educational activities (such as discussion boards), as well as to assist with managing and facilitating learning (such as spaces for submitting assignments and giving feedback to learners). VLEs can also provide online access to resources from outside the physical premises of the educational organization, extending the places and times when learning can happen.

Web browser

A software program that enables users to display content from the world wide web. Examples include Microsoft Internet Explorer, Mozilla Firefox and Google Chrome.

XML (Extensible Markup Language)

A set of rules for encoding documents (often web pages) in machine-readable form.

Note

This glossary has been compiled from a number of sources including:

CNET (2010) *CNET Glossary: terms for the techie*,
    http://reviews.cnet.com/4520-6029_7-5741404-1.html?tag=eye.
Planet eBook (2010) *Ebooks Glossary 1.0*, www.planetebook.com.
South Western College (2010) *eBook Glossary*,
    www.swlearning.com/ebooks/glossary.html.
Wikipedia (2010) www.wikipedia.org.

Top tips from the contributors

A number of the contributors to this book have provided their own essential tips on how to create and make the most of a library collection of e-books, and these provide a very useful starting point for those who are new to this area of work.

Part 1: The production and distribution of e-books

Choosing a supplier (Anna Grigson)

With so many different suppliers offering so many different business models it can be difficult to compare like-for-like when choosing a supplier. Create a checklist of the criteria that are important to you - for example, whether you need access for multiple simultaneous users - and use it to compare and rank vendors' business models, pricing and licence terms to find which ones are the best match for your requirements.

Making good use of Google Books (Kate Price, with thanks to Joseph Ripp)

Use the Advanced Search facility on Google Books to limit the search to 'Full view only' in order to identify texts that are freely available in full. (Note that this setting reverts back to 'All books' with each new search.)

For those with a Google account, it is possible to set up, organize and annotate a virtual bookshelf on Google Books, which can then be shared with other users by sending them a link, or embedding it within a web page. This may be useful for supporting groups of students with specific projects, or for guiding readers to frequently requested material that is not available within the local library collection.

Part 2: Planning and developing an e-book collection

Providing a good range of material (Martin Palmer)

The single most important contributory factor to the success of public library e-book services (assuming that all of the technical details have been sorted out!) is much the same as that for a print collection – the range and amount of material on offer. Readers will be encouraged to return if there appears to be an abundant choice of material, but if the service does not have a critical mass of titles available for use from day one, then a major promotional opportunity will have been lost.

Planning an e-book collection (Karen Foster and Emma Ransley)

Strategic decisions: Decide how having e-books will enhance the current collection and for what specific reasons e-books should be included. If the strategic decision is to go ahead with the development of an e-book collection then you may also wish to consider the following tips.

Collection management: Create a stock management policy that deliberately and clearly includes e-books. This will provide a framework for staff, and raise the profile of e-books across the institution. The policy should acknowledge the differences between e-books and traditional resources and identify how the collection will develop in the future.

Staffing: Identify what tasks are needed to acquire, manage, develop and promote the e-book collection successfully. Then consider the members of the team and how the tasks will be allocated – for example, some people have a flair for promotion whilst others are great with statistics. As well as allocating tasks, remember that there will be a time impact on the team.

Budgets and finance: Ensure value for money by analysing and reviewing usage statistics regularly. In this way you can see which texts are being used most and perhaps increase e-bookstock in this area, whilst identifying opportunities for further promotion where there is poor usage.

Considering a patron selection plan for e-books (Jim Dooley)

Libraries have traditionally acquired materials in anticipation of use – 'just-in-case'. Advances in library and vendor systems have now made it possible to acquire materials in direct response to expressed patron need – 'just-in-time'. E-books are particularly suited to acquisition in this manner; therefore libraries should seriously consider a patron selection plan for e-books.

Part 3: Delivering e-books to library users

Cataloguing e-books (Anna Grigson)

Be prepared to make a compromise between quality and quantity when cataloguing e-books. Aim for the best metadata that you can achieve at a reasonable cost, but do not aim for perfection. It is better to have 'good enough' records for most of your e-books than to have perfect records for just a few.

Getting academics on board (Karen Gravett)

Give guidance to academics as to the benefits of e-books in general, and as to which titles are available in their subject area in particular, and once on board they will help to engage and encourage students. Ask academic staff to let you know if they see any new e-books that they would like purchased, and always check texts to see if they are available in e-format, asking academics if they would like the e-book as well as or instead of the print version, and then ensuring that these titles are included on their reading lists as e-books. Coutts MyiLibrary offers a great 'slipstream' service for the notification of new e-books, which can be e-mailed to academic staff.

Part 4: Engaging readers with e-books

E-book promotion in public libraries (Martin Palmer)

When using e-books as the basis for a reading promotion, it is vital to select the audience carefully. Offering e-books to people who have no interest in reading anything other than print is not only likely to be a waste of time, but may well be counterproductive, with the danger of active opposition to e-books and negative feedback affecting other people who may otherwise be open to using them.

Engaging students in further education with e-books (Sue Caporn and Lee Bryant)

Get them early! The research at City of Bristol College clearly shows that study habits are formed early on. Delivering an e-book session at the start of the first year of study will help make e-books a first choice resource for students. In addition, work closely with teaching staff to ensure that any e-book training sessions link directly to an assignment, so that any research undertaken using e-books is valued by students. Better still, convince teaching staff to build an assignment around the use of e-books so that they have to be used!

Incorporating e-books into VLEs (Karen Foster and Emma Ransley)

Embed links to the core e-books related to a course in the teacher's subject-specific VLE page. This will provide instant access to the most relevant resources and act as a constant reminder that e-books form part of the huge amount of information available to learners for their course. Consider adding an image of the book cover next to the link for the e-book; this will make it easier for learners to relate to the idea that the online book contains the same content as the physical copy and should make them more inclined to click on the image to access the material. Finally, ensure access is as simple as possible. A user education programme on the use of Shibboleth or Athens to access resources off-campus is essential.

Engaging students in higher education with e-books (Anne Worden and Timothy Collinson)

Persuade lecturers that information literacy sessions benefit all students, even the most technically competent! Even if students have used e-books before, they are unlikely to have discovered more than the basics. However little time you get, include a demo of e-books. Also, examine your usage statistics and give feedback to lecturers about which e-books are being used the most and by whom – there may be some surprises.

Checklist for e-book acquisition

When making collection development decisions regarding e-books, information professionals may wish to evaluate the following:

1 Business models
2 Licensing
3 Technical issues
4 Collection management considerations
5 The user interface.

1 Business models

a) What is the business model for purchasing/subscribing to the material?
b) How many simultaneous users are allowed, and what happens if this limit is reached?
c) Does a one-off payment confer rights to perpetual access?
d) By how much is a subscription cost likely to rise in the future, and on what basis (e.g. if more titles are added, is there an increased cost involved?)
e) Is there a platform charge in addition to the cost of the material itself, and is this one-off or ongoing?
f) Is the material available through a consortium deal?
g) Are any discounts available for volume purchases?
h) Is the supplier on the parent authority or institution's 'approved' list, or will it be necessary to undergo a formal procurement process?

i)   Is the material subject to VAT, and at what level?

2   Licensing

a)   Does the licence allow the upload of parts of the text into a VLE, use of the text in printed course packs, and reproduction of parts of the text for the purposes of assignments and theses (if applicable)?

b)   Does the licence allow 'walk-in' use for visitors to the library building who are not members of the institution?

c)   Does the licence allow reproduction of parts of the text for the purposes of interlibrary loans?

d)   Does the licence allow access to readers based overseas (such as distance learners and students based at partner institutions)?

e)   Does the licence allow access to staff and students at associated institutions and/or alumni?

f)   Does the licence grant permission to archive titles locally for the purposes of continuing access should the supplier withdraw material or go bankrupt, or does the supplier deposit material in a dark archive such as CLOCKSS or Portico?

3   Technical issues

a)   Which access management (log-in) route will be used?

b)   Will additional software or permissions be required to enable the e-book or platform to function on an institutional network?

c)   Can the titles be integrated into federated search systems and/or pre-harvested (web-scale) search systems?

d)   Are titles compatible as a source and/or a target for use with a link resolver?

e)   Can the material be uploaded to a mobile e-book reader device? If so, what percentage of the text can be uploaded, and is a charge made for this by the e-reader service provider?

f)   Can information from the resource be exported to relevant bibliographic referencing software?

g)   Is support available by telephone or e-mail from a local office, and is this available to readers as well as library staff?

4 Collection management considerations

a) Is the subject coverage appropriate for the library's readers?
b) Is the material at the right level for the target audience?
c) What is the selection mechanism for individual titles or subject collections?
d) Is the material up to date, providing the latest editions?
e) Are relevant usage statistics readily available?
f) Are MARC records available in a format that is compatible with the library management system in use, and is there a charge for these?
g) How often are MARC records updated (for collections)?
h) How quickly are full MARC records available after purchase (for individual titles)?
i) Can MARC records be customized by the supplier/library as appropriate?
j) How are collections updated when new titles or editions become available?
k) How are library staff informed of any additions or deletions?
l) Does the supplier provide promotional material?

5 User interface

a) Is the information organized in a clear and consistent manner?
b) Is access to text and navigation through the resource intuitive?
c) Is it possible to perform both easy and advanced searches?
d) Are the use of graphics and colour appropriate?
e) How are data, graphics, audiovisual and interactive materials presented?
f) Can the non-text elements be downloaded and/or printed out?
g) Is it easy to reference the text for academic purposes?
h) Is the resource accessible for readers with additional needs? Is it possible, for example, to change the font size, page size, background and font colours? Can keyboard shortcuts be used? Is the resource compatible with screen readers and other accessibility software? Is there a 'read-aloud' function integrated into the resource?
i) Is there support for non-English languages and non-Roman scripts?

j) Are there appropriate online help screens, tutorials and contacts for further assistance?

k) Are functions such as copy and paste, downloading and printing easy to use?

l) Are there additional functions such as the ability to highlight, bookmark and share text?

m) Are there DRM restrictions in place, and what impacts will they have on the reader?

Selected e-book suppliers

Please note: this is not intended to be an exhaustive list, and the information given is subject to rapid change and development. Many more organizations (such as learned societies, professional bodies and specialist publishers) supply e-books, as do library and educational consortia. Inclusion of a supplier is not intended as a recommendation.

Library suppliers

Askews www.askews.co.uk
Dawson www.dawsonbooks.co.uk
EBSCO www.ebscobooks.com
Swets www.swets.com
W. F. Howes Ltd. (Clipper DL) www.wfhowes.co.uk

Aggregators

Ebook Library (EBL) www.eblib.com
Ebrary www.ebrary.com
MyiLibrary www.myilibrary.com
NetLibrary www.netlibrary.com
OverDrive www.overdrive.com
Public Library Online www.publiclibraryonline.com

Specialist suppliers

Alexander Street Press http://alexanderstreet.com
Books@Ovid www.ovid.com
Books24x7 www.books24x7.com
Credo Reference www.credoreference.com
Engineering Information www.ei.org
iFlow Reader www.iflowreader.com/bookstore.aspx
Knovel http://why.knovel.com
ProQuest www.proquest.co.uk
Safari Books Online www.safaribooksonline.com
STAT!Ref www.statref.com

Online vendors: consumer sales

BooksOnBoard www.booksonboard.com
Diesel eBook Store www.diesel-ebooks.com
eBooks.com www.ebooks.com
Google Books http://books.google.com
Kobo www.kobobooks.com
Questia (also sells to libraries) www.questia.com

Booksellers: consumer sales

Barnes & Noble www.barnesandnoble.com/ebooks
Blackwell's http://bookshop.blackwell.co.uk/ebooks
Borders www.borders.com
Foyles www.foyles.co.uk/ebooks.asp
Waterstone's www.waterstones.com
WHSmith http://ebooks.whsmith.co.uk

Online vendors: e-books for handheld devices and mobile phones

Amazon Kindle www.amazon.co.uk
eReader.com www.ereader.com
iBook and other book apps www.apple.com/itunes
iFlow Reader www.iflowreader.com/bookstore.aspx

Mobipocket www.mobipocket.com
Sony Reader Store http://ebookstore.sony.com

Publishers: fiction, children's and consumer titles

Dorling Kindersley www.dorlingkindersley-uk.co.uk
Pan Macmillan www.panmacmillan.com/Categories/EBooks
Penguin www.penguin.co.uk/epenguin
Random House www.rbooks.co.uk/ebook.aspx
Simon & Schuster http://ebooks.simonandschuster.com

Publishers: academic monographs, textbooks and reference works

ABC-CLIO http://ebooks.abc-clio.com
Biz/ed premier www.bized.co.uk/premier
Blackwell Reference Online www.blackwellreference.com
Brill http://ebooks.brillonline.nl
Britannica Online www.britannica.com
CAB ebooks www.cabi.org/cabebooks
Cambridge University Press www.cambridge.org/online
CRCnetBASE www.crcnetbase.com
Elsevier SciVerse Science Direct www.sciencedirect.com/science/books
Emerald eBook Series www.emeraldinsight.com/products/ebookseries
Gale Virtual Reference Library www.gale.cengage.com/gvrl
McGraw-Hill www.mhprofessional.com
Morgan & Claypool www.morganclaypool.com
Oxford University Press www.oxfordonline.com
Palgrave Connect www.palgraveconnect.com
Sage Reference Online www.sage-ereference.com
SpringerLink Books www.springerlink.com/books
Taylor & Francis www.ebookstore.tandf.co.uk
Wiley Online Library http://onlinelibrary.wiley.com

Publishers: international bodies

European Union http://bookshop.europa.eu

IMF eLibrary www.elibrary.imf.org
OECD iLibrary www.oecd-ilibrary.org
United Nations http://unp.un.org
The World Bank eLibrary http://elibrary.worldbank.org
World Health Organization www.who.int/publications
World Tourism Organization www.wtoelibrary.org
World Trade Organization http://onlinebookshop.wto.org

Accessible e-book services in public libraries

Denise Dwyer, Development Officer (Access to Publishing), RNIB

1 Why is it important to have an accessible e-book service?

There are three main reasons why it is important for libraries to have an e-book service that is accessible to people with print disabilities.

1.1 Restricted choice

We estimate that fewer than 5% of books published are made available in alternative formats such as large print, so readers with sight problems or other print impairments (i.e. difficulties with reading printed text) have restricted choice.

In 2009, 133,224 new books were published in the UK. Charitable organizations such as RNIB convert books to alternative formats such as audio, braille and large print, but only have the capacity to transcribe a small proportion of books published.

1.2 Potential of e-books to improve access to books

Accessible e-book services have the power to transform access to books for people with sight problems or other print impairments, giving them access to the same book, at the same time as everyone else. Books in electronic format are inherently more accessible than print, as they have the potential to allow the user to adapt the content to their individual needs. The number of new and existing books being made available in e-book format is growing every day, dwarfing the number of titles available in alternative formats.

1.3 Legal position

Libraries have a statutory duty to promote equality of opportunity and not to discriminate against people with disabilities.

Any public library planning to deliver an e-book service should carry out an impact assessment under the Disability Equality Duty (DED) on the effect that such a service would have on blind and partially sighted people. They should then take steps to minimize any negative impact or to make alternative proposals.

If a library's existing e-book service is inaccessible to people with disabilities they would need to make alternative arrangements to fulfil the reasonable adjustments duty under the Disability Discrimination Act (DDA).

2   What is an accessible e-book service?

An accessible e-book service is one that allows users to engage with all aspects of the service in a way that suits their individual needs. This includes:

- logging on to the service
- searching for and selecting a title
- accessing the e-book content
- navigating within the e-book.

You will find descriptions below of the various ways people with print impairments access e-books. User needs differ depending not only on the print impairment, but also on the individual, so it is advisable to test any e-book service with a number of readers who have different needs and preferences. You will need to check that they can perform all the functions listed above in a way that suits their needs, using the technology and/or methods described below.

2.1 Alternative ways of reading e-books

2.1.1 Text-to-speech

Text-to-speech software programs read digital text out loud by converting it to synthetic speech. Many readers benefit from this software, including people with low vision, who struggle to see the text, and people with dyslexia, who can see the text but have difficulties processing its meaning.

2.1.2 Screen readers

A screen reader is software that allows users to access the contents of a computer screen and navigate around its structure using synthetic speech. It is more advanced than text-to-speech programs, as it not only reads out digital text, but also provides navigational and structural information, allowing a reader who has little or no vision to navigate through the different sections of a website, program or document.

2.1.3 Colour and contrast

The ability to adapt the colour and contrast of screen interfaces can be a huge benefit to people with sight conditions or dyslexia. Many software packages also allow customization of text and background colours to improve readability and contrast.

2.1.4 Screen magnification

Screen magnification software can magnify the text, menus and icons on a computer screen up to 32 times. The software is designed to enlarge images but minimize distortion. Additional options include the ability to zoom in and out, choose different colour contrasts between text and background, show split screen navigation and provide larger-sized pointers and cursors.

2.1.5 Keyboard access

Someone with low vision or motor difficulties may rely on keyboard navigation. This means that they will use the keyboard to access all the controls and functions of the software, rather than the mouse.

3   Questions to ask about the accessibility of e-book services

E-book service providers may claim that their products are accessible and compliant with the DDA, but it is worth probing further to find out exactly what they mean by 'accessible'. Ask specific questions to get a fuller picture of the type and level of accessibility.

3.1 The e-book service interface

In what ways is the service interface accessible to people with disabilities? For example:

- Does it support navigation using the keyboard only?
- Is there a 'read out loud' or text-to-speech function for the menus and navigation system?
- Is it possible to use this service with a screen reader, text-to-speech and screen magnification software?
- Are all hyperlinks appropriately described (is the link, for example, 'Adult non-fiction' as opposed to 'For adult non-fiction click here')?

3.2 Reading e-book content

In what ways can readers access the e-book content? For example:

- Can the text font size and style be personalized?
- Can the colour of both the text and background be personalized, and in particular can the colours be reversed to display light text on a dark background?
- Is it possible to alter contrast and brightness?
- Will enlarged text reflow to fit the page and avoid left/right scrolling?
- Is there a table of contents that enables users to navigate around the book quickly?
- Is there a 'read out loud' or text-to-speech function for all e-books?
- Will the reading software work with access technology such as a screen reader, text-to-speech or screen magnification software?

- Is all e-book text stored as text rather than images? For example, e-books in PDF format can be image-only PDFs or text-based PDFs. E-books available in JPEG format should also be available as a text stream for screen reader users.

3.3 Support

How does the e-book service provider support libraries to ensure that readers with disabilities can access their service? For example:

- Do staff members who are supporting the service have awareness or experience of supporting users of access technology?
- Are there alternative facilities in place for users who cannot access the system with their technology (see section 'What to do next' below)?
- Are other assistive technology tools available to support the reader? There are many free and open-source software tools that can support users – see www.techdis.ac.uk/getlibraryguides for more information.

4   What to do next

Once you have assessed the e-book services on offer and have taken into account accessibility considerations, you may find that an e-book service is accessible to some users, but not to others; for example, it may be accessible to those who use screen magnification, but not to those who use a screen reader.

Alternatively, you may find that an e-book service allows someone who uses a screen reader to log on to the service, search for and select a title, but will not allow them to access the e-book content with their technology. This is often true of e-book services that depend on third-party platforms. For example, OverDrive's e-book service uses Adobe Digital Editions, which does not currently support screen readers or text-to-speech software, so readers who rely on these methods will be locked out of the e-book content.

Once you know which areas of the e-book service are inaccessible, take the following steps:

- Ask the service provider what their timescale is for improvements.
- Ask the service provider what support services are available in the meantime to fill this gap; for example, can they provide DRM-free e-books for those who cannot access the e-book content with their technology? If the catalogue is inaccessible, is there an alternative way to access it?
- Include accessibility in any staff training on the e-book service, including what the service's limitations are and what workarounds are available in the short term.
- Have an accessibility statement that incorporates information about the new service, so readers know in advance whether it is accessible to them, and if not, what back-up is available to help them access it.

Remember, workarounds are only a short-term solution: e-book service providers may not currently offer services that are fully accessible, but should have a roadmap in place to make their service accessible to all users.

5   Resources

For more information on the accessibility of e-book platforms, and the potential benefits and obstacles of e-books for people with print impairments, visit the following:

JISC TechDis (2010) *Towards Accessible E-Book Platforms*,
     www.techdis.ac.uk/getebookplatforms.
RNIB (2010) *eBooks*,
     www.rnib.org.uk/livingwithsightloss/readingwriting/ebooks/Pages/ebooks.aspx.
RNIB Centre for Accessible Information (2008) *Ebooks Review: review of ebook players, formats and service providers - Autumn 2008*,
     www.rnib.org.uk/aboutus/research/reports/inclusive/pages/ebooks_review.aspx.

Supplementary reading

Resources for e-book collection development and management

Berglund, Y. et al. (2004) Appendix F: checklist for the evaluation of free e-books. In *An Investigation into Free e-Books - final report*, http://ota.ahds.ac.uk/documents/ebooks/report/FreeEbooks.html.

Books for All (2010) *Learning Materials in Accessible, Alternative Formats*, www.booksforall.org.uk.

Cleto, C. (2008) *ATG Special Report - 10 steps to implementing an ebook collection: a guide for librarians*, www.against-the-grain.com/TOCFiles/10Steps_p47-48v20-1.pdf.

CLOCKSS (2008) *CLOCKSS: a trusted, community-governed archive*, www.clockss.org/clockss/Home.

COUNTER (n.d.) *Counting Online Usage of NeTworked Electronic Resources*, www.projectcounter.org/index.html.

Dooley, J., Hruska, M., Stambaugh, E. and Tanji, L. (2008) *Guiding Principles for Collecting Books in Electronic Format: report of the Collection Development Committee Task Force on E-books*, http://libraries.universityofcalifornia.edu/cdc/taskforces/ebooks_final_report.pdf.

Edeserv (2010) *E-book Finder*, http://ebookfinder.labs.eduserv.org.uk.

EPIC (2009) *E-resources Toolkit: tips & tools for making the most of your e-resources*, www.epic.nz/training-resources/e-resources-toolkit.

JISC (n.d.) *Academic Database Assessment Tool: compare ebook platforms*, www.jisc-adat.com/adat/adat_ebooks.pl.

LOCKSS (2008) *What is the LOCKSS Program?*,
www.lockss.org.
McSherry, C. and Cohn, C. (2010) *Digital Books and Your Rights: a checklist for readers*, www.eff.org/files/eff-digital-books.pdf.
Portico (2010) *Portico - a digital preservation and electronic archiving service*,
www.portico.org.
RNIB (2010) *Ebooks*,
www.rnib.org.uk/livingwithsightloss/readingwriting/ebooks/Pages/ebooks.aspx.
Turcic, A. (2010) *MobileRead Wiki*, http://wiki.mobileread.com.
UKSG (n.d.) *The UKSG E-resources Management Handbook*,
www.uksg.org/serials#handbook.

General reading about e-books

Anson, C. and Connell, R. (2009) Executive Summary. In *SPEC Kit 313: e-book collections*, www.arl.org/bm~doc/spec-313-web.pdf.
Armstrong, C. (2010a) *Social E-books*, www.ukeig.org.uk/factsheet/social-e-books.
Armstrong, C. (2010b) *Writings about E-book Publishing 2009*,
www.i-a-l.co.uk/resource_ebook2009.html.
Armstrong, C. (2010c) *Writings about E-book Publishing 2010*,
www.i-a-l.co.uk/resource_ebook2010.html.
Chief Officers of State Libraries Agency (COSLA) (2010) *COSLA: e-book feasibility study for public libraries*,
www.cosla.org/documents/COSLA2270_Report_Final1.pdf.
EDUCAUSE (2010) *7 Things You Should Know About . . . E-readers*,
http://net.educause.edu/ir/library/pdf/ELI7058.pdf.
JISC (2009) *JISC National E-books Observatory Project: key findings and recommendations*, www.jiscebooksproject.org/reports/finalreport.
JISC (2010a) *E-books for FE Project*, http://fe.jiscebooksproject.org.
JISC (2010b) *Migrating to e in UK Further Education*,
www.jisc-collections.ac.uk/Documents/migrating_to_e_in_FE_report.pdf.
New Media Consortium (2010) *2010 Horizon Report*,
http://wp.nmc.org/horizon2010/chapters/trends.
Newman, N. (2009) *Highwire Press: 2009 librarian ebook survey*,
http://highwire.stanford.edu/PR/HighWireEBookSurvey2010.pdf.
Overdrive (2010) *Digital Library Blog: bright ideas for your virtual branch*,
http://overdriveblogs.com/library.

Polanka, S. (2010) *No Shelf Required: blog*,
    www.libraries.wright.edu/noshelfrequired.
Springer (2010) White papers for librarians (eBooks,usage and ROI),
    www.springer.com/librarians?SGWID=0-117-6-958921-0.

Index

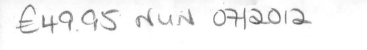